YOU CAN
ALWAYS
SELL MORE

YOU CAN ALWAYS SELL MORE

How to Improve Any Sales Force

JIM PANCERO

WILEY

John Wiley & Sons, Inc.

Published by John Wiley & Sons, Inc., Hoboken, New Jersey.
Published simultaneously in Canada.

For general information on our other products and services or for technical support,
please contact our Customer Care Department within the U.S. at (800) 762-2974,
outside the United States at (317) 572-3993 or fax (317) 572-4002.

Wiley also publishes its books in a variety of electronic formats. Some content that
appears in print may not be available in electronic books. For more information about
Wiley products, visit our web site at www.wiley.com.

Library of Congress Cataloging-in-Publication Data:

Pancero, Jim.
    You can always sell more : how to improve any sales force / Jim Pancero.
      p. cm.
    ISBN-13: 978-0-471-73915-9 (cloth)
    ISBN-10: 0-471-73915-4 (cloth)
  1. Selling. 2. Sales management. 3. Sales personnel. I. Title.
    HF5438 .25 .P35   2005
    658.3'044—dc22   2005012278

Printed in the United States of America.

10 9 8 7 6 5 4 3 2 1

To my daughter Kate:
way too young yet oh so wise
and to my Mother Jane:
way too wise yet oh so young

I am so proud and I love you.
I want to be just like both of you when I grow up.

CONTENTS

Acknowledgments   *xi*

Introduction   *xiii*

**Section I   Are You and Your Sales Organization
                  Good Enough to Get Better?**   **1**

CHAPTER 1   Why Is It So Hard to Improve a Sales Force—
             and Why Do We Tend to Lose It Once We
             Change It?   5

CHAPTER 2   Is Your Senior Management Creating and
             Supporting a Positive Sales Culture That
             Allows Your Sales Team to Be Successful?   17

CHAPTER 3   The Six Commitments Necessary to Generate
             Long-Term Change and Success Within a
             Sales Force   23

CHAPTER 4   Applying the Concepts of *ISO 9000* to
             Improve the Consistency and Quality of Your
             Sales Team   41

**SECTION II   Strengthening Your Central Leadership
               Values to Increase Your Personal Sales
               Leadership Skills**   **49**

CHAPTER 5   Are You Prepared, and Have You Earned the Right
             to Coach and Lead a Sales Team?   53

CHAPTER 6   Mastering Your First Central Leadership Value:
             Being a Leader instead of Just the Lead Doer   59

CONTENTS

CHAPTER 7   Mastering Your Second Central Leadership Value—
             Being Balanced as a Coach, Disciplinarian, and
             Number Cruncher   69

CHAPTER 8   Mastering Your Third Central Leadership Value—
             Having Empathy, Loyalty, and Trust in Your
             Sales Team   87

CHAPTER 9   Mastering Your Fourth Central Leadership Value—
             Being a Leadership Visionary   93

CHAPTER 10   Mastering Your Fifth Central Leadership Value—
             Believing in the Structures of Selling   101

SECTION III How to Improve Your Personal Sales
             Leadership Skills   107

CHAPTER 11   Using the *Sales Leadership Evaluation* to
             Evaluate, Prioritize, and Develop Your Sales
             Leadership Abilities   111

CHAPTER 12   Evaluating Your Sales Leadership Abilities as
             an Administrator, Problem Solver,
             and Disciplinarian   119

CHAPTER 13   Evaluating Your Sales Leadership Ability to
             Build and Retain a Sales Team   127

CHAPTER 14   Evaluating Your Sales Leadership Abilities   137

CHAPTER 15   Evaluating Your Sales Leadership Ability to
             Be a Coach and Strategist of Your Selling Process   145

CHAPTER 16   Suggestions to Improve Your Sales Leadership
             Skills and Effectiveness   167

SECTION IV   How to Improve a Salesperson's Selling
             Skills and Abilities   169

CHAPTER 17   Evaluating a Salesperson's *Operational Selling
             Skills and Abilities*   173

Contents

CHAPTER 18   Evaluating a Salesperson's *Tactical Selling Skills
              and Abilities*   189

CHAPTER 19   Evaluating a Salesperson's *Strategic Positioning
              Selling Skills and Abilities*   211

CHAPTER 20   Suggestions to Improve a Salesperson's *Selling
              Skills and Effectiveness*   227

SECTION V   **Developing a Successful Sales Team
                 Improvement Strategy**   **229**

CHAPTER 21   *Evaluate* Your Sales Force in an Open and
              Honest Environment   233

CHAPTER 22   *Design* Your Ongoing Sales Improvement Strategy   243

CHAPTER 23   *Implement* a Learning Growth Strategy for
              Each Sales Team Member   253

CHAPTER 24   *Track* Sales Team Members' Improvements by
              Utilizing a Comprehensive Sales Performance
              Tracking System   267

CHAPTER 25   *Lead* Your Sales Team by Ongoing Coaching
              of Your Defined Selling Best Practices   271

SECTION VI   **Are You and Your Sales Team Ready to
                 Get Better?**   **285**

CHAPTER 26   So Now What?   287

Appendix   291

Index   295

ACKNOWLEDGMENTS

Please allow four quick thank-yous for a collection of individuals who have profoundly changed and continue to change my life for the better.

To Pat Schmidt, my VP of Marketing and Paul Pyle, my VP of Operations for all of their years of loyalty, creativity, intelligence, hard work, and loving support.

To my support group—my closest friends. George Landreth, Krissi Barr, Jerry Fritz, W. Mitchell, Dr. Carl Hammerschlag, Sue Hershkowitz Coore, and Sarah Layton who continue to help me evolve by example into a higher life-form through their love, brilliance, and challenges.

Two individuals no longer with us have had the most profound impact on my life. My father, Howard Pancero, who lived every day of his life based on the values of ethics, professionalism, love of family, and the Masonic belief that true success in life is founded on helping others. And to my first, and most profound mentor, Bill McGrane Sr. Bill taught me that only through a complete and unconditional love of self and commitment to lifelong enlightenment can we ever achieve inner peace, happiness, and success.

And finally I thank my clients who have trusted me enough to share the intimate realities of their businesses and their lives allowing me to learn, help, and be a part of their journey as they continue to work toward their goals. If it wasn't for them, I would have had to go out and get a real job years ago.

You Can Always Sell More: How to Improve *Any* Sales Force

As an experienced sales manager, how do you improve your team's performance? Which selling skills, if strengthened, could generate the greatest impact on your revenues and profitability?

You, as sales manager or leader, are the most critical member of a sales team. You are high enough in the organization to see the bigger picture and what needs to change to improve success but are close enough to the selling front line to actually coach and lead your sales team to improved performance. The sales manager is the guide, the coach, the encourager, and the pacesetter of the sales force. A weak sales team guided by a strong and skilled sales manager can and will grow into a successful sales organization. A strong salesperson cannot impact an entire sales team if there is weak sales leadership. Yet as critical as the sales manager is to an organization, more than 95 percent of current sales managers are untrained and uncoached in the functions of their job.

Increasing sales and profitability as well as providing service and support to long-term customers are the two most important goals of corporations today. Thousands of books have been published on selling to help achieve these goals. But almost nothing has been published on the topic of sales management or how to improve a sales force. A recent search on Google of "Books on sales" generated 15,400 hits ("How to sell" generated 1,210,000 hits). But a search on "Books on sales management" generated only 70 hits ("How to manage sales people" generated 26 hits).

Training sales managers is a challenging task. The majority of companies have too few sales managers to justify investing in their own in-house or *consultant led* training programs. This is why some trade association annual conventions include speeches and seminars on sales management for member companies too small to afford their own training.

About *You Can Always Sell More: How to Improve Any Sales Force*

A note of caution: This book offers questions, tests, and evaluations to help you assess your sales team and selling processes. All are meant to help improve your company as you move forward, not to assign blame and/or responsibility for what hasn't happened in the past. It is critical you keep all conversations about your sales team *positive forward* focused instead of *assigning blame and responsibility, looking back.*

You Can Always Sell More will guide you through a proven step-by-step system to help you evaluate, design, implement, track, and lead your sales force to a position of market dominance. You will learn how to implement a simple, yet effective evaluation and improvement planning process that benefits even your most successful salespeople. This book is based on the processes and methods proven successful by my clients in a wide array of industries. It will also show you how to improve your coaching skills and lead a team of sales professionals. You know your team is good—but are they good enough to get better?

You Can Always Sell More is designed to assist you in communicating to the rest of your management team so they share your vision of how to rebuild and refocus your sales team. Section Overviews are included at the beginning of each section of this book to provide short explanations of the concepts covered within each section.

A Note about Section Heads

The brief Section Overviews at the beginning of each of the six sections of this book provide a brief summarization of the section including the major concepts being covered.

There are four goals of these brief overviews. The first goal is to introduce you to the major ideas being discussed in the section so you preview what you will be learning. The second goal is to provide you with a detailed guide to help you be able to locate and review specific concepts after you have completed this book and are working to implement these ideas within your sales team. The third goal is to provide an efficient way for you to revisit the major concepts covered in *You Can Always Sell More* at a later time.

The fourth and final goal of these overviews is to provide you with a way to share these ideas with your senior management, especially if you hope to enlist their support of your efforts. Even if a senior manager doesn't have time to read this entire book you can still ask them to read just the section overviews to understand what you are trying to accomplish in your efforts to build and improve your sales team.

Need more explanation? Find something you want to learn more about or have clarified? Well then, you'll just have to read the book.

Section I (Are You and Your Sales Organization Good Enough to Get Better?) explains how to evaluate if your organization, and senior leadership, are capable of supporting and maintaining an improved sales force.

Section II (Strengthening your Central Leadership Values to Increase Your Personal Sales Leadership Skills) outlines the five Central Leadership Values every leader of a sales force needs to understand and believe if they want to be successful.

Section III (How to Improve Your Personal Sales Leadership Skills) offers a detailed 20-question sales leadership evaluation tool to help you analyze and then prioritize your skills as a manager/leader of a sales team. This section will help you clarify both your current leadership skills as well as the best practices of leadership that, if improved, can help increase your ability to impact a sales organization.

Section IV (How to Improve a Sales Person's Selling Skills and Abilities) offers a detailed 20-question *Sales Evaluation* tool to help you analyze and then prioritize the selling skills of each member of your sales team. This evaluation tool will also help you quantify your understanding of the specific selling skills that can most impact the overall performance and success of a salesperson.

Section V (Developing a Successful Sales Team Improvement Strategy) shows you how to organize all of the information and awareness gained in the first four sections into a comprehensive step-by-step process that can generate long-term improvements in your sales force.

Section VI (Are You and Your Sales Team Ready to Get Better?) finally discusses how to achieve a successful implementation of these ideas within your team.

Visit www.GreatSalesSkills.com, the companion website to this book.

Both of the 20-question evaluations detailed in this book are also available as a free online interactive evaluation at www.GreatSales Skills.com. On this site you, or members of your sales team, can complete either evaluation and then receive a free multipage customized report offering additional information and suggestions to help you improve your skills. These reports are immediately available upon completion of your online evaluations. A comprehensive selection of training materials from top sales experts are also available on www.Great SalesSkills.com to help you expand the selling, or sales leadership skills highlighted with each question.

> *You Can Always Sell More* is the result of more than 35 years of selling, research, and training.

I accepted my first sales job in 1969 and founded my own sales and sales management consulting company in 1982. Each year I invest more than 30 days of research in clients' offices interviewing their leadership teams as well as riding with and observing professionals sell. All of the individuals and companies discussed in this book are drawn from these observations and experiences.

> You know you're good; are you now good enough to get better?

Dramatic improvements of sales organizations are rare. Most sales leaders attempting to change either don't have the time, don't have the awareness, don't have the commitment and support of the rest of their organization, or don't have all the other components necessary to implement and then maintain successful long-term change. The ideas in *You Can Always Sell More* can help you overcome these obstacles and achieve significant improvements in the skills, competitive positioning, and profitability of your sales force.

And let me hear how you are doing! You can e-mail me at Jim@GreatSalesSkills.com. I would love to hear your stories, successes, and challenges as you improve your sales force.

I hope you enjoy the process.

Section

Are You and Your Sales Organization Good Enough to Get Better?

Section Overview

CHAPTER 1 **Why Is It So Hard to Improve a Sales Force— and Why Do We Tend to Lose It Once We Change It?**

Most sales teams are not performing at the levels management wants and needs. Unfortunately most attempts to change and improve a sales force do not work. Successful, long-term change requires you and your team to invest significant amounts of effort to make changes in your sales leadership, your company, and all the members of your sales team.

You Can Always Sell More has been written to provide you with proven, straightforward solutions for you and your team to increase your awareness, guidance, structures, and philosophies of successful selling.

This first chapter will share the four most widely accepted but invalid leadership assumptions that are often responsible for hindering your management team's understanding of, or desire to, improve your

1

sales team. Organizations that believe in these invalid assumptions are normally not interested or committed to any type of long-term positive change and are not willing to invest either the money or the time in their sales force to actually generate the type of changes that lead to long-term improvements.

CHAPTER 2 Is Your Senior Management Creating and Supporting a Positive Sales Culture That Allows Your Sales Team to Be Successful?

Every organization and worker in business today has a bias toward one of the three major aspects of business: technical, financial, or sales. Though the best organizations are balanced in their focus, most management teams tend to support one bias, tolerate a second, and ignore the third.

A management team without at least some focus on sales tends to offer little support, investment, or encouragement to a sales team. A sales organization needs senior management's support and involvement to ensure that attention, funding, and priority are all in place to allow for growth and success.

You don't have to have a strong bias toward sales as a senior manager to realize that strengthening your sales team's skills and competitive advantage will directly impact the profitability and long-term success of your company.

CHAPTER 3 The Six Commitments Necessary to Generate Long-Term Change and Success Within a Sales Force

Changing a sales force involves more than just motivation and skills training. The long-term improvement of a sales team requires that the sales leadership adhere to, or at least consent to, the six simple, yet critical commitments to a team's long-term success. Attempts to change the processes and procedures of a sales force will likely fail if even one of these six commitments are not established, agreed to, or in alignment within your entire team.

Improving a sales organization takes the agreement and commitment of every member of the team including the sales leadership, upper management, and all sales representatives. Only when all six of these commitments are in alignment can you increase your sales team's productivity and success.

CHAPTER 4 Applying the Concepts of *ISO 9000* to Improve the Consistency and Quality of Your Sales Team

ISO 9000 is a quality program utilized in a number of manufacturing and services industries. Though *ISO 9000* was not developed for sales organizations, the basic concepts can have profound value and relevance to sales teams.

Applying the philosophies and goals of *ISO 9000* is a central philosophy of this book. Your sales leadership needs to first identify and start measuring where your sales people's skills and awareness are today, then identify the selling best practices that can increase your selling success. Next, you need to train, coach, and track your salespeople as they work toward your newly defined best practices. And finally, raise the best practices expectations you have in place as a way to continue increasing your competitive advantage.

Improving the selling effectiveness of your sales team as well as your abilities to lead a sales force are ongoing processes that are never completely finished. This is why the concepts of *ISO 9000* have such potential to help improve your sales team.

1

Why Is It So Hard to Improve a Sales Force— and Why Do We Tend to Lose It Once We Change It?

Does this sound like your sales organization?

George was flying home after having spent time riding with the last members of his new sales team. He had recently joined his industrial equipment manufacturing company as the VP of Sales. Having spent his life selling in this industry, he was confident he understood what it would take to be successful in this competitive a market.

On his flight home George is thinking about the first few months he has spent riding with all 12 of the sales reps who now report to him. He is glad he had felt it was so critical to get out and meet their larger customers as soon as possible and to assess the skills and experiences of his new sales team.

George is laughing as he thinks about his new situation. He wonders if his glass is half full or half empty. On the positive side he has a sales team he thinks he can work with. His assessment is that he has four real pros on his team: years of experience and strong sales numbers but with a collective "just leave me alone unless I ask for help with shipments and pricing" attitude. These four are generating about half his total sales. They have a lot of really strong larger customer relationships in (for the most part) stable territories, are proficient at maintaining these relationships but do not cultivate a lot of new growth, he thinks.

Two sales reps are probably not savable. While they are nice people who have been in their territory several years, they aren't selling much of anything and don't even seem to be trying. They deserve a fair shot, he thinks, but they are both clearly in over their heads.

He was surprised to learn he also has two brand new "rookies" to outside sales; each has less than a year in the job. Both moved up in the company through the customer service side but were completely green to outside selling and territory management.

His final four reps are "middle of the pack" types. Not your best performers but still doing okay. George saw lots of opportunity with this group and the rookies as well, but they are also in need of a lot of work and attitude adjustments.

Now for the heavy lifting to start, George thinks. He is going to have to meet with Maggie, the president of the company and his boss to begin discussing what would need to change to achieve the kind of growth expectations Maggie identified when he was hired.

Why is change so damned hard? He knows his team is good, and he knows, for the most part, they are good enough to get better. He just isn't seeing a real clear path of how to get himself and his team there, and then to maintain that level of performance.

Does George's situation share any similarities to the sales team you are leading? Is your sales team performing at the levels you want and need? What techniques have you employed in your efforts to increase the success and profitability of your sales team? How well did those techniques work?

After almost 25 years as a sales and sales management consultant researching, training, and coaching sales teams like George's, I've seen a significant number of attempts to change that have not worked.

Want to increase the professionalism, skills, and selling success of every member of your sales team? The majority of sales situations can be improved, but they will require you to invest a significant amount of effort to make the changes necessary in you, your company, and all the members of your sales team.

Though you can lead this process, you cannot successfully complete it alone. Want help? This book has been written to provide you with proven straight answers of what it takes for you and your team to increase your awareness, guidance, structures, and philosophies of successful selling.

Throughout this book there are a series of informal tests for you to administer to various members of your team. The expected responses from your team are also identified as well as suggestions of how to begin leading your sales team to increase your competitive success.

This first chapter offers several very specific tests you can administer to members of your sales team to validate the assumption that the majority of the Invalid Leadership Assumptions that follow are present within your company.

Next, we discuss guidelines to create the best possible environment for your sales team to be successful. Then we cover how to evaluate both yourself and each member of your sales team to understand the current sales (and leadership) levels of your entire team. Once you have a clear and quantified understanding of your current level of performance you can get to work designing, then implementing a learning growth strategy for all members of your team.

You will also learn how you can track various aspects of your team's improvement through the implementation of a Selling Skills Performance Plan and then finally how to lead your team, with their new skills and awareness toward a more successful future.

A note of caution as you proceed with evaluating your company's answers to both these questions and the other evaluation tools provided in this book. All of the evaluation questions asked in this book are meant to help improve your company as you move forward, not to assign blame and/or responsibility for what hasn't happened in the past. As you evaluate and discuss these questions with others in your organization you will need to work to keep all conversations *positive looking forward* instead of *assigning blame and responsibility looking back*.

Evaluating each of these questions alone will most likely only be restating the obvious. The real value to your organization will be if you can ask these questions to several in your company. The more members, from numerous departments, who provide their opinions, the more help you and your company will receive to define and improve the bias and direction of your business. The goal is to generate discussions and awareness so your entire organization is working and supporting your efforts to build a stronger and more profitable competitive position within your market.

To help you generate this change, you first need to see if you as a sales leader believe in any of these invalid leadership assumptions.

Invalid Leadership Assumption #1   Believing that experienced = trained.

How do you grow your salespeople's skills and success if they don't feel they need any sales training or coaching? The sad reality is that most salespeople selling today have never been through any type of formal sales training at any time in their careers, yet they still feel they don't need any additional training due to their seniority and experience levels. How many times have you heard managers say ". . . we don't need to provide any sales training because we only hire experienced salespeople"?

Coaching Question #1   Do you want to know if your sales team believes that experienced = trained?

Test: *(Ask each sales rep) How much "nonproduct specific" sales training have you had in the past year? How many books on selling have you read or seminars have you attended that were not provided by your company?*

Expected Results: The majority of experienced salespeople have done nothing to improve their training or awareness of selling in the past 12 months. Even though they are in a job where if they sell more they'll make more, most don't invest in the skill building efforts necessary to increase their proficiency and total revenues. They believe that experienced = trained.

The majority of attendees of my advanced "business to business" sales training programs enter the room assuming (1) there is nothing new in selling, (2) with their experience they have heard it all before anyway, and (3) with their seniority and success they should be the ones teaching the class, not attending it. Does this describe any of your more senior salespeople?

8

This book outlines a system to help you evaluate your sales team, shows how to design and implement an ongoing sales skill building process, explains how to track each team member's progress, and helps you strengthen your sales leadership abilities.

> **Invalid Leadership Assumption #2** The majority of my sales team already knows how to sell our products.

Most salespeople assume they can sell anything to anybody. But how many members of your sales team actually demonstrate organized, structured, and consistent selling skills? Have you ever had a salesperson explain his or her technique by saying, "I can't really explain it but I just know what to say when I get in front of a customer?"

Strong intuitive selling skills are important for anyone involved in selling. But the vast majority of salespeople feel their intuitive skills are all they really need to be successful. Most experienced salespeople see selling as an intuitive art instead of a structured, repeatable science. Their sales calls have no structure or consistency. On one call they are persuasively brilliant, but on the next they "crash and burn." They believe each sales call is so different and unpredictable that they just "wing it" on each call hoping that when they open their mouths they will say something persuasive.

Coaching Question #2 Want to see if your sales team has any understanding of the most basic structures of selling?

Test: (Ask each sales rep) Write down the steps of a sales call.

Expected Results: Salespeople who see selling as a structured science will think and plan out their sales calls following a specific series of steps. If they have been trained, know what they are doing, and have some type of process that works for them, they will be able to write down all of their steps in a minute or less. How long did it take each member of your team? And how clear and effective were the steps they identified?

Though this is one of the most basic questions in selling, the majority of sales reps, even the more successful ones, cannot write down the steps of a sales call because they were never taught, have forgotten what they learned years ago from a lack of use, or just see each sales call as being so completely different they don't even understand or see how there could be any kind of consistent steps identified or followed.

Test: *(Ask each sales rep) Describe what you plan to accomplish during a sales call.*

First, ask each salesperson to identify their best accounts or new growth opportunities. Next, ask them three questions. It's important to allow a salesperson to fully answer each question before asking the next.

Question #1: "What do you plan to accomplish on your next call to this account?" Write down all the things they identify.

Question #2: "What do you plan to accomplish on your second call to that account?" Again, write down anything they say.

Question #3: "What do you plan to accomplish on your third call to this account?"

The majority of sales reps, even the more successful ones, tend to have a strong set of answers to the first sales call question. But the two most common answers to the second sales call question is, "Whatever I don't get done on that first call . . ." or "How am I going to know what I'll do on the second call until I see how far I get on the first call?"

Only a few will have an answer for the third sales call question. How did your sales team do?

Expected Results: A salesperson who plans out their calls and thinks ahead will be able to answer these questions with little thought. But a sales rep who relies on an intuitively biased selling process will answer with a lot of ". . . it depends," or ". . . we'll have to see when we get in there."

Most salespeople are like the "Hellarewe" bird. "Hellarewe" birds are three-foot birds living in four-foot grass and spend their entire lives saying, "Where the hell are we?"

How many moves ahead are your sales reps thinking and planning? Most sales reps spend their entire careers thinking only what their next move will be.

The benefit of thinking multiple moves ahead can be related to playing a game of chess. Your opponent is thinking only one move ahead, but you are consistently thinking two or more moves ahead. How many games will you win? Unless you make a major error, you will win all of them due to your thinking more moves ahead. So how many moves ahead are your salespeople thinking and working? Would getting your team to consistently think more moves ahead help increase your team's competitive advantage?

Randy is an experienced janitorial and cleaning supplies salesperson. He has a solid set of accounts and normally performs in the upper half of the sales team. Randy has always believed that really exceptional salespeople are born that way. "Either you've got it or you don't," has always been how he accounted for the success of the best salespeople.

But Randy's manager Sandy has some concerns and feels that Randy could be generating a lot more sales from the territory he is managing. Randy works hard but does not seem to have any account plans or structure to his selling efforts. His entire plan each week is to work his territory, respond to customer questions, and solve any problems that come up. "Keep tracking your customer until they order something," seems to be his only sales strategy. Sandy has ridden with Randy on several occasions and has noticed some inconsistencies. On some calls Randy is brilliant, but on others he just wastes his customers' time with idle chitchat. He can provide great answers after a call as to why it was successful but never seems to be able to accurately predict what will happen before going into a call.

Randy is a solid performer but could be so much better. Sandy sees that Randy lacks any consistency in his selling and territory management skills, but she can't seem to figure out how to help Randy improve his performance and success.

Coaching Question #3   Do you have any salespeople performing at Randy's level?

Selling doesn't have to be this inconsistent and disorganized!

> **Invalid Leadership Assumption #3**   Even without ongoing management leadership and involvement our sales reps will all be working on opportunities to proactively grow their territories.

The job of a sales rep is to proactively grow sales, but the majority of salespeople, like Randy, tend to only reactively work their territory.

Are your salespeople rainmakers looking for and making things happen in their territories? Or are they only reactive weathermen/women just waiting for the customer to give them business? Too many salespeople spend their days servicing existing accounts and working hard on their personal relationships hoping their customers (or company management) will tell them of additional business opportunities. "How many of your sales reps have recently complained you are not giving them enough sales leads?"

Relationships are a critical component of any salesperson's success, but too many salespeople view maintaining relationships as the only way to grow their territory. By maintaining client friendships, they hope the customer will think of them and ask to buy something. The proactive salespeople continue working their relationships but also are actively searching, questioning, and proposing new business opportunities.

So many salespeople are so busy reactively supporting their existing accounts that they invest no time in activities they initiate on their own.

Coaching Question #4 Want to evaluate how much your salespeople have invested in proactively growing their territory?

Test: *(Ask each sales rep) "How much new business prospecting have you conducted in the past three months?*

Expected Results: Most salespeople do little prospecting. They also tend to focus on responding to customers' requests rather than on going out and initiating actions to either stabilize their existing customers or to look for new business opportunities.

Don't just ask if they have made any new sales calls. Ask them to explain their ongoing system for new business prospecting. Do your people seem to only talk about their new business generation efforts as "random prospecting events" or are they able to explain the specifics of their new business generation system?

Test: *(Ask each sales rep) How many additional support and/or new selling activities have you initiated at your best accounts within the past 60 days?*

Expected Results: Most salespeople initiate efforts toward acquiring additional business only from an existing account after first being asked by the customer. Much of their time is instead spent managing difficult accounts rather than soliciting new business from the accounts that are lower maintenance. How many members of your sales team seem to give your more irritating customers, the ones who complain all the time, a better level of support just because they keep asking and demanding?

Proactive efforts are a strong way to identify and develop new business opportunities both within new prospects as well as existing accounts. If you want to move your sales team to a stronger competitive position, you will need to make sure every member of your team is initiating proactive efforts to prove to their customers their value and the value of their product.

> **Invalid Leadership Assumption #4**   Your sales team doesn't need to invest in a strong manager/leader because you already have a tightly organized sales organization functioning as a solid team.

Are you managing a group of mountain men guerillas or are you leading a SWAT team? Excuse my choice of terminology here; however, the more politically correct "mountain persons" just doesn't seem to make much sense. Assume for a moment your company is a fort in the wilderness and you have hired a bunch of mountain men guerillas (aka salespeople) to keep your fort fed. They are a fiercely independent group, each bringing their own weapons, each with their own hunting style, and each convinced they are the best and don't need any help from you or the rest of the fort.

They have all disappeared into the woods and right now you have no idea where any of them are except for hearing the occasional gunfire or catching a glimpse of smoke. Once in a while one of them comes out of the woods dragging game they have shot. Food supplies have been increasing, so your mountain men have been doing a good job.

Even though you are their manager, they really don't seem to be interested in listening to your suggestions or directions. When you ask to ride with them, their first response is to ask, "Why are you picking on me?" and to remind you that you will not only slow them down but will probably get hurt because this is a rough territory and you are a soft manager.

How much communication is there among a group of mountain men? What is the potential that if one figures out a better way to hunt, he or she will share that idea or experience with the others? And what's the likelihood they will share the mistakes they made to help other members of their team to avoid those same errors?

Mountain men/women salespeople think they are in competition with the other members of their team, feel any coaching and/or training assistance is a sign of weakness, and fear they will lose face in front of the rest of the team if they share any mistakes or errors they made in their own selling efforts. How many of these mountain men/women do you have on your sales team?

But it doesn't have to be this way. Compare the mountain man team approach to a police SWAT team. SWAT teams are constantly in training to insure they function as a single team. All team members are in constant radio contact and have a central leader to direct all activities. They also debrief as a team after each assignment to identify what went wrong and to identify how they can do better the next time. SWAT teams have a motto: "What one learns, benefits all."

Coaching Question #5   Are you managing a team of mountain men/women or are you leading a SWAT team?

Test: (Ask yourself and your sales leadership team) How often do you, as the leader of your sales team, conduct account strategy planning sessions with multiple members of your team?

Expected Results: Most sales managers conduct only "operational" or "transactional" planning sessions to identify what their sales reps' "next best sales steps" need to be. How often do you conduct longer-range account planning sessions where you involve multiple salespeople in a discussion/planning session of what your overall account plans and strategies need to be?

Test: (Ask yourself and your sales leadership team) How often do you, as the leader of your sales team, conduct "account loss review" meetings when a significant selling effort is not successful or a major account was lost?

Expected Results: Most sales managers, and their teams, tend to focus only on positive future planning and avoid debriefing to identify why an account was lost. Accounts lost to your competitors are some of the best learning tools a sales team has but because of strong sales egos the efforts that contributed to a lost account tend to never be discussed with the entire team. Are you and your team learning from team members' mistakes and omissions so that what one learns benefits all?

Coaching Question #6   Is your sales leadership contributing or inhibiting your success?

Too many times companies promote their best salesperson to sales management, give them no training or direction, and yet expect them to know how to lead a team. After all, you assume, they were a great salesperson so of course they will also be a great sales leader.

Test: *(Ask yourself and your sales leadership team) What is the definition of the job of a sales manager/leader?*

Expected Results: Most sales managers have no idea what the description of their job is, or should be. Remember almost all sales managers have never been trained on how to manage or lead others. Most managers when asked this question will supply you with a list of responsibilities they have to do (hiring, firing, special pricing, problem solving) but cannot describe their core focus or strategic responsibility to their sales team.

When sales managers can describe their job, most identify the main objective as "to make sure all of my people are performing above minimum." Consider what George, the VP of Sales mentioned earlier, should do about strengthening his sales team.

Look at George's challenges. Where should he invest his time over this next year? Which of his 12 sales reps should get the most attention? What would you do with four senior but plateaued reps generating half your sales, four "middle of the pack" reps, two rookies, and two most likely not able to improve and stay with his team?

George decided he needed to first invest his time where it was most critically needed—with the two in trouble and his two rookies—but he also realized he couldn't just ignore his top performers. He knew if he centered all of his time on just fixing the two he doubted would make it and his two rookies, he might only actually impact a small percentage of his company's total sales. Every one of his team needed, and could benefit from at least some of his help and direction. George realized the best description of the job of sales manager is *"to help each of your people achieve more than they would have achieved if just left alone."*

What sales management definition and strategy are you following?

Coaching Question #7   What have you learned about your current sales team based on their answers to these coaching questions and tests?

How did you and your team do with these four leadership assumptions and eight tests? The common reality is the vast majority of sales teams do believe in the majority of these assumptions and do fail the majority of these tests.

As a sales and sales management consultant, I have observed that organizations believing in these invalid leadership assumptions are neither interested nor committed to any type of long-term positive change to their sales organization or selling efforts. When they do implement training, they aren't willing to invest either the money or the time to actually generate the type of changes that lead to long-term improvements.

You now have a choice. Do you want to just be a manager of a sales team working to maintain and hopefully randomly grow your sales, or do you want to be a proactive team leader helping them redesign and redefine their selling success?

You Can Always Sell More will lead your team through this exciting Sales Improvement Strategy to help increase your competitive advantage and selling success. We know you and your team are good. Are you good enough to get better?

2

Is Your Senior Management Creating and Supporting a Positive Sales Culture That Allows Your Sales Team to Be Successful?

Though every company is biased toward one particular aspect of business, most managers aren't aware of the true bias of their organization. There are three principal biases of any organization: Your company either has a sales, technical, or financial bias.

All businesses need to have all three bias represented within their organization, but the average company tends to focus all of its attention and funding on one area, tolerates a second area, and tends to ignore the third area as much as possible.

Coaching Question #8 **Can you identify your company's principal bias?**

There is a simple test to identify where your company's principal bias lies. Assume your accounting department just discovered an extra

$100,000.00 in funds. Also assume that if the money doesn't get spent by the end of the year it will be lost. Where will your company invest the funds?

A technically-biased organization would invest in research or production equipment to improve the quality or diversity of its products. A financially-biased company would either pay down debt or drop the funds down to their bottom line so they could increase their total profits for the year by $100,000.00.

What would a sales-biased organization do? Throw a party of course! Or hold a sales contest, attend another trade show, invest in a promotional item, or hire another salesperson. As a consultant I have observed that the principal bias of a company is immediately identified by how they answer this funding question.

A few years ago I encountered an organization that was extremely technically-biased. A manufacturer of uniquely engineered high technology components for the transportation and aviation industries was considering my sales training programs for their team. For decades the success of this company had been based on their ability to design, patent, and manufacture highly engineered and complex technology components. The VP of Sales bragged that all of his sales people were engineers.

As we talked I learned that in the past eight months the president of the company had decided not to replace 2 of the 10 outside salespeople who had recently left the company for better opportunities. He had also laid off the three administrative salespeople responsible for managing the administrative, ordering, and billing components of the sales department. These tasks were now the responsibility of the reduced outside sales force. The reason given for all the cutbacks was unavoidable budget tightening, but the sales team was still expected to increase sales 20 percent that year. That same year the president had also hired three more design engineers and had invested in new manufacturing robotics. As you would expect, the VP had been unable to get the funding for the sales training approved and the team also had missed their sales quota by a significant percentage.

There is no one best bias to have. The most successful organizations maintain a balance among the amount of emphasis and effort expended within each area. Long-term success for any organization comes from the balancing and investing in each of these three areas. If one area is underinvested in or unsupported, it will lead to weakened overall performance. It is nearly impossible to develop and/or strengthen a sales organization if your executive leadership and the rest of your company are not supportive of your sales team. An additional reality of business is that smaller and independently owned businesses are more likely to be biased and unbalanced than larger, public companies.

The Impact of Your Senior Management and Company Not Supporting Your Selling Efforts

So what if your leadership team is not supportive of your sales team and selling efforts? Even if senior management does not support its salespeople's efforts, it is still possible to achieve some level of success in the short term, but they will not be able to achieve the level of long-term success they could be achieving with the help of their leadership and the proper tools.

An unsupported sales team is like a car going 90 miles an hour but still in first gear. Though it is achieving significant speeds and distance, it will not be able to maintain this high a performance level in such an inefficient gear for any length of time. An unsupported sales team has to work twice as hard, or spend twice as much time to successfully sell and/or support their accounts. They also tend to lose a higher percentage of selling opportunities due to the lack of technical and executive support that hinders their ability to prove their value differential to potential clients.

Sales teams who have to provide extensive nonselling customer support such as administrative, technical problem solving, or installation support also produce less than satisfactory results since a large portion of their days are spent completing these other tasks. Why use experienced sales professionals to provide extensive billing, technical, or order expediting efforts? Every hour they spend wasted on those efforts prevents them from selling more business. Is it easier for you to hire and train another administrative assistant or another experienced sales professional?

A company's success and even its competitive advantage can result from the collaboration of a leadership team supporting a sales team's efforts. Salespeople are some of the most expensive people to replace and train. An established and skilled salesperson can significantly increase their selling efforts with the proper support and leadership guidance.

When a sales team is provided with effective sales leadership, administrative, and technical support, even an otherwise average performer can perform at a much higher and more profitable level. With support and coaching leadership selling time frames can be shortened, closing percentages can be improved, and larger revenue accounts can be successfully pursued.

Coaching Question #9 Is your sales team being supported and affirmed by the rest of your organization?

Is your company actually helping your sales force? A sales force cannot achieve long-term success without the support and involvement of the rest of the company. There are several questions you can use to evaluate how well your company's leadership and support structures are either contributing or inhibiting the overall selling success of your company.

How Strong Is Your Senior Management's Support?

Coaching Question #10 Are your salespeople getting the proper respect and recognition from your senior managers?

Test: (Ask each sales rep) Is your senior management helping you achieve more than you would have achieved if just left alone?

How would your sales team evaluate the consistency of your senior management's honesty, trust, openness, and respect toward them? Does your sales team feel that your senior leadership is contributing or inhibiting their success?

If your team's answers to these questions are not positive, you will most likely face a significant challenge. Most competent sales professionals will quickly leave for another job if they feel their leadership does not respect them or is not being completely honest or supportive of their efforts.

Coaching Question #11 Is senior management and your company funding and leading the development of new products/services as well as ongoing quality improvement of existing products/services?

This question is really asking if your company has somewhat of a technical bias. The vast majority of markets are aggressively competitive with little differentiation among competitors. Only organizations that continually invest in value strengthening as well as quality improvement efforts can stay competitive. No sales professional, no matter how skilled, can sell profoundly inferior products or services.

This is a critical area that will be evaluated by the more competent sales professionals who are either considering joining your team or contemplating leaving for a better job. No one wants to sell a product the market deems either inferior or generic. This is also an area that, though critical to the success of your sales team, is most likely not one of the areas you can change. A commitment to product and service excellence combined with continually investing in competitive advances is something that has to be identified by the senior leadership or ownership of your company.

Coaching Question #12 Is senior management encouraging and supporting ongoing skill building and training for the sales and customer service teams?

In the first chapter you were asked if you and your team subscribe to the invalid leadership assumption "experienced = trained." This is a great question to ask senior leadership as well. Most companies do not believe sales training is a valid or needed investment for an experienced sales team. I have observed that more than 90 percent of all sales training is done solely on product and industry knowledge. Little is done to actually train and improve the selling skills of a sales force. How much have you spent on sales skill training for your experienced sales team lately?

How does your senior management view sales training? The weakest companies view sales training as an expense, something they have to occasionally offer, especially to new sales hires. The more knowledgeable organizations view sales training as an investment, something that, when properly designed and implemented, results in an exponential return on investment. The most enlightened companies view their sales training as part of their competitive advantage. When properly evaluated, planned, implemented, and coached, sales training provides a sustainable competitive advantage in the marketplace. How do you and your senior management team view sales training for your team?

Changing Senior Management

Coaching Question #13   **How can you change the bias of your executives, especially if you are not an owner or senior manager?**

The first suggestion is to speak with senior management to help them understand that improving the skills and coaching of a sales team will positively impact the overall results of your company. Also make sure your sales team also recognizes the positive contribution sales training can have with even an experienced sales force.

The second suggestion is to have each member of your sales team and senior management complete the 20 question *Sales Evaluation*—filling it out on your reps—outlined in this book and on the companion website www.GreatSalesSkills.com. Having an accurate and comprehensive evaluation of the skills of your sales team allows you to both identify and plan the sales skills training that will have the most impact on their selling success.

3

The Six Commitments Necessary to Generate Long-Term Change and Success Within a Sales Force

Though all sales leaders want increased sales, profits, and success, most don't know how to begin leading a team through change. Improving a sales force involves more than just motivation and skill training.

The long-term improvement of a sales team requires leadership to implement, or at least consent to, six simple yet critical commitments or contributors to a team's long-term success. As a consultant, I have seen attempts at long-term change fail because at least one of these foundation commitments was not established, agreed to, or in alignment with the entire team.

Like a lock with six tumblers, only when all six tumblers are in alignment will the key actually work to open the lock. With the six commitments, if even one commitment is ignored or out of alignment, nothing happens; the sales force stays unchanged.

Accelerating the long-term change of a sales organization takes the agreement and commitment of every team member. You need the commitment of you, upper management, and all sales representatives. The six commitments necessary to change, improve, and align a sales organization are:

1. *Commitment to values.* Are the values of everyone on your team in alignment?
2. *Commitment to leadership.* Will your team agree to follow your leadership?
3. *Commitment to communications structures.* Does everyone on your team agree and support your required communications structures?
4. *Commitment to responsibilities and expectations.* Does everyone on your team understand and agree with their responsibilities and expectations?
5. *Commitment to rewards and consequences.* Does everyone understand and agree to the identified rewards for success? Do they also understand and accept the consequences of not achieving the assigned goals?
6. *Commitment to focus and strategy.* Are all members of your sales team "rowing in the same direction"?

First Commitment of Change Agree and commit to the shared values of the team and organization. Are the values of everyone on your team in alignment?

A successful team with a consistent focus begins with a sharing of values. This is the most fundamental component of all long-term success. If all team members do not share a common set of values, there will be guaranteed conflicts and disagreements on how to progress and how to define success. This becomes especially critical when an existing team experiences a change of leadership, company ownership, or the merger of different companies or divisions.

Mike had been VP of Sales for only eight months when he was fired. When asked why he let Mike go, Tom, the President, summed it up with one word: values. Mike's values about work, leadership, and customer relationships were not in line with Tom's, the company's, or the members of the sales team he managed. Tom had sensed there were problems and spent the last month meeting with each of the salespeople to learn where things really were. Tom was impressed with the commitment and loyalty of the team. They were all hard workers and were always pushing other departments to do what was best for their customers. Mike seemed to have more of a "take whatever you can get" attitude. He did not seem to respect the customers and kept disagreeing with the reps when they insisted upon doing the extras their customers most valued. He also did not seem concerned or interested in building up the energy and commitment of his team.

The six sales reps were a close-knit team who had been working together for several years. Their quarterly meetings, when all the reps traveled to the corporate office, were important communications and connection times for the reps. But Mike didn't seem to care about these meetings. In seven months he had shown up only for one of three meetings. Mike's actions at this last meeting were the issue that finally caused Tom to let Mike go.

Mike had hired me as a sales consultant to work with his sales team at that final meeting. The goal of this particular day was to help the sales reps see how they could increase their customer focus and competitive advantage. It was agreed that a number of selling and customer support decisions would be made during this day. But Mike didn't even show up for the meeting. "Urgent customer business" was his vague excuse to the team when he called the morning of our training to announce he wouldn't be there. Of course very little was accomplished in our day together because most of the decisions to be made required the approval and support of Mike.

When Tom learned that Mike hadn't even attended the training, he knew it was time to finally make the change. Tom explained that he had even counseled Mike of the need for him to be "more involved and connected" to his team. Tom also regretted not more accurately defining or predicting his conflicting values about work, customers, and leadership during Mike's initial hiring interviews

Coaching Question #14   What do you need to do to insure your sales team's values are in agreement?

Values are the most fundamental and most difficult to change commitments of any individual. What are your shared values regarding work ethics? Professionalism? Work efforts? Peer and leadership relationships? Customer respect and relationships?

What can Tom do next time during his interviews for a new VP of Sales to better identify and clarify a candidate's values?

- *Idea #1*   One of the first and most critical initiative is that Tom and his team define what values are most important and non-negotiable within their company and team. The more certainty you have about what you and your organization believe and value, the easier it is to recognize these shared traits and values in others. It is also critical to identify what specific beliefs and values will never be tolerated.

- *Idea #2*   The second initiative is to make sure you discuss and communicate the company's most important shared values on a regular basis to insure that these values are respected and remembered by all team members. It is also important to spend time discussing values during job interviews. Most job candidates spend little time in interviews being asked about their values.

What can you do to insure you and all members of your team either share or are comfortable with a common set of values?

Second Commitment of Change   Agree and commit to your team's leadership and support structures. Will your team agree to follow your leadership?

As simple as this sounds, a number of organizations fail to change or improve due to a basic lack of commitment to their sales leadership. If a leader is perceived to be inexperienced or an outsider, or does not have the commitment of the team, change will not take place. Directives will be ignored, and little will be done to generate success for the team. Leadership of a team can also be lost if any team members feel their leader has violated any of the six commitments of change discussed in this chapter. The only way you can be the leader of a team is if all members of the group individually agree to follow. Do you have the commitment and support of your entire sales team?

Coaching Question #15 What do you need to do to insure all of your team's leadership and support structures are in agreement?

Leadership power can come from three sources: personal, informational, and positional power.

Personal power is the strongest and most effective source of leadership power and comes from one's ability to persuade and attract a group of followers. Have you ever noticed how some members of your team have the attention and respect of the rest of the organization? Experience, success, or the ability to create an affirming and supportive team environment can all generate a strong level of personal power for a leader. People tend to be drawn to competence and excellence. However, personal power is also the hardest type to develop and earn within a team. You either have the respect and support of a team or you don't. Personal power cannot be assigned or demanded; it can only be earned.

The second type of leadership power is informational power. Team members gravitate and listen to those who are able to provide new information and/or insight. The person with the most information that benefits others tends to be viewed as a leader by the rest of the team. How are you helping your team see, learn, and achieve more than they would have achieved without your involvement and assistance?

The third and least effective source of leadership power is positional power. Positional power is the assigning of job titles or responsibilities by other, more senior management. "You will follow me because the boss put me in charge," is a positional power statement. Positional power is the easiest of these three power sources to achieve (because it is the only one actually assigned), yet it is also the weakest long-term source of power. Just because you have been put in charge doesn't mean the rest of the team will listen to you or even follow you.

The inherent weakness of positional power is the reason children of company owners (or senior management) put in a position of leadership have such a difficult time earning the respect and following a team. How effective will you be as a leader of a sales group if the majority of your team feels you are only in charge because "Dad" gave you the job? The difficulty of being a credible "CEO" (Children Employed by

Owners) is why most family business consultants strongly suggest any children of owners interested in working in the family business spend at least a few years working for another company to strengthen their awareness, skills, and credibility.

Working outside the family business for a few years also increases the unique "informational power" you bring back to the family business. A family member coming with outside experiences from another company to join the family business will have more credibility and power than will a family member who has worked only for the family company. How much have you been relying on positional power for your leadership success?

Coaching Question #16   What do you need to do to get your team to follow and respect your leadership?

You will increase your team's interest and commitment to following you if you can increase any and all of these three levels of power.

1. *Make sure everyone knows you have the support and commitment from senior management.* You will not be followed if your team suspects you do not have the full support of upper management.

2. *Increase your informational power.* What can you do to learn as much as possible about your job, your company and products, your customers, and the selling process? If you want to increase your leadership skills, you need to increase your knowledge and ability to provide insights and wisdom to others. How many books on selling have you read, how many seminars have you attended? How much research have you done on your buyers and why they buy from you and your competitors? If you know more about what is happening than the members of your sales team, you will also increase your strengths as a leader. The more value, awareness, and assistance you provide, the more likely your team will want to follow you.

3. *Check your ego.* People do not want to follow someone who appears to be in this for themselves. A critical component of leadership is humility and openness. If you make a mistake you need to identify your error instead of trying to hide it or blame it on others. People need to be aware you are genuinely interested

and open to their feedback before they will accept your direction and coaching leadership. An old leadership philosophy states that a successful leader always gives credit for success to their team members but also always takes personal responsibility for any loss by their team. How important and supported do you make your team members feel?

4. *Increase your personal power.* This is the most important way to increase your leadership power. Start working with your more junior or less skilled team members to help them increase their competency and success. The best way to increase your personal power is to increase your wins and success stories. It's also easier to work with your newer or less skilled team members since they are most likely to embrace any help you provide. This will also give you a solid experience base as you work to improve and strengthen your more senior team members.

Third Commitment of Change   Agree and commit to your communications structures. Does everyone on your team agree and support your required communications structures?

An organization increases their success rate and ability to lead when it has more accurate, current, and complete information. So the dilemma exists in most sales teams where management constantly demands more information and reports while the sales team keeps complaining about the excessive reporting and paperwork required by management that prevents them from spending more time in front of their customers. How much agreement and support is your sales team giving to you and your company's information demands?

Salespeople tend to be loners. Most experienced and successful salespeople take pride in their independence. Often senior sales professionals also pride themselves on not needing the help of their management to be successful.

Many salespeople also feel they are creating job security by sharing as little as possible about their accounts and new business opportunities. It's a lot harder for their manager to fire them if no one else knows their customer contacts or are unaware of potential new business opportunities being developed.

Salespeople also believe that keeping management in the dark about their territory activities helps them look more professional. After all, if a sales call crashes and there is no manager around to notice, does it count? Similarly, random success will always be claimed as "preplanned success on purpose" after the fact.

Most sales professionals also have a strong ego. A strong ego is one of the best defenses against all the risk and rejection inherent in selling. But a salesperson with a strong ego also tends to take both their wins and losses personally. It doesn't matter how much the entire team contributed to the success of a sale. A salesperson will feel success was only really achieved due to their personal efforts.

Because of their large egos a significant percentage of salespeople also do not want to keep management updated on their plans and progress with an account. Their belief is that if they tell you about their plans, you will be able to identify why they were not able to completely implement those plans. Large egos tend to be the reason the majority of salespeople see their customer losses as personal signs of defeat. Most salespeople want to ignore a lost sale and move on. Ask a salesperson to analyze why a large sale was lost and the majority will answer that it was caused by anything except their personal efforts: "The customer only bought on price," "our competitors bought the business," or "the buyer was a jerk who didn't know what they were doing."

How often have you heard a salesperson identify the reason for their lost sale as being due to their inability to communicate a stronger value message or because they did not effectively reach the correct decision makers? The larger a salesperson's ego, the less likely they will be to want to help identify how their ineffective efforts or lack of awareness were major contributors to the lost sale.

An account loss is one of the best and most critical opportunities to learning how to get better. A good leader will learn more from a loss than from a win. An effective leader will be involved in the ongoing selling process, acting as a coach and strategist to help provide additional value and insight to even the most experienced salespeople.

How active are you in communicating with your salespeople as they plan and implement their selling efforts? How are you helping your team get better by analyzing losses to help identify areas that could be improved in future sales efforts? How well do you understand your complete selling process so you can predict and help plan the best selling course of action?

Coaching Question #17   What do you need to do to insure that your team's communications structures are in agreement?

1. *Review all of the regular requests for information being made of the sales force by you and your management.* Are all reports being turned in on time? Are the submitted reports complete and accurate? Do you have to constantly follow up for information requests, reports, or account updates? Evaluate the relevance of each information request and identify what may be generating the strongest resistance from your team.

2. *Test the openness of your team, especially of your most senior players, to see how open they are to discussing and receiving coaching assistance with their current selling situations.* Are they receptive to your selling and strategy questions? How do they receive your suggestions and ideas that might improve their selling efforts? Do they feel your questions and requests for updates about their new business opportunities are valid and worthwhile investments of their time and attention?

   Any negative responses to these questions and evaluations could be a sign they are not accepting your communications requirements, or it could mean you don't have enough personal leadership power or support from your team. Consider reiterating why your requests for information and updates are so critical to the team's success. You also might need to review how others have benefited from this process to prove the validity of your requests.

3. *Review what you see are your responsibilities as their team leader and how you want to help them achieve more than they would achieve if just left alone.* If you are encountering opposition to your information requests, this might be a battle that needs to be fought. It will be almost impossible to build a strong sales team if they are not supportive of your leadership and communication requirements.

Fourth Commitment of Change   Agree and commit to all the responsibilities and expectations. Does everyone on your team understand, agree, and affirm their responsibilities and expectations?

Everyone who is involved with your team, from as high up as senior management to your front line customers all have responsibilities to your team as well as expectations of what you and your team will provide. Responsibilities and expectations have to coincide. The responsibilities of the team member have to match the expectations of the manager, and the responsibilities of the manager have to match the expectations of the team members. How clear are all of these responsibilities and expectations?

Do your team members understand their personal responsibilities and what is expected of them? Do you and your upper management understand and consistently provide the tools, resources, and support required (and expected) by your sales team and customers? Do your customers understand and accept their responsibilities to be timely, fair, and accurate in their loyalty and treatment of your team and company? Do your sales team members step up and take responsibility for errors or problems caused by them and/or your company? Problems will develop if any of these responsibilities are not identified and accepted.

And what about everyone's expectations? What do you and your upper management expect from your sales team? What does your sales team expect from you and the rest of the management team? How are you making sure all of these expectations are communicated, understood, and accepted? How consistently are your customer's expectations being met?

These are simple questions to ask. But defining and making sure everyone understands and accepts their responsibilities as well as having their expectations from others accepted and affirmed are some of the most critical aspects of being a leader.

Consistency and clarity are essential in communication. Salespeople have to understand and trust that their responsibilities are fair, defined in advance, consistent, and predictable. They also need to have confidence their expectations of others in the company are also being fulfilled. A team falls apart when they are surprised with lack of support from others in the company, especially their management.

Does everyone understand his or her responsibilities? Are the expectations others have of you clearly defined and understood by all? If not, your team will become ineffective and weakened.

Coaching Question #18 What do you need to do to insure all of your team's responsibilities and expectations are in agreement?

This is one of the reasons employee performance plans and sales expectations have to be in writing and published for all members of your sales team to see and understand. Subjective "only verbally communicated" responsibilities may be challenged and cause conflicts. We all have selective memories. Both responsibilities and expectations need to be explicit and put in writing to insure any discrepancies or misunderstandings do not cause a conflict. These responsibilities and expectations also need to be reviewed and discussed on a regular basis to insure everyone understands and shares a common focus and awareness.

If not already in place, implement an annual performance plan system for your team. It is critical to review both their assigned responsibilities and their progress to date several times a year as well as to review your team's written assignments and responsibilities on a regular basis.

Ken Blanchard, coauthor of the *One Minute Manager* (William Morrow, 1982), has said, "The things that get worked on first tend to be fixed first." Are you working and reviewing these areas of responsibility and expectations on a regular basis to insure your team is functioning under a "no surprises" philosophy?

Fifth Commitment of Change Agree and commit to the rewards and consequences. Do all team members understand and agree to the identified rewards they will receive for their successful efforts? Do they also understand and accept the consequences of not achieving their assigned goals?

I believe in a simple concept of motivation: "the greater the risks and expectations you have for someone, the greater the rewards need to be offered for their success."

The way to generate extraordinary efforts from a team is to provide extraordinary rewards for those efforts. Why would anyone take significant risks if there were not also significant rewards available for success?

Too many sales management teams expect their members to generate major accomplishments even though minimal rewards are offered.

A bank trust department I was consulting with implemented a new sales contest (against my recommendations). All trust officers were paid a salary with an annual raise tied to the accuracy and effectiveness of their work. The head of the trust department decided to implement a sales contest to help motivate his team to sell more services and to work harder. The announced contest stipulated that anyone increasing their revenue at least 10 percent for the year would receive a $4,000 end-of-year bonus. Some of the workers seemed excited about the new program but a lot of the more senior people just ignored the incentive opportunity. I asked Paul, a senior trust officer whom I had a personal friendship with why this contest was generating such little interest. He shared in confidence how he viewed the program:

> Last year my salary was about $65,000.00. And though I would like to make more money, let's keep this $4,000.00 bonus opportunity in perspective. I have two small kids at home. To increase my sales over 10 percent will require me to work at least two more hours each day for the entire year. Do the math. About 260 business days divided by the $4,000.00 bonus means I would earn an extra $15.00 per day if I met my goals. That's $7.50 per hour or $3.25 per child per hour for me to be home investing my time with them. Watching my kids grow up is worth more than $3.25 per hour!

Paul also explained that he expected no negative consequences if he didn't make his 10 percent increase goal. Though you may not agree with Paul's lack of motivation, it is easy to understand his logic and his decision to ignore the bonus opportunity. To him, the potential payoff was just not worth the extra work and commitment to achieve the contest prize, and the consequences of not making his goal were perceived as minimal.

What are the risk-to-reward calculations for your contests, promotions, and programs? What are the established consequences of not making any of the assigned goals or assigned expectations? Are the payoffs in balance with the risk and commitments being asked?

Coaching Question #19 What do you need to do to insure that your team's rewards and consequences are in agreement?

Each industry and type of market is unique. A bank trust officer is normally not seen as an aggressive sales position. Some environments that pay a salary to salespeople need only small bonuses or contest opportunities to generate an increase in efforts. But some sales environments require a stronger payoff for the assumption of stronger work efforts or greater risk. How valuable a bonus do you need to offer for your team to generate extra efforts and results?

Money has found to be a poor long-term motivator but you still need to be competitive. Are your salaries, commissions, and bonus programs in line with the rest of your industry?

Don't condone incompetence or underperforming. All salespeople have "off" years, but are all members of your team working hard or at least trying? Most salespeople define their job security as not based on the top performers but rather based on those performing below their current position. If a sales rep sees that a peer is performing at half the level they are and the peer's job is still safe, what is the pressure for that sales rep to improve? A low level performer can affect an entire sales team by proving how minimal performance or low efforts are tolerated. An underperformer needs to be immediately dealt with and placed on some type of improvement program.

There needs to be accountability for your sales team and their efforts. Lower performance levels need to be identified and tied to lower income and recognition levels. How much accountability do you and your company demand of your sales team?

Remember the goal of any commission, incentive, or bonus program is to help your salespeople achieve more than they would have achieved without the program. How are your incentive or "stretch" programs helping your people work harder to achieve more than they would have achieved without the program in place?

Sixth Commitment of Change Agree and commit to the focus and strategy. Are all members of your sales team "rowing in the same direction"?

Let's assume your team has values that are aligned (1st), support you as their leader (2nd), is committed to your communications structures (3rd), has a clear understanding of their responsibilities and expectations (4th) as well as the rewards and consequences (5th) of their job.

You now have a motivated and energized team. But are they all motivated and energized in the same direction? Most sales teams do little to discuss their selling focus and strategy yet assume all members of the team are selling the same way to the best customer opportunities.

Coaching Question #20   What do you need to do to insure that your team's focus and strategy are all in agreement?

There are three questions you can ask your sales team to learn if they share a common selling focus and strategy. Privately ask each team member (and each management team member) the following four questions. If your entire team shares the same selling focus and strategy, then all answers will be consistent. But if your team, like the majority of sales teams, is unfocused and inconsistent with their selling strategies, their answers to these strategic questions will vary significantly.

Question 1. *Define the attributes or shared values of our core customers.* "Core" customers are the ones who take maximum advantage of your company's unique value offerings. Even if core customers put their business out to bid, you would still most likely win due to your ability to perfectly fit their needs and requirements compared to your competitors. Just because you have a large account doesn't mean they are a core customer.

Probable Answer.   The majority of salespeople will not be able to answer this question. Most experienced salespeople define their best accounts by the name of the account. When I ask this question, they tend to tell me the names of their best relationships, not the attributes. What are the unique values or support issues you can provide an account so they want to buy from you versus any of your competitors, even if you are a higher price?

Who are the next best prospects for your sales team to go after? A lack of consistent identifiable attributes can lead to a decrease in sales. Defining a solid set of identified attributes that best describes your most loyal and satisfied customers can have a positive effect on the success of your sales team. Finding a prospect with those same requirements will both speed up your selling process and increase your odds of winning the business.

Question 2. *How would you answer a prospect who asked, "You're the fifth vendor I've talked to about this product/service this week. Why, based on all the competitive alternatives available to me do I want to buy from you?"* This question will identify what value and/or uniqueness your salespeople feel you and your company provide the market compared to your toughest competition. How clear and consistent a set of answers does your sales team provide your prospects and existing customers?

Probable Answers. You will most likely encounter three problems with the answers to this question. The first problem is that each salesperson tends to have a different set of answers. Even though you all work for the same company and sell the same stuff, most sales reps have completely different answers to this question.

The second problem is that when they do have the same answers, they will most likely center on these four responses: Why do you want to buy from me? Well because of (1) my high quality products, (2) my strong levels of support, (3) my competitive prices (we're not the lowest but we are still competitive), and (4) you get me! What's wrong with these four answers? It's most likely what all of your competitors are saying. How unique and competitive could you be if your four responses are all generic responses your competitors are also offering?

The third problem is that their answers are all "me, the salesperson" focused instead of "you, the customer" focused. Most sales reps when asked this question talk about how great their company and support offerings are, how long they have been in business, and how many satisfied customers they have. All "me, the seller" focused answers.

There's a concept my father taught me as a kid. He always said, "You don't go into a hardware store to buy a drill. You go into a hardware store to buy the opportunity to make holes!" Are your sales team's answers focusing on your "drills" (your products and what you will do for them) or are you focusing on the customers "opportunities to make holes" (what you can do for them)? "Me" focused language centers on all you provide (like 24-hour service) but "you, the customer" focused language would focus on how your customer can get help any time they need it.

Question 3. *What business do you not want?* Under what conditions are you not the best choice for a customer? Most salespeople come from a position of desperation. They go after anything that moves or will talk to them. How many new customers have you won but were not able to keep because they just wanted more or different things from what you were best at providing?

Probable Answers. Most sales reps when asked this question answer only with a "credit check" type of response. "We don't want to sell to anyone who won't pay their bills." If your sales reps can't agree on the definitions of what business you don't want, they will most likely be pursuing prospects you will either have low odds of winning or will have an expensive time trying to support and satisfy. How clear are you and your team as to what prospect attributes are not the best for you to want as a customer?

Coaching Question #21   How did your sales team do with the coaching questions and tests covered in this chapter?

How consistent is the focus and selling strategies of your sales team? Are they all "rowing in the same direction" or are they all scattered in their focus and beliefs as to why their best customers buy from you?

The vast majority of sales teams are all over the place with their answers to these questions. When was the last time you and your management team worked with your sales team to define or clarify these questions? If the sales team's management has not helped define the answers to these questions why would you be surprised that each team member seems to have a different response when asked?

Meet with your team to discuss and identify the best answers to these three questions. The only way you will get both clarity and consensus with their answers is if you and your team work through what the best and most unique answers will be.

> Summary: Is your sales team in alignment for maximum performance and success?

38

Only when all six of these commitments are in alignment will the key actually work to open the lock of your sales team's productivity and success. Is your team in alignment in each of these six areas?

Once all members of your team are in alignment with these six commitments, then the next steps are to begin working to increase the skills of your sales leadership and the selling skills of your team members.

4

Applying the Concepts of *ISO 9000* to Improve the Consistency and Quality of Your Sales Team

About half of the companies I consult with and train are *ISO 9000* certified. *ISO 9000* is a quality program utilized in a number of manufacturing and services industries. ISO stands for "International Organization for Standardization" and is an international network of national standards institutes. The ISO website (www.iso.org) describes ISO (International Organization for Standardization) as the world's largest developer of standards.

To become *ISO 9000* certified a company works with trained independent ISO consultants who help realign and improve their quality and consistency. An *ISO 9000* certification confirms that a company has proven consistency in the production and distribution of their products or services. Many large corporations will not buy from a company that is not *ISO 9000* certified.

Using the Concepts of *ISO 9000* to Improve Your Sales Team

Though *ISO 9000* was not developed for sales organizations, their basic concepts can have profound value and relevance to sales teams and their leadership. *ISO 9000* basically follows four simple steps to improving your quality:

1. *Identify and start tracking what your people are currently doing.*
2. *Identify the "best practices" you wish they were doing.*
3. *Train, coach, and track your people to get them closer to your best practices.*
4. *Raise the bar to move to a higher level* (Continuous Quality Improvement).

ISO 9000 Step One   Identify and Start Tracking What Your People Are Currently Doing.

Bill works as the VP of Sales for a machine tool company. They design and manufacture the large million-dollar computer controlled laser cutting machines used to cut out parts from sheets of steel up to one inch thick. His team of 10 sales reps are experienced professionals who have all been selling at least 15 years for their company. His industry has gone through several years of a challenging economy and increasingly aggressive competitive markets.

He knows his and his team's long-term survival (and success) will be achieved only if they become more competitive and effective in their selling efforts. The reality of the large equipment machine tool industry, like most other industries, is that market advances have removed most of the uniqueness and differentiation among the major players in the market. Now more than ever a competitive win will be based in large part on the selling and positioning skills of their sales team.

Bill's experienced pros are doing a good job but he knows they can definitely get better. He has always described the members of his sales team as a bunch of race cars all going 90 miles an hour, but most are still in first gear and only firing on six of their eight-engine cylinders. So where does he start? He knows he needs to push them, but from what and to where?

How do you measure the skills of an otherwise experienced and successful sales team? Though each member of the team is unique in their personal selling styles, they are all basically persuasive and have formed strong customer relationships. It's the lack of more advanced skills that seem to be slowing his team down. They start off strong with a new business opportunity but seem to stall out getting lost in a kind of fog about halfway through their selling process and always seem to get nailed on price by their customers and competitors. They seem to be weakest in positioning and communicating their competitive uniqueness, so their customers are not aware of, nor see the value of, paying more for a better supported piece of equipment.

Bill wasn't sure what specific skills needed to be improved and also wasn't clear on what the "best practices" were that he should be steering his team toward. As I discussed in the first chapter, his team all felt that, as experienced sales professionals, they really didn't need any sales training. "Just give us lower prices and increase our service levels if you want us to sell more" was the solution as they saw it.

Have you ever seen this sales leadership model within a sales organization? The managers/leaders of the sales team share a passion for wanting their team to become more successful and to sell more and more profitable business. They continue to push their team to, in their words "get better." But there are two major gaps in their implementation strategy.

The Two Critical Gaps of Most Sales Leadership Models

The first major gap in Bill's sales leadership model is that he continues to push his sales team to "get better" but has no definition of what "getting better" involves. Like the majority of all sales teams, Bill and his team have not even qualified or defined what the members of his team have consistently done to win business.

The second major gap in their sales leadership model is that Bill and his team also have not defined their "best practices" he wishes all of his team were trying to achieve.

The Concepts of *ISO 9000* Can Help

It is shocking how many sales managers want their salespeople to improve, yet aren't keeping track of where they currently are and haven't identified how much better they want them to be.

Coaching Question #22   What can you do to better measure the current selling skills and structures of your sales team?

The only way you can start improving a sales force is to first begin measuring where they are now. How will you know if your sales team is getting better if you don't first establish a base line of where they are now? And how will you know if you are getting better and more effective as a sales team leader if you also don't have some type of base line skill measurement of where you are as their manager?

To continue your process of improving your sales team complete the 2 "20 question" evaluations outlined later in this book. Complete the 20 question Sales Leadership Evaluation *on yourself and a 20 question* Sales Evaluation *on each of your salespeople. To validate your evaluations and to provide additional feedback you might also consider having your senior management complete a* Sales Leadership Evaluation *on you and your sales management skills and to also complete a* Sales Evaluation *on each of your salespeople. Having them complete these evaluations can help you understand both where your team is now and what all need to do to get better.*

Another positive activity to implement at the beginning of your sales improvement process is to have each of your sales reps complete a Sales Evaluation *on themselves as well as a* Sales Leadership Evaluation *on you. This is a great way to bring your entire sales organization into your improvement process and to help them understand what and why you are initiating this growth effort. One of the best ways to strengthen your selling team is to have them provide you with feedback on your skills as you work to help them improve theirs. The more open and receptive you are to their feedback and observations, the more likely they will be to receive your suggestions. Remember to keep the discussion positive moving forward and not negative looking back to assign fault and blame.*

After all the evaluations have been completed, sit down individually with each of your salespeople and discuss both your and their evaluations of their selling skills and your leadership skills. Discuss the discrepancies and similarities in both your evaluation as well as theirs. The goal here is not to have you both agree on the 1 to 5 rating identified for each evaluation question but instead to generate a dialogue about why you and they either agree or disagree with their skill evaluation and rating.

This is also a good time to start tracking any relevant sales numbers like your wins, losses, and the number of proposals issued. What are your closing ratios? How many initial conversations do you need to generate one sale? How many proposals do you have to issue to make a sale? These are important numbers to start measuring so you can potentially spot trends and future improvements.

When you have completed your inventory of where you and your team currently are, you will most likely not be satisfied with your team's newly quantified current selling skill levels and competitive positioning strengths. Don't panic! The goal of this process so far has been only to identify and quantify where your people currently are with their skills. The next step is to begin your growth and improvement process by helping them identify where they need to be by identifying and quantifying the selling "best practices" they need to be working toward to increase their selling success and profitability.

Coaching Question #23   What tools can you utilize to help you analyze and track the selling skills, structures, and processes of you and your people?

Tools Available for You the Sales Leader—Section III—How To Improve Your Personal Sales Leadership Skills, Chapters 11 to 16 and our companion website www.GreatSalesSkills.com will provide you with a detailed sales leadership 20 questions evaluation as well as a free detailed and customized action report to help you evaluate your skills as a sales leader. These tools will provide you with a comprehensive and detailed identification of your current leadership skills as well as a plan to help you improve your management and leadership effectiveness.

Tools Available for Your Entire Sales Team—Section IV—How to Improve a Salesperson's Selling Skills and Abilities, Chapters 17 to 20 and our website www.GreatSalesSkills.com will provide you with a detailed sales skills 20 questions as well as a free detailed and customized action report to help evaluate the skills of each member of your sales team. These tools will provide you with a comprehensive and detailed identification of the current selling skills for each member of your sales team as well as a set of plans to help each team member improve their selling skills and competitive advantage.

> ***ISO 9000* Step Two**   Identify the "best practices" you wish they were doing.

Once you start tracking and measuring your sales team's current selling skills and structures, you can start to identify the "best practices" they should be implementing. What are the components of a successful sales call? What are the critical points to make during a tour of your plant or offices? What are the important points that need to be in every proposal you issue?

Success in selling is based on increasing the structures and consistency of your sales team and their selling efforts. But to improve their selling structures and make them more consistent, you need to first take the information you gained from the first step of the *ISO 9000* structure as identified previously and combine it with the second *ISO 9000* step by identifying the set of structures or "best practices" you wish they were doing.

Are You Intuitive *or* Structured about Your Selling Skills?

The majority of sales teams are able to identify few best practices. Most salespeople are intuitive in their selling skills. They don't think about the steps or structures of selling, they just do it. There are salespeople who are successful just by being intuitive in their selling efforts. But intuitive salespeople are rarely consistent 100 percent of the time.

Intuitive salespeople also believe best practices are impossible to define because every sales call is different and each sales rep sells differently. Though it is true each sales call and each sales person is unique in some way, and even though every customer's personality and challenges are different, there are still structures and consistencies that, when applied or followed, can make you a more consistent and successful salesperson.

Have you ever noticed how commercial airline pilots always go through their laminated check list cards for the equipment they are flying? Even if the same crew has taken off and landed several times that day in the same jet, they will still complete their checklist off that card before every flight. Why do they so consistently complete those check lists? Because omitting something or making a mistake could cost them their lives. Do you think salespeople would be more consistent and concerned about their selling structures if there were more significant consequences of "crashing and burning" on a sales call? How complete are your definitions of your selling best practices?

Coaching Question #24   What can you and your team start doing to define and clarify what your selling "best practices" need to be?

Ask your salespeople if they can define any of the "best practices" your sales team should be implementing. Some of your team will not even see the value in defining these concepts. And others will feel this is a simplistic exercise because "everyone already knows what they are."

Your job, as a leader, is to help them identify and learn how they can apply your newly defined selling best practices in their daily selling efforts. Which skill areas do team members most need help with right now? What are the individual skill components for each member of your sales team that, when fixed or improved will generate the greatest payoff for themselves and your company?

You will learn how to identify and define your sales leadership and selling "best practices" as you complete both of the 20-question evaluations covered later in this book.

> **ISO 9000 Step Three**   Train, coach, and track your people to get them closer to your "best practices."

Throughout this book you will be offered extensive suggestions and resources to help you in your training and coaching to help move your team closer to your newly defined selling "best practices."

> ***ISO 9000* Step Four** Raise the bar to move to a higher level ("continuous quality improvement").

Improving both the selling effectiveness of your sales team as well as your abilities to lead a sales force are ongoing processes never completed. This is why the concepts and four steps of *ISO 9000* have such potential to help improve your sales team. By following the four steps of *ISO 9000* you can move your team toward a competitive uniqueness in your markets.

Coaching Question #25   When will I know it's time to start raising my expectations of our selling best practices?

Once you feel your team has really improved and are functioning at a stronger competitive level closer to your defined "best practices," it is time to raise the bar by increasing your expectations of your team's skill and structures moving them to a higher level. You will know it is time to raise your standards when your team gets comfortable and is consistently utilizing the skills (or best practices) you have been promoting. The goal is to always have a stretch path and program identified and in place so your team is being guided and encouraged to constantly want to get better and more successful. This constant movement/improvement of your "best practices" standards is referred to as "continuous quality improvement."

So Now What?

The rest of this book provides a step-by-step series of evaluations and processes, in combination with our companion website www.Great SalesSkills.com, to help you evaluate, plan, and lead your sales team to a stronger level of success. *We know you and your team are good. Now are you good enough to get better?*

48

Section

Strengthening Your Central Leadership Values to Increase Your Personal Sales Leadership Skills

Section Overview

CHAPTER 5   Are You Prepared, and Have You Earned the Right to Coach and Lead a Sales Team?

Improving a sales force requires that you first evaluate, and then improve the skills and focus of your sales leadership team. The challenge for most sales leaders is that they are not prepared, nor have they earned the right to coach or lead a sales team.

The definition of a sales manager's job is rather simple. *The job of a sales manager is to help each of their people achieve more than they would have achieved if just left alone.*

Having a background in sales does not guarantee success as a sales leader. In fact the majority of ineffective sales managers have a successful selling background but have no idea how to effectively lead a team.

There are five Central Leadership Values or philosophies that, if adapted and implemented, can dramatically increase the success of any sales leader, even if they have never personally sold before.

CHAPTER 6 Mastering Your First Central Leadership Value: Being a Leader Instead of Just the Lead Doer

All positions within an organization can be classified into one of three categories: Doers, Doing Managers, and Managing Managers.

A *doer's* job is to do things. A *doing manager* is someone who is responsible for some type of personal production (like selling) but is also in charge of leading others. A *managing manager* is someone who leads their team in accomplishing their assigned responsibilities. Most sales leaders are doing managers.

Doing managers who have not been trained in how to lead will approach their management job as the lead doer. There are also a lot of upper-level managers and owners who do not recognize or understand the value of having a sales manager or leader whose sole responsibility is to coach and lead others to achieve more. Successful sales leadership occurs when you actually lead your team instead of just being the lead doer.

CHAPTER 7 Mastering Your Second Central Leadership Value: Balancing Your Roles as a Coach, Disciplinarian, and Number Cruncher

Sales leaders tend to have a bias toward one of their three roles: coach, disciplinarian, or number cruncher. A manager with a bias towards coaching concentrates on working with their team to achieve more. A manager with a bias toward number crunching concentrates on keeping score to monitor their team's progress and profitability. A manager with a bias toward being a disciplinarian focuses on maintaining the discipline, deadlines, and consistency of their team. The more balanced your environment, the more stable, productive, and successful your team will be. But the more out of balance your team is, the less productive and effective they will be.

To manage the various biases within your company you need to serve and satisfy four separate masters. Your entire environment will collapse if any one of these four masters becomes dissatisfied or disillusioned with your leadership efforts.

Completing the 20-question sales leadership evaluation covered in Section III (Chapters 11 to 16) can help you identify your biases and skills so you can prioritize which areas will benefit most when strengthened.

CHAPTER 8 Mastering Your Third Central Leadership Value: Having Empathy, Loyalty, and Trust in Your Sales Team

Success in leadership begins when your team members believe you are on their side and truly care about them and their personal success. A successful sales leader offers more than suggestions, critiques, and ideas. They also offer support and affirmations. The most successful leaders have achieved a balance between the amount of positive and negative feedback they provide to their sales team.

Another way to strengthen the loyalty and trust of your team is to make sure your team members get the credit when they are successful. Your team needs to believe you are on their side and will help them fight their battles. That includes helping divert some of the negative consequences if things don't go right, and intensifying the positive outcomes for your team when things go right. You cannot effectively lead a team until they first have decided they want to follow you as their leader.

CHAPTER 9 Mastering Your Fourth Central Leadership Value: Being A Leadership Visionary

Visionary leadership is your ability to combine staying proactively focused as a leader while also maintaining a future focus in your communication and planning efforts. Even though it seems obvious that all members of your sales team should be proactive, the reality is that most sales people are almost completely reactive in their selling efforts.

Part of being a visionary leader requires making sure your team sees you as a proactive initiator. Reactive leaders believe their job is to make sure everyone is performing above minimum. Reactive efforts tend to at best maintain stable results, but proactive efforts tend to create growth opportunities.

In addition to being more proactive, a visionary leader also needs to be more future focused in their thinking and planning. Even though they cannot change the past, most reactive managers tend to be *today* and *history* focused rather than concentrating on improving the future.

CHAPTER 10 Mastering Your Fifth Central Leadership Value: Believing in the Structures of Selling

The majority of salespeople are intuitive by nature, seeing selling only as an art instead of a science. Helping your people understand and apply the steps and structures of selling can significantly increase their consistency of selling and also improve their competitive advantage and selling success. Helping them utilize these structures is also one of the most important foundations of sales coaching leadership.

There are three skill sets essential to sales success: Operational, Tactical, and Strategic. The only way you can effectively coach experienced and successful sales professionals is if you understand more about these skills and structures of selling than they do. You don't have to be a better salesperson than your people in order to help them, but you do need to understand all of the steps, structures, and philosophies of how selling works so you can coach even your best people to become better than they are now.

5

Are You Prepared, and Have You Earned the Right to Coach and Lead a Sales Team?

Improving a sales force requires you to first evaluate, and then strengthen the skills and focus of your sales leadership team. Are you and your management team prepared and have you earned the right to coach and lead a sales team?

In Chapter 1 I identified the first and most invalid leadership assumption for either a sales person or a sales leader: to believe that experienced = trained.

Jill was facing a real challenge as the new head of sales for her family's restaurant supply business. She was younger then all the sales reps she was leading, was the only female on the sales team, and had never worked in sales before. And even tougher, although she had been working in the corporate office for the past five years, this was her first managerial position. The president, her father, felt it important she take over the sales leadership function for a few years to help groom her to one day run the company.

Most of the five reps were dismayed that Jill was now in charge of the sales team. They didn't mind when she was working in other departments but now, as head of sales, she was getting too close for the comfort of the more experienced salespeople. "Anyone could do a better job as sales manager than the boss's kid," was the comment overheard in the sales room. Though Jill was intelligent and a hard worker, she just wasn't sure how to approach her new responsibilities. Her team had already assumed their defensive positions, doing everything they could to avoid her and to work around her.

During her initial one-on-ones with the sales reps, each asked her how she planned to help them sell more if she didn't even understand how selling actually worked. "Kind of like the high school nuns trying to teach sex education," was the common joke with the team.

What would you do if you were in Jill's current situation? How would you progress to win over her rather hostile sales team?

The Critical Role of a Large Ego in Selling

Salespeople, especially experienced ones, feel they are part of a unique breed. They believe their jobs require a higher risk taking mentality, demand more creative ongoing efforts, and involve longer hours and harder work than the rest of the employees of their company.

Having a large ego is a critical component of a successful sales career. Sales reps spend their lives hearing customers and prospects tell them no. It takes a strong ego to maintain a positive attitude with the ongoing rejection and negative responses that are a normal part of every sales job.

But the presence of a strong ego also creates a challenge for their leader. People with larger egos tend to live in a very hierarchical world where they constantly rank everyone they meet. You are either taller or shorter than they are, make more or less money, or are better or worse at selling. It is usually hard for an employee with a large ego to accept advice and direction from someone they view as less knowledgeable or experienced in selling. "To accept ideas from you means you are better than me" is a common high ego feeling. This hierarchical ranking or comparing is definitely not healthy behavior, but is still a normal part of most sales teams and needs to be considered by anyone leading such a group.

Most experienced sales reps also believe it is impossible for a manager to successfully lead a sales team if they have not worked as a salesperson first. Their reasoning is that a manager could not possibly understand the unique challenges and demands a sales rep faces if they had never actually sold.

As a professional sales trainer the first question I am constantly asked is "so what have *you* actually sold as a sales rep?"

Why It Is important for a Sales Manager to Have Sold Some Time in their Career

There are three driving reasons it is important for a sales manager to have actually sold some time in their past.

1. *If a sales manager has sold, they gain credibility.* Salespeople tend to have an "us versus them" mentality. Anyone is considered an "us" if he has ever worked as a sales rep. A sales manager who has sold for several years prior to going into management will have significant credibility even if his experiences were outside the industry and customer mix of the current sales team. But the manager's credibility increases significantly if she has either successfully sold within the sales team's industry or for a more prestigious outside industry or product line.

   Salespeople will tend to be more open and trusting of a manager who has previously "done my job" and "truly understands my unique environment and challenges."

2. *If a sales manager has sold, he is assumed to have an understanding of the job.* Most business to business selling requires a mastery of rather complex steps, structures, and strategies. If someone has not sold before he may not understand or appreciate the finer nuances or challenges of selling. A sales team expects their leader to quickly understand, and then offer useful, credible advice to help win a sale.

   An experienced sales professional will expect to answer to a sales leader who has more experience or awareness than she has. Most salespeople question how a manager or leader will be able to support or defend them if that manager or leader has never actually sold before. Where are your current selling skills and awareness compared to the members of your sales team?

3. *If a sales manager has sold, she can actually add value and contribute to the sales team.* Most experienced sales reps view their sales manager as either being able to speed them up by helping them be more effective and efficient or to just slow them down by requiring excessive explanations and being unable to contribute or add value to the team. A leader with a nonsales background will be viewed as someone who will only hamper the team's efforts and not know enough to contribute anything of value.

   If the definition of the job of a sales manager is to help all of his people achieve more than they would have achieved if just left alone, a sales manager who has never personally sold will have a challenging time helping his people, especially the more experienced ones, to achieve more because of their involvement.

In Chapter 2 I explained how all organizations are biased toward one aspect of business. They are either sales, technically, or financially biased. Sales reps assume and demand that their sales managers be sales biased so they understand what the reps require to achieve success. But a sales manager/leader who has never sold before tends to be either technically or financially biased rather than sales biased.

Coaching Question #26   What can you do to improve your abilities to lead a sales team if you haven't sold before?

There are two issues needing to be identified. First, having a selling background does not guarantee your success as a sales leader. The majority of ineffective sales managers have successful selling backgrounds but no idea of how to effectively lead a sales team.

The second issue is you can still be a successful sales leader without any personal experience selling.

Coaching Question #27 What can Jill do to help her become a more effective leader of her sales team?

She can increase her success if she first works to understand the best practices of how to be an effective leader of a sales team. Next, even though she has never personally sold before, she can become a student of selling, doing everything she can to learn more about the skills, structures, and philosophies of selling. She also needs to work to master all five of the Central Leadership Values covered in this section.

6

Mastering Your First Central Leadership Value: Being a Leader instead of Just the Lead Doer

There are five Central Leadership Values or philosophies that, if adapted and implemented, can dramatically increase your success leading your sales team. Though any sales leader can benefit by focusing on these five efforts, the less sales experienced you are, the more critical these invested efforts become.

This chapter will also help you and your upper management decide if you can be a more productive leader, and do more to impact the total sales and profitability of your company by becoming a full time managing manager sales leader.

The Central Leadership Values Required for Success as a Sales Leader

Each sales manager tends to lead a sales team in a different and unique manner or style. But there are five Central Leadership Values critical to all successful sales leaders. Your success potential grows as you become more proficient in practicing each of these five ideals in your daily dealings with your sales team. The five Central Leadership Values are:

1. Being a leader instead of just the lead doer.
2. Being balanced as a coach, disciplinarian, and number cruncher.
3. Having empathy, loyalty, and trust in your sales team.
4. Being proactive and future-focused.
5. Believing in the structures of selling.

How many of these philosophies or values do you communicate on a daily basis to your sales team? What can you do to incorporate more of these five attributes in your personal leadership style?

The First Central Leadership Value: Being a leader instead of just the lead doer. When you forget about job titles there are only really three positions in an organization: doers, doing managers, and managing managers.

---

1. *Doers.* A doer's job is to do things. They have no leadership responsibilities and are only measured based on their personal production. Anyone working in an office, warehouse, or sales department that has no direct or indirect reports is a doer.

2. *Doing Managers.* A doing manager is someone with split responsibilities. They are responsible for some type of personal production but are also in charge of leading others.

    Rob runs a machine tool press at a metal forming company. He is the most senior of the six tool press operators and has the job title of Tool Press Foreman. He has a production quota that is about 80 percent of the output of the other tool press operators. The additional 20 percent of his time is expected to be spent being the leader of the tool press work area. He is responsible for all training and safety issues for the team and makes sure all members are working hard. His split role of both a worker and a leader makes him a doing manager.

60

A sales manager who personally carries territory is also a doing manager. For part of his week he makes sales calls on assigned accounts while also making sure the other sales reps on the team are productive and effective. More than 75 percent of the sales managers I have met as a consultant are doing managers.

3. *Managing Managers.* The third and final job category is called the managing manager. The job of a managing manager by definition is to do nothing. A managing manger is not successful based on what she personally does but on how she helps her team accomplish their assigned responsibilities.

I doubt if the head of General Motors will build any cars today or help sell anyone a car. A managing manger's job is a pure leadership responsibility to make sure all of the people he is leading have the training, resources, tools, opportunities, and shared corporate vision necessary to achieve their assigned goals.

Why are there so many doing sales managers?

The most common reason a sales manager is functioning as a doing manager who personally manages accounts is because his sales force is not large enough to warrant a full time manager/leader. Each sales team has different demands and requirements of their leader, but the total revenues of smaller companies are likely not great enough to be able to afford a full time sales manager. An accepted standard of sales leadership is that managers responsible for less than six reps do not need to be full time managers, but can devote some time to their own territories.

There are exceptions to this rule. If you are starting (or restarting) a sales team and have six new sales people, then leading and training them will definitely need to be a full time responsibility. Another exception would be a company selling multimillion dollar contracts to large customers. Even though you have six (or less) salespeople, the customer demands for your presence as a sales manager could be so great as to prevent you from being able to spend any selling time with your own accounts.

There are also geographic reasons for a sales manager to carry accounts. Ralph was the VP of Sales for an automotive component parts manufacturer. He managed eight experienced sales reps who all worked out of their homes throughout North America. Ralph also personally carried a rather large account. When asked why he was also selling he explained the account was headquartered in his hometown of Boston and his closest sales rep was in Philadelphia requiring travel expenses to handle the account. Ralph also explained that he and his wife have three small children and by handling this important local customer he was able to justify spending an additional three or four nights home a month—something of critical importance to a father of younger children.

> *But why do so many sales managers function as doing managers, carrying their own accounts?*

Having too few salespeople is a great reason for a sales manager to act as a doing manger personally carrying accounts. But there are also a number of invalid reasons sales managers personally sell. Most of these invalid reasons are because so many sales managers came out of sales positions and never left their sales mentality.

The sales rep as super doer. A very common belief of almost all experienced sales professionals is that they can do almost anything better for their customers by just handling it themselves than to hassle with trying to get others in their company to help. An old joke among salespeople says the job of a sales rep is *to protect my customer from the incompetence of the rest of my organization.*

The vast majority of sales reps have had problems at some point with someone in their company not following up and supporting the customer as much, or as fast as they thought was needed. Because of being let down in the past, most knowledgeable salespeople will personally fulfill as many client requests as possible. This is why salespeople believe successful account management can be accomplished only by acting as a super doer. "If you want it done right you might as well do it yourself," is the mantra of most salespeople.

Look at the career evolution of the typical super doer sales rep. Bill had worked for an industrial gas and welding supply distributor for more than 12 years until he was promoted to VP of Sales for their 10-

person sales team. This was a job title he had spent his entire business life working to achieve, and he felt honored to be recognized for his skills by Howard, the company owner and president.

But Bill's company was a local small business and never even considered investing in any kind of sales management, coaching, or training. Howard, who really didn't understand selling, instead focused all of his attention on production and office matters. Bill's large ego had also led him to believe he did not need any sales management training.

This is the career path of the majority of sales managers. They excel in their sales job and demonstrate the potential to be a leader/manager. They are then promoted into sales management, given no training in their new job, yet are expected to be successful because they have spent their lives in sales.

How much sales management training and coaching were you given when you moved into sales management?

When I ask this question in my seminars, I find that, on average, more than 95 percent of a sales management audience has never received any type of sales management training or coaching. We are back to the invalid leadership assumption that experienced = trained covered in Chapter 1.

If you were Bill, how would you have approached your new leadership position? As expected Bill jumped right in, but more as a doer, than a manager. He immediately tried to do everything himself. He wanted to take over all of the important customer accounts and quickly earned the reputation among his sales team as someone to not take on a sales call. With his "doing" mentality he didn't see himself on the call as the VP of Sales with the responsibility of supporting the sales rep sitting next to him, he saw himself as the "best sales rep" on the team and would immediately try to take over the sales call as the lead sales rep. His attempts at selling not only confused customers but also tended to make the reps feel unimportant and not trusted by their manager.

Invalid Reasons for a Doing Manager to Personally Carry Accounts

Have you ever worked for a doing sales manager like Bill? In addition to the valid reasons already mentioned for sales managers to carry accounts there are also several invalid reasons for "doing manager" biased managers to be personally selling. How many of these invalid reasons do you use?

Doing manager rationale #1. "I need to be able to personally keep my finger on the pulse of our customers" This is the most common reason I hear when I ask doing managers why they still carry accounts. The "super doer" mentality believes the only way they could possible understand their customers would be by personally acting as a sales rep to some accounts.

Coaching Question #28 Can you pass the "super doer" sales management test?

The "super doer" sales management test *Do you have this tendency as a manager? Are you primarily carrying accounts so you can "Keep your finger on the pulse of your customers?"*

Let's assume you are spending 80 percent of your time as a sales leader managing your team. The final 20 percent (at least one day a week) you also spend personally handling three accounts. These three customers see you as their only rep with full responsibility for their business.

Which approach will give you a better understanding of your customers and industry? Spending 20 percent of your time working in-depth with three accounts or assigning those three accounts to a sales rep and investing your now freed-up 20 percent by visiting with every customer who buys from your company over the next year?

Consider the doer mentality of most sales managers. They believe the only way to understand their customer base is by personally working in depth with a few accounts instead of being able to communicate with the majority of their company's customers. Are you approaching your job as a managing manager leader of your sales team, or as the lead doer of your team?

Doing manager rational #2. "This account is just too important to turn over to someone less skilled than I am" This is the second most common reason I hear when I ask "doing managers" why they are still personally carrying accounts. Managers with super doer mentalities also assume they were promoted and are now in charge because they are indeed the top dog or best sales rep on the team.

There are three problems with this doing manager style of leadership. The first problem is they are assuming they were promoted to leadership because of their doing sales skills rather than their potential leadership skills.

This mentality contributes to the second problem with doing managers: They actually believe their job as the leader of a sales team is to sell. Even if you currently are the best salesperson on your team your job as a leader is not to sell (a doing mentality). The job of a leader is to help the members of your team to become better salespeople (a managing or leadership mentality).

In sports this is called "playing your position." It's the salesperson's job to sell. If you as the sales manager visit a customer, you are not there as a salesperson but as a representative of your company and the salesperson's manager. You don't create value trying to be another salesperson to that customer; you create value by showing your customer how interested and concerned your company's management is about their business and satisfaction.

The job of a sales manager is also to support your salesperson by being the next tier in customer negotiations. As a sales manager you gain more power negotiating price and terms than a salesperson does. But your value to the negotiations process is to help your sales reps take the negotiations to a higher level than they were able to achieve on their own. Your job as a sales manager is to also help your sales reps get higher, wider, or deeper within the account than they were able to achieve on their own. All of these functions, as a manager, are meant to increase the power, profitability, or visibility of your sales reps within their accounts. These activities enhance the selling efforts of your team but do not involve you actually doing any account selling with their customers.

The third, and most significant problem with the doing manager mentality of personally carrying accounts is that your presence as the sales rep actually reduces the support your customer receives. Even if you are the best sales rep on your team your covering an account reduces the total support your customer receives.

When you call on an account as a selling manager, your customer will still see you only as a sales rep. Customers have learned that job titles don't mean anything. Many full time doing sales reps have job titles of "Account Manager" or "Regional Sales Manager." Customers know that if you act like a salesperson and you talk like a salesperson, they won't care if you are really a sales manager.

What kind of upper management support are you able to provide your accounts? Who goes with you to your account when you want to impress them by bringing in a manager?

Imagine the alternative of you're acting like a managing manager or sales leader: You assign your accounts to another rep, who might even be a junior salesperson on your team. You stay actively involved as a coach and make calls as a manager but make sure you help your sales rep build their own presence with their customer. Now, when you go into that account the customer is receiving support from both a sales rep and their manager instead of a single sales rep. Are there any accounts you are currently covering that could benefit from an increase in support by having both an assigned sales rep and a manager actively involved?

Doing manager rationale #3. "How else do you justify my salary?" This is the third reason I hear from doing sales managers who are still carrying accounts. This reason may be based on either their thinking or that of their upper management.

Most doing managers don't really understand how to motivate and lead a sales team. They hang onto their own accounts because even though they don't know what they are doing as a manager, they feel they can't be fired because they still personally sold two million dollars worth of business last year.

Unfortunately a lot of sales managers continue to carry a territory only because of expectations of upper management. Does your boss understand the contributions a sales leader/manager is supposed to make to a sales team? Though the job of a sales manager is to help each individual to achieve more than he would have achieved if just left alone, there are still upper managers and owners who do not understand, or see the value in your helping and leading others to achieve more.

Coaching Question #29   What can you do to help change the "sales managers need to sell" expectations of your upper management?

It is critical to start changing upper management's perspective if they do not see your value as a coach and leader and see you only contributing based on your personal selling. One suggestion to help you change their thinking is to get them to read this book or at least the overviews that begin each section. Another is to track the individual sales numbers of each sales team member and then prove how much you would need to increase total sales to justify turning your accounts over to someone else. Getting a commitment from your company leadership that you would need to reach certain sales levels to become a full time manager, coach, and leader could help quantify to them (and your team) how you as a coach and sales leader are contributing to the growth and improvement of your sales team.

Coaching Question #30   Is it acceptable for you to be carrying your own accounts as a doing sales manager?

There are a number of factors that go into considering whether you should be carrying accounts. No matter what the justification, though, your company still might not be ready to have you as a full time sales leader, either due to staffing issues or the financial impact of losing your personal sales production. Even if you cannot make the change to full time sales leadership, you and your upper management can at least identify and analyze the potential costs that exist with you still spending time personally selling. You might also be able to begin a discussion of the payoffs to your company of your starting to move to full time sales leadership.

This is a transition that will require time and effort. The first goal of improving any sales organization is to make a clear and accurate evaluation of where you and your sales team are today. The second goal (following the *ISO 9000* concepts from Chapter 4) is for you and your upper management to identify the "best practices" for how your sales and sales leadership structures should function to maximize growth and selling success. Only after accomplishing these first two goals can you start to actually shift your leadership style and sales team toward your newly defined "best practices."

Coaching Question #31   What can you do to transition toward being a leader instead of just the lead doer?

It is important for you to first find out where your team really is by completing the evaluation of your sales leadership skills (Chapters 5 to 10) and the selling skills of each member of your sales team (Chapters 11 to 16). Only then will you be able to begin to identify, and then start moving toward increased levels of selling.

Once your evaluations are complete you can also start to define and focus on the "best practices" both you and your team need to be implementing. Once your goals or "best practices" are defined it is time for you, as the sales leader, to lead your team in the skill building necessary to successfully implement a "best practices" approach to selling.

7

Mastering Your Second Central Leadership Value— Being Balanced as a Coach, Disciplinarian, and Number Cruncher

The second of the five Central Leadership Values or philosophies involves your ability as a sales leader to balance the responsibilities of being a coach, disciplinarian, and number cruncher.

Chapter 2 explored how each organization is biased toward sales, technical, or financial aspects of business when making decisions and communicating their corporate values. It also addressed how most organizations, and their senior leaders, tend to have a bias toward one aspect, tolerate the second, and completely ignore or devalue the third.

We can apply this concept of being biased to your role as an effective sales leader by using a slightly modified set of biases. Which one of the three roles of coach, disciplinarian, or number cruncher do you personally value the most and in which would you like to see your company invest more effort? Even though all leaders are biased toward one of these three roles, the reality of your success as a sales leader will be based on your ability to provide at least some emphasis on each of these three functions.

Coaching Question #32   How balanced are you as a coach, disciplinarian, and number cruncher?

There is a simple test you can take (or administer to others) to help identify your personal bias. You will improve both the value and accuracy of this test if you complete this exercise before reading further in this book. Reading what to do with your answers in Step 2 before completing your answers will bias your results.

> *Step 1:* Write down in bulleted form all of the responsibilities and/or jobs of a sales manager.
>
> *Step 2:* Assign to each of your bulleted answers one of the three following roles or biases:
>
> - *Coaching bias.*   Your focus is to coach and lead each team member to do better and achieve more.
> - *Number crunching bias.*   Your focus is to keep score and to monitor the progress and profitability of each member of your team. This involves tracking and evaluating all sales and financial reports prepared by your sales team and other departments in your company.
> - *Disciplinarian bias.*   Your focus is to maintain the discipline, deadlines, and consistency of each member of your team. This involves making sure everyone meets their assigned deadlines, shows up on time, follows all of the assigned rules, and works hard with the proper attitudes.
>
> *Step 3:* Add the total number of responsibilities identified within each of the three roles. Is your listing blended in the three areas or have you identified where your personal bias lies?

This is only the first step of the *ISO 9000* improvement process covered in Chapter 4. Also consider giving this test to your boss to learn about their bias and how they expect you do your job. Ask them to complete this exercise by writing down all of the areas he or she expects you to manage as a leader of your sales team.

You can also complete this test with the members of your sales team, asking each of them to also build a list of all the duties for which they perceive you are responsible.

Determining the expectations and biases of both your boss and your team members can provide you with important insights into how others may define your success and where they may expect you to invest your efforts. You will significantly increase your success as a sales leader if you understand how others define that success.

Expect that you, your boss, and your sales team members will all have biased and incomplete definitions of what success means for the leader of a sales team. Now that we have defined the biases all members of your organization have about what it takes to be a successful sales leader, you can now move onto step two based on the ISO process and begin identifying what the "best practices" need to be for your job as sales team leader.

What is the best bias balance for a successful sales leader?

There is no one best bias for a leader of a sales team. Your business environment is like a giant jigsaw puzzle with your sales leadership piece being the last to be inserted in the middle of the puzzle. The shape of your jigsaw piece (or leadership bias) need to be defined by where others are and what they are missing.

For any leader of a team, the more balanced a leadership environment you can create, the more stable, productive, and successful your team will be. The more out of balance your team is, the less productive and effective you will be. The most successful sales leaders are those who are able to adjust their attention to provide what will complement the organization's current biases, instead of only focusing on their own personal bias. If your team is sales and coaching focused you may need to increase your role as disciplinarian and number cruncher.

One of the reasons the job of leading a sales team is so challenging is that a sales leader has four separate masters they need to serve and satisfy. Your entire environment may collapse around you if any one of these four masters becomes dissatisfied or disillusioned with your leadership efforts. The four masters a sales leader has to serve and satisfy are (in no particular order of importance):

Master #1: Your Boss and the Rest of Your Company's Upper Management

If Your Boss and the Rest of Your Company's Upper Management Are Too Focused on Coaching

A boss with a strong coaching bias will believe the most important job of a sales manager/leader is to coach and lead each member of their team to do better and achieve more.

Executives that have a tendency toward coaching others are constantly calling you, the sales leader, to offer suggestions on what your people could be doing better or how they can improve the service, support, and quality levels they are providing to your customers. They may also second guess you by telling you what they think you should have done or complaining about how long it took you to take action on a particular issue. In worst case situations these upper managers may take it upon themselves to personally tell your people what they are doing wrong, how they could be doing better, and which ideas should be implemented. Coaching executives can cause significant problems by taking away, or undermining, your leadership of your team.

Are you working for or with any of these coaching senior executives? If so, one of the first decisions you have to make is if you are willing to take a risk by standing up to your boss, a senior executive in your company.

The next step is to go to your boss and share your concerns with him, explaining how the outside interference with your coaching efforts is distracting the team and compromising your authority. You will also need your boss's support and agreement if you are to take on someone higher up than you are in the company. Never fight this type of battle alone. Protecting you from the other departments and senior executives is one of the critically important jobs of your boss. If at all possible you want your boss fighting this battle for you instead of trying to solve it yourself.

You also want to meet with your sales team and make sure they understand what your expectations are and your concerns about the outside advice being communicated to your people. You also want to make sure your team members understand how you expect them to handle a senior executive getting too involved and giving them orders. They need to understand that it is your job, not theirs, to take on or disagree with a senior executive's involvement and directives, and that their only first response after getting too much help and guidance is to contact you so you can get involved.

If Your Boss and the Rest of Your Company's Upper Management Are Too Focused on Number Crunching

Someone with a strong number crunching bias will believe the most important job of a sales manager/leader is to provide upper management and the rest of the organization with detailed, timely, and accurate information on the progress and profitability of each sales team member. Both the demands for and proliferation of information within an organization tends to grow uncontrolled unless specifically managed.

Several years ago (before the availability of most company information online) Paul was hired to take over the sales team of an investment company. After he started work in his new job he was amazed at all of the computer-generated reports he saw around the sales office. A number of these reports were several inches thick and he rarely saw anyone using them. In his second week in the job he demanded all reports coming into his sales team's office be personally delivered to him. He told all his team members he was glad to let them use any of the reports he received; they just had to get them from his office.

Within 30 days he discovered that more than 60 percent of the reports produced were never used by anyone in his department. He was able to save tens of thousands of dollars annually in internal computer charges to his department by just eliminating unused and useless reports.

The problem was that 18 months later his report reduction accomplishment was still his only success. Having a focus on number crunching made him great at improving the numbers and information flows of his department; he just never did anything of significance to improve the selling processes utilized by his sales team. After a year and a half of not making any significant sales improvements, he was replaced as head of sales.

A boss who is focused on numbers will be constantly demanding too much information on a too frequent basis. Valid and timely information is needed to run any business, but there has to be a balance between the value of the information being demanded and the opportunity costs of the time your salespeople devote to producing the requested reporting. Too many sales leaders are dealing with so many extensive information demands from upper management and the other departments that they and/or their salespeople have little time left to actually sell.

This is also the same problem that exists today with e-mail. Some reps get as many as 30 to 60 e-mails a day from other departments within their company requesting detailed, time burning information. Some sales reps are spending as much as three hours a day responding to company generated e-mail requests for information. How are the number crunching biased executives and other departments within your company slowing down the time available for your sales team to actually be selling?

Most of the Customer Relationship Management (CRM) computer systems being installed in businesses today are designed to reduce the paperwork and information demands being made of sales teams. The goal of an effective CRM system is to provide a centralized collection of data on each customer that is available to the entire sales organization. Data being tracked for each customer or prospect includes information on the customer contacts, calling activities, orders processed, current project details, and future selling plans. CRM systems organize in-depth information on all activities within an account reported by, and accessible to, all sales team members. CRM systems when properly managed can offer significantly improved customer tracking and communications tools to the entire sales team.

But you, as the sales leader, need to make sure your old reporting systems are actually being eliminated now that you are using the more current CRM software. Any CRM computer program will demand more time from a sales force compared to the old tracking systems to enter and maintain all of the information required of these customer tracking programs. But the worst-case scenario occurs when the new customer tracking software increases the sales workloads without also removing any of the old tracking and/or reporting systems.

Are you working for or with senior executives who have a number crunching bias? If you do, you need to develop a plan to effectively reduce their sales time demands.

First, do your homework and evaluate how much information is being demanded from your team and how much time they actually spend generating the requested reports. It is the universal truth of salespeople that they always feel they are asked to generate too much paperwork and your demands for information are excessive. You need to address their reluctance to providing this information and collect valid quantified data on their efforts and time investments to decide if the information requests from within your company are either valid or excessive.

Assuming the information being requested is excessive, you need to evaluate how much time (and the associated labor costs) are being invested in each of the information requests in question. With a quantified summary of how much sales time is being lost by your team and how much this time loss is costing your company you can go to your manager to discuss potential solutions. Bringing valid researched data on the actual costs of the current information requests should give your boss the ammunition she needs to help you fight this battle. Remember that the only way to successfully win a fight with a number cruncher is by providing valid and detailed data.

If Your Boss and the Rest of Your Company's Upper Management Are Too Focused on Being a Disciplinarian

Someone with a strong disciplinarian bias will believe the most important job of a sales manager/leader is to control the naturally undisciplined sales team by providing the necessary discipline, deadlines, and consistency so the entire sales team meets their assigned deadlines, shows up on time, follows all of the assigned rules, and is working hard.

Senior managers focused on being a disciplinarian tend to remind you to get tougher with your sales team and encourage you to put your foot down. They also tend to communicate from a negative perspective wanting to tell you what is wrong or what wasn't done rather than point out the positives and opportunities.

These senior managers believe with more discipline comes more effort, more commitment, and more results. Because of this they also try to increase the rules, procedures, and consequences whenever possible and look for opportunities to provide negative feedback (they call it constructive criticism) directly to your salespeople whenever given the chance.

As with the number crunching senior managers discussed previously who were getting too close to your leadership responsibility, you need to first go to your boss, share your concerns, and ask for help to allow you to be the leader of your sales team. To be safe you also want to start a private log of any senior manager's "too close" efforts. One instance can always be dismissed as an exception, but multiple incidents by an intruding senior manager reprimanding members of your team may mean this is an ongoing problem that needs to be corrected. You also need to meet with your sales team to discuss your concerns regarding the senior manager's efforts to insure that your team keeps you informed of these activities. It is critical for your team to understand how you want them to handle these situations.

Master #2: Your Customers

If Your Customers Are Too Focused on Coaching

A customer with a strong coaching bias tends to believe the most important job of a sales manager/leader is to coach and lead each member of their team to provide more consistent and timely support.

These customers are constantly calling you, the sales leader, directly to offer their ideas on what your people could be doing better or how they want/expect them to improve the service, support, and quality levels currently being provided by your company.

Having customers who tell you what they want and what you can do to improve their buying experience is a positive, but when customers become too focused on coaching you or your team, they tend to go overboard constantly telling your salespeople how to do their job, telling you how they expect you to change your leadership, or ordering your team to conform to their expectations.

Similar to dealing with "too involved" senior executives discussed earlier, it is important to make sure your sales team is aware of your concerns about these surprise inputs and directions they might be receiving from their customers. You want to make sure they understand how to best handle these situations as they arise. Also remind your team that it is your responsibility, not theirs, to address a customer's involvement and that their response to customers demanding changes in protocol should be to contact you so you can get involved.

If Your Customers Are Too Focused on Number Crunching

A customer with a strong number crunching bias believes the most important job of a sales team is to provide detailed and constantly updated information about products, order schedules, and usage volumes.

A customer requesting more usage, product, or tracking information can be a good thing unless it becomes disruptive or if the information demands become excessive. How much extra time do you and your salespeople have to invest in preparing all of the financial and product usage data that is being requested?

These customers are constantly calling you and their salespeople asking for additional, unusual, or complicated reports. Making customized information controls and reports available to customers is a positive unless the customer demands and reporting efforts are greater than the profitability their account is generating. The reality of most customers who focus on number crunching is that they tend to ask for the most reporting while still expecting to pay the lowest prices.

Does this sound like any of your team's current customers? If you suspect a customer's demands for information are becoming excessive, you need to first evaluate the information requests from the customer's perspective. Is their request valid? Too often customers' requests are considered excessive or unnecessary because they are the only customers requesting a particular action. Determining how to efficiently provide a customer's information requests can result in discovering alternative methods of providing better information, thereby creating a competitive advantage for your company.

If their requests are identified as too excessive, you have some options as to how to proceed. One option is to simply tell your customer you will not be fulfilling their information requests, and potentially compromise the relationship. Another option more likely to ensure a more positive outcome would be to continue fulfilling their requests and just adjust their prices.

Instead of saying no to a customer, you can explain that the information requests are greater than those your company normally provides or has ever agreed to. You need to reaffirm you want to continue to be responsive to their requests, but can only do so by applying a 5 percent pricing increase. You may not be able to get more money for your sales-people's efforts, but you can at least negotiate for something in return for the increased time required to satisfy their information demands. If this solution does not work, you need to decide if the extra labor expended on number crunching is worth the business at its current level of profitability. It might be best for you and your company to part ways with these excessively demanding customers.

If Your Customers Are Too Focused on Being the Disciplinarian

Customers with a strong disciplinarian bias believe they need to help you, the sales leader, to manage your sales team. These customers may even retract orders or demand extra discounts if they feel their sales rep has either made a mistake or is not being responsive enough to their demands. Similar to the biased senior managers focused on being disciplinarians, these customers feel they need to implement stronger expectations of discipline from the salespeople, and to help straighten out any salesperson not measuring up to their high expectations.

One of the best ways to handle a customer's focus on being a disciplinarian is to play along in your conversations with them so they feel they are appreciated and respected. As a sales leader you may need to tell the customer what discipline you plan to give the offending sales rep because of a wrong made against this customer, even if you feel the salesperson was doing what needed to be done. Next, all you have to do is tell the sales rep how you solved the problem and to be aware that as far as the customer was concerned they were reprimanded.

Master #3: The Other Departments and Workers within Your Company

If the Departments and Workers within Your Company Are Too Focused on Coaching

Other departments or workers in your company with a strong coaching bias believe your main job as a sales manager/leader is to coach and lead your team.

These types of individuals are constantly telling you, as the sales leader, how you and your sales team could be selling more or doing a better job supporting your customers. In extreme cases they communicate ideas, feedback, and even orders directly to your salespeople without your knowledge or consent.

Though it is usually beneficial to receive assistance and feedback from other departments, your salespeople and the rest of your company need to understand you are in charge of the sales team and are the final decision maker on the discipline, structures, processes, and direction of your team.

As with the too involved senior executives or customers discussed earlier you need to make sure your sales team understands how you expect these types of situations to be handled and when it is appropriate for them to involve you.

It is important to be sure others within your company understand that you are open to feedback, both positive and negative, but you also need to make sure they understand that the best way to structure this communication is for them to provide positive ideas and feedback directly to your sales team members, but provide negative feedback or concerns directly to you so you can then handle the feedback and changes of sales behaviors yourself.

If the Departments and Workers within Your Company Are Too Focused on Number Crunching

Someone with a strong number crunching bias believes the most important job of a sales manager/leader is to provide the rest of the organization with detailed, timely, accurate, and complete information on the progress and profitability of each sales team member.

This is a scenario you will likely face from the other departments within your company: A standard philosophy of most employees is that "My department is the most important department within this company. If it wasn't for us this company would have collapsed a long time ago." Along with this belief they tend to also believe all of the other departments should be providing them with all the numbers and reporting that they need to be a success, even if this work detracts from the other departments accomplishing their own goals and responsibilities.

Though this is a common attitude held by most workers, this mindset tends to put excessive reporting and information collection demands on the sales force. These demands become stronger if any department feels they are working harder (or earning less) than the sales force. Since a sales team is often away from the office meeting with customers, many of these number crunching individuals aren't aware of how much work your salespeople do on a daily basis.

One of the best ways to handle these types of excessive information demands is to begin assigning a "sales hours required to fulfill" number for each report demanded of a sales team. How many hours will this information request take to complete by the entire sales team? What is the opportunity cost of this information request?

Despite the amount of time these demands can take, it is critical you still affirm the importance of the information being requested. Challenging the validity of information requests tends to increase the amount of demands and resistance. If you feel the need to involve higher management to resolve excessive demands, then you do not need to challenge the validity of their information requests. Just point out the excessive amount of time necessary to collect the requested information. Now you are fighting a financial fight and are more likely to get your upper management to support your challenge.

Another alternative is to utilize your negotiations skills. Instead of agreeing to the entire information request, is there a way you could provide only part of the information they have requested but with a much lower investment of sales time?

If the Departments and Workers within Your Company Are Too Focused on Being Disciplinarians

Those with a strong disciplinarian bias believe the most important job of a sales manager/leader is to control what they perceive as an undisciplined sales team by providing the necessary discipline, deadlines, and consistency so the entire sales team meets their assigned deadlines, shows up on time, follows all of the assigned rules, and is working hard.

These individuals from other departments expect you to get tougher with your sales team. Like the suggestions offered earlier with handling a disciplinarian senior executive, when these other workers attempt to discipline your team, you want to first get the support of your boss. Make sure you document multiple instances of times when the other individuals or departments are getting too involved. You will also need to meet with your sales team to alert them to your concerns and to instruct them in how you want them to handle these situations in the future.

Master #4: The Members of Your Sales Team

As we discussed in Chapter 3, the second commitment necessary to generate long-term change and success within a sales force is for each member of your sales team to accept you as their leader and to agree to follow you.

If the Members of Your Sales Team Are Too Focused on Coaching

One of the components of a successful sales team is to have a strong sales leader who acts as a coach and strategist. Your objective as a sales leader is to coach each member of your team to perform better and achieve more.

Having a sales team that is too focused on coaching is rarely a problem. Most sales reps are so independent that they brag about not needing any coaching from anyone. You can identify a sales team that is too coaching driven when all they seem to want to do is to meet with you to plan, debate, and discuss what they should be doing or working on next. Planning is a beneficial component to leading a team, but it is possible to spend so much time planning that no one is actually going out making sales calls. One of the ways salespeople can delay having to call on a customer is to keep asking questions and discussing alternatives with their manager.

What can you do as the sales leader if your sales team is too focused on coaching? The first suggestion with any team out of balance is for you, as their leader, to lean to the functions they are avoiding and to downplay the functions they are strongest at performing.

If your sales team is too coaching biased you need to allow the coaching efforts to continue but with an increased focus on discipline and questioning on how and when any kind of implementation will occur.

If your sales team is not focused on coaching, you need to increase your dialogue about their efforts and plans for selling to their accounts.

Many more ideas on how to increase your coaching of a sales team are covered in the rest of this book.

If the Members of Your Sales Team Are Too Focused on Number Crunching

One of the responsibilities of a sales team is to provide information to their sales leadership and the other departments within your company. Your number crunching task as their sales leader is to track the progress and profitability of each team member including evaluating all of the sales and financial reports generated by either the sales team or other departments.

Being too concerned with number crunching is also rarely a problem for most sales teams. The reality is most salespeople despise all paperwork and report generation. The third commitment covered in Chapter 3 is the need to gain the sales team's commitment to your required communications structures. Since salespeople by nature tend to be loners and most experienced and successful salespeople feel they create job security by sharing as little as possible about their accounts and new business opportunities, they tend to withhold information. This underreporting of territory activities also helps them appear more professional since you can't see the details of their lack of account controls and plans.

How complete and timely are all of the territory reports from your sales team? Are their call reports complete, detailed, and insightful? Are their expense reports thorough and submitted on time?

You can tell if a sales team is too focused on number crunching by analyzing how much time they spend on their reports, customer tracking information, and e-mails. A team too concerned with number crunching tends to use their data preparation and analysis time as an excuse to not be out selling.

What you can do as the sales leader if your sales team spends too much time crunching numbers? You may be laughing about even the possibility of a sales team actually "reporting" too much information but it does exist, especially within highly technical or engineering biased sales teams. The more technical and/or engineering biased you are, the more uncomfortable you will tend to be selling and especially prospecting. Also the less sales focused, experienced, or comfortable you are about selling the more you might rely on excessive reporting and data analysis as a way to reduce your selling and prospecting time.

John was the new VP of Sales for his engineering design and consulting company. He was hired for a position where his primary responsibility was to increase the sales volumes of his company, especially the new account sales volumes.

John immediately directed his sales team to initiate a new business prospecting program. He indicated he wanted each of his seven sales reps to start spending at least 20 percent of their time prospecting for new accounts. John made a slight oversight though. He had not evaluated where his team's current selling skill levels were and, even more important, he had not recognized the team's focus on number crunching.

After John's new business program had been in place for three weeks, he sat down with each team member to evaluate their new business progress and to offer coaching assistance. John quickly discovered no one had yet made any prospecting calls but all had spent a great deal of time researching all of the possible new prospects on the Internet and had been generating detailed new business action plans.

If your sales team spends too much time number crunching you may need to conduct an information reporting review with your team. Collect copies of each report that is either being given to your sales team or they are producing, and evaluate the complete information reporting structures currently in place for your sales team. What reports are producing redundant information? What data being collected is just not important enough to invest time generating instead of selling and working with clients? What outside departments are asking for excessive levels of reporting detail from your sales team? What information, being collected or processed, might be completed by someone outside your sales team?

One of the ways to get a sales team to reduce their dependence on information management is to first evaluate their current information production levels, identify the best data to be producing and analyzing, and work with each team member to help them understand the importance, and benefit of modifying their information generation efforts. Notice this is just directing you to implement the first thee steps based on the *ISO 9000* improvement process.

If your sales team is not focused enough on number crunching, you may need to increase your expectations and requirements for information. Complete the exercise above where you organize all of the data analysis demands and reporting being handled by your team. Evaluate if the current information being provided to your sales team and also being generated by them is sufficient for you to have the necessary aware-ness and vision of your team's efforts.

Once you identify the "best practices" of the information controls you want in place, then you need to educate your team members and the rest of your company as to the benefits of your new information gener-ating "best practices." Once you have decided on the information pro-duction levels, you need to track and coach your people to fulfill your assigned deadlines and accuracy requirements.

If the Members of Your Sales Team Are Too Focused on Being Disciplinarians

A component of a successful sales team is their ability to be well orga-nized, efficient, and effective in their assigned responsibilities. Is your team disciplined and consistent in their efforts? Your job as their sales leader is to make sure your team meets their assigned deadlines, is show-ing up on time, follows all of the assigned rules, and is working hard.

An undisciplined sales team wastes tremendous amounts of time. How often do your sales meetings start and end on time? If your weekly meetings are consistently starting 10 minutes late because of tardy team members, then you are wasting hours each month with your team members just sitting around waiting for your meetings to fi-nally start. That's hours of opportunity cost that could have been spent selling or prospecting!

How disciplined and efficient are you and the members of your sales team? Like excessive number crunching, excessive discipline is rarely a problem in a sales team. Most sales managers are constantly fighting the lack of discipline and structures within their team.

A team too focused on discipline is usually that way due to the in-fluences of upper management or the style of their past sales leader. A team too discipline biased will be so focused on doing everything exactly by the book that they become less productive or effective. Motivational sales trainer and speaker Zig Ziglar is quoted as saying, "Are you spend-ing so much of your time trying to do things right that you aren't even doing the right things?" A team that is too disciplined and structured will be so focused on the details of *how* they are supposed to be doing their jobs that they might miss opportunities of *what* they can be doing to increase their sales.

If you have a sales team of disciplinarians, you need to find out why. Though I am sure they do exist, I have never seen a sales team that was too focused on discipline on their own. Their too disciplined behaviors are most likely based on the demands or requirements of others. You want a disciplined sales team, but you also want them loose and responsive enough to react quickly to new opportunities and to be projecting a positive image to your customers.

Meet with each sales rep discussing what the rules and expectations are of the sales team. Your goal is to first identify what they perceive the rules and procedures are and then decide if that is the level of discipline and control you feel will be best for the team and their overall success.

And getting back to reality . . . if your sales team is not disciplined enough, you need to increase your expectations and requirements for their behaviors. Conduct a team meeting where you define the deadlines, rules, and procedures you expect all team members to follow. It is critical to explain why each requirement is important and how it contributes to the overall team's stability and success. Most managers assign new rules and procedures without explaining why they are important and contribute to the overall success of a team. It's important to allow for ventilation and disagreement. Finally, discuss what the consequences will be for not following or fulfilling these assigned disciplines.

Be careful not to tighten up the rules and requirements too fast. Discipline is something that has to be developed. You will fail and be rejected if you try to force too many new rules into place with too drastic a set of consequences. You need to ease a sales team into conformity and acceptance of new rules and procedures. Rushing new disciplines might cause your sales team to become so distracted and distressed that their overall selling effectiveness and success is effected.

> How balanced are you as a sales leader and what can you do to insure everyone else is also showing balance?

Success in sales leadership is based on your ability to balance your own biases and to adjust your biases to balance the rest of your sales organization. Increasing your awareness of the natural biases of your senior management, co-workers outside of sales, your customers, and your sales team is the first step for you to strengthen your organization.

The next step to help strengthen your sales organization and sales leadership is to complete the 20 question sales leadership evaluation covered in Section III. This will help you identify the balance of your skills and can help you prioritize which of your leadership skills will benefit the most when strengthened.

Working to strengthen your Central Leadership Values covered in this section can also help you define and implement the sales leadership best practices that will generate the strongest success levels for you and your entire team. Remember this entire improvement process is based on the idea, *I know you are good; this is the process that can help you to get even better.*

8

Mastering Your Third Central Leadership Value—Having Empathy, Loyalty, and Trust in Your Sales Team

The third of the five central leadership values critical to all successful sales leaders involves your ability, as a leader, to be open and empathetic to your staff. There is an old leadership motivational phrase that says, "People will not care to learn until they learn you care."

A major component of successful leadership occurs when your team members believe and understand you are on their side and truly care about them and their personal success.

Robert was the Senior VP and head of the trust department of a major bank. Now 61 years old, he has spent his entire career working through the leadership levels of banking trust. Robert was a true expert in both business and personal trust but was a weak and disconnected leader of his trust officers. In banking the position of trust officer is really a selling position with responsibility to either grow their assigned trust accounts or to help develop new trust business.

Robert considered himself a great leader and felt his trust team valued him and his leadership style. It was amusing to hear him brag about how much his people loved him when in reality he was not trusted and was severely disliked by the majority of the trust officers reporting to him. A common complaint about Robert was expressed by a trust officer who said, "Robert never tells you anything positive about what you have accomplished and only seems to dwell on what you didn't do or what you could have done better. He never makes you feel like you are doing a good job and hasn't given anyone a compliment in years."

Chapter 2 discussed how all employees and organizations tend to have a bias toward the sales, technical, or financial aspects of business. Robert focused most of his efforts on financial matters but had weak communication and interpersonal skills. One problem Robert had was that he believed he was very funny, but no one ever understood his humor. He would say something he thought was funny but it was received by his trust officers as either cutting or negative. Robert was the kind of leader who assumed all of his team members already knew they were doing a good job so he didn't need to waste time affirming or saying anything positive to his people.

What percent of your communications is positive versus negative? Evaluate the last 10 conversations you had with your sales team. How many of those conversations involved your saying anything to your sales rep that was either affirming or empathetic?

Bert was one of the newer trust officers working for Robert. Bert also had been assigned to work with Mrs. Slate, one of the larger, and more difficult personal trust account customers. No matter what or how hard Bert tried, it seemed he could never completely satisfy Mrs. Slate and her expectations. Robert was meeting with Bert to help develop a course of action based on a recent telephone conversation Robert had with Mrs. Slate. During Robert and Bert's conversation it became evident Robert had sided with Mrs. Slate and was criticizing Bert for not being responsive enough with her account. Even though Bert complained about all the extra efforts he had been investing in this account, Robert kept coming back to his standard statement of "Well then, it's evident you are still not doing enough to satisfy your customer."

Bert left Robert's office completely dejected and demotivated thinking Robert just didn't seem to appreciate how tough Mrs. Slate was being with her demands and how hard he was working. But even as Bert left feeling dejected and unappreciated Robert actually thought he was able to provide good ideas to help Bert with Mrs. Slate.

A successful sales leader offers more than suggestions, critiques, and ideas. She needs to also offer support and affirmations. The most successful leaders are able to maintain a balance between the amount of positive and negative feedback they provide to their sales team members. Salespeople receive enough negative comments and feedback from their customers and the other departments within their company. Where do they get their positive inputs and encouragement?

Coaching Question #33   What can you do to reevaluate your personal balance of positive to negative comments?

Listen to the conversations in your office. Most sales leaders spend as much as 90 percent of their total communications on negative issues and feedback.

You will be ineffective as a leader if you only provide either all positive or all negative feedback. Successful leadership requires a balance. Consider working to communicate your empathy and affirmations for the person and how hard they are working while still working to help them improve their current efforts. You can provide feedback without being negative. Ken Blanchard, author of the *One Minute Manager* suggests, "Catching your people doing something right instead of only looking for them to be doing something wrong."

> But what about those times when you do need to communicate negative information to a salesperson?

The reality of business is that there will definitely be times when you need to communicate your concerns or the unacceptability of team members' actions. This is not suggesting you just become the positive pumper in your office ignoring and avoiding anything negative or a problem. The key is to make sure the overall communications is positive to keep your salesperson motivated and excited about their work.

For example, you learned that Jane, one of your newer salespeople missed an important customer appointment. You learned of her missed appointment because of a 20-minute, angry phone call from her customer. You call Jane into your office to share your concerns and to impress upon her that you expect her to never miss this important a meeting again. Here are two scenarios.

In the first scenario, you handle the initial conversation with Jane as most managers would, dealing with your concern for her missed appointment.

"Jane, you missed a really critical appointment today and your customer is very upset. Missing this important an appointment is completely unacceptable and you need to understand I expect it to never happen again."

How would you feel if you were Jane and you were just told this by your manager? How positive would you feel about your job? How would you think your boss felt about you and your future?

Most salespeople would feel completely negative about this conversation. It is critical that you, as sales leader, make sure your team members understand the consequences and problems caused when they make a mistake. But you also need to be a leader doing everything you can to help your people be hard workers and excited about their job. How hard do you think Jane worked the rest of the day?

The alternative to giving Jane that feedback involves your separating the individual from their actions. Bill McGrane Sr., a self-esteem consultant from Cincinnati, Ohio, identified that most people do not have strong enough self-esteem to separate themselves from their actions. So if Jane's self-esteem is not as complete as it needs to be this negative conversation from her boss about her mistaken actions could be perceived by her as meaning her boss doesn't like her. Now that her self-esteem has been challenged, she will also tend to not work as hard and not be as positive as she needs to be with her customers.

The solution Bill identified is that you, as her sales leader, need to give her straight feedback as to the problems she has caused her customer and your company, but in such a way that you don't destroy her motivation or self-esteem. Consider this second scenario with Jane.

"Jane, I know you're working hard but you missed a really critical appointment today and your customer is very upset. I have watched how much extra effort you put into doing a good job for all of your customers, but missing this important an appointment is completely unacceptable. I know you can do a better job of managing your time. You are a promising young salesperson and I expect you to achieve tremendous success in your selling career with this company."

How would you feel if you were Jane and your boss had given you this second set of feedback? Notice that the same negative comments about Jane's actions were present in both statements. But in the second statement, there were also affirming comments about Jane's potential and how hard she has been working.

Do you think both statements communicate to Jane how upset you were with her actions? Now consider which of the two statements would generate more long-term efforts and positive attitudes about her job. You can keep an even negative feedback session positive by affirming the *person* while communicating your concerns or the problems their *actions* have caused.

Your job as a leader is to give your team members the credit but you take the responsibility.

Another way to strengthen the loyalty and trust of your team is to make sure your team members get the credit when they are successful.

Several years ago I was presenting at the annual national sales meeting of an electronics parts distributor. Mike, the VP of Sales picked Wendy, one of his more promising salespeople to give a brief presentation at the meeting. This presentation was a big opportunity for Wendy to be showcased in front of all her company's senior management. Both Wendy and Mike were nervous about her presentation and they had worked on her speech for several weeks. Mike had personally coached Wendy to insure she did a good job.

Wendy did a fantastic job when it was her turn in front of the microphone. That evening at the group dinner Mike, in front of Wendy, told everyone how proud he was of Wendy and the great job she had done—just the way he had taught her to do it. Watching this all unfold, it was evident how Wendy felt Mike sabotaged her. How much loyalty do you think Wendy now has for Mike after he publicly took her success away from her?

How would you have handled the dinner with Wendy?

91

The job of a sales manager is to help each of your people achieve more than they would have achieved if you just left them alone. Mike's job was to make sure Wendy did the best job possible in front of everyone. But his job was also to make sure Wendy felt empowered and positive by her experience. Mike's biggest error with this situation was he put himself in front of his salesperson.

If Wendy had messed up, it would have been appropriate for Mike to take the responsibility for not coaching her enough to insure her success. But Wendy did a good job. Now Mike's job should have been to help make sure Wendy got all of the positives she deserved for her great presentation.

One of the best ways to build loyalty and support within your sales team is to make sure they understand you are on their side and will help them fight their battles. That includes helping to divert some of the negatives if things don't go right, but it also includes making sure you help intensify the positives for your team when things do go right. What can you do to make sure your team members are getting more positives from the rest of your company?

Coaching Question #34   What can you do to communicate your empathy, loyalty, and trust in your sales team?

Your success as a leader is based on your ability to help your team members feel you care about them, show empathy, and communicate your trust and support of them and their efforts. You can do this by making sure your communications are more positive and that you blend positive comments about the person with the negative comments that are needed to address their actions.

Remember you cannot effectively lead a team until they first have decided they want to follow you as their leader.

9

Mastering Your Fourth Central Leadership Value—Being a Leadership Visionary

The fourth of the five central leadership values critical to your success is your ability to be a visionary leader. "Visionary leadership" is your ability to combine staying proactively focused in your leadership efforts while also maintaining a future focus in your conversations and planning efforts.

Coaching Question #35 **What percent of your sales leadership time over the past 30 days was based on your initiating proactive actions?**

Are you spending more time being proactive or reactive? Proactive efforts are anything you initiate. Reactive efforts are those efforts initiated (or caused) by someone else. A sales rep calling on a new prospect is proactive. Making a sales call on a new prospect following up on a lead someone gave you is reactive. Contacting a customer to express concern that a shipping problem might have occurred and requesting your customer to allow you to double-check their order is proactive. Calling on your customer to take an inventory because they called saying their order wasn't complete is reactive.

Which will make you a better sales leader, announcing to your team your door is always open (reactive) or scheduling time with each team member to discuss and help plan their future selling efforts for each of their most active accounts (proactive)?

A consistent problem with both salespeople and sales leaders is that they spend the majority of their work day in reactive mode. How many times have you come into work on Monday with a detailed list of To Dos but went home at the end of the day with your original list untouched, and an additional 20 items added to it? Most people spend the majority of their job just responding to others instead of being the one who initiates the efforts.

The majority of sales managers are only reactive transaction managers. The majority of their conversations with their team are based on solving transaction based problems such as:

"Can you help me get a special price for this customer?"
"Can you help me expedite this order?"
"Can you help me straighten out this customer invoice?"

These are all transactional questions asked by salespeople. What are you and your sales team doing to gain a competitive advantage in your marketplace? Few organizations are able to gain a sustainable competitive advantage because of their reactive selling efforts.

Which of these two situations could actually increase your account loyalty and your competitive advantage? In the first situation a customer calls to tell you he is having a crisis. Last night he had a major warehouse fire and all of your products they inventory for resell to their customers were destroyed. Your customer called you to ask for an emergency reshipment so they can continue to fulfill customer orders. You schedule an emergency shipment and your company delivers the new products by the end of the day. Were you proactive or reactive in your efforts?

Now consider the second situation where, learning of your customer warehouse fire on the morning news, you drove straight from home to check on your customer's situation. Seeing that your products were destroyed in the fire, you call your office and begin arranging for an emergency shipment. You find your customer contact and share your discovery of your destroyed products and your already started efforts to replenish your inventory by the end of today.

Which situation made a more significant impression on the customer? Which situation would have helped increase your competitive advantage with your customer? In both cases you were the hero getting them products by the end of the day. But look how much more impressive the second example is over the first. In the first all you did was reactively respond to a customer's problem. But in the second example you initiated the efforts without being asked.

Symptoms of Reactive Behaviors

Though it makes sense that all members of your sales team should be proactive, the reality is most salespeople are almost completely reactive in their selling efforts.

Coaching Question #36   How do you know when a salesperson is being too reactive?

You know your sales reps are too reactive if

- They are always coming to you saying they need to be given more sales leads.
- They begin their week each Monday by opening their mail, reading e-mails, and checking voicemail messages to decide what they need to work on for the week.
- They are doing little to no new business prospecting.
- They ask only these five questions (in order) when on an existing customer sales call:
  1. "Everything okay?"
  2. "Any problems or concerns you need my help with?"
  3. "Any new opportunities or projects I can get involved in?"
  4. "When do you want me to call on you again?"
  5. "Is there anything else I can do to be of help or assistance?"

Coaching Question #37 **How can you tell when a sales manager is being too reactive?**

You know you are too reactive as the leader of a sales team if

- You wait for a sales rep to ask for help with an account before you get involved.
- You assume all of your sales reps have a plan in place for each of their assigned accounts even though you have never asked about it.
- You believe your customer relationships as a manager are so strong that your customers will call you if they don't feel their sales rep is doing a good job.
- You believe all of your sales reps are so experienced that you do not need to conduct any training (experienced = trained from Chapter 1).

So how reactive are you and your sales people? What can you do as their sales leader to increase your proactive efforts?

The Proactive Aspects of Being a Visionary Leader

Part of being a visionary leader is to make sure your team sees you as a proactive initiator. Reactive leaders feel they need only to check the current levels to be effective. They believe their job is to make sure everyone is performing above minimum. A reactive leader will also put little support into one of their higher performing sales team members, believing they don't need any help. Reactive efforts tend to at best maintain stable results.

If you want to be more proactive as a leader, consider strengthening these skills/efforts:

- *Commit to being a proactive coach and helping each of your people get better and achieve more.* Instead of just waiting for them to ask for help, go to them and ask to discuss their territory and growth plans. Ask them to describe what their plans and strategies are for their top, most important accounts. Help them identify and clarify their account strategies and upcoming plans.

96

- *Continually evaluate and check on all areas you are responsible for.* A proactive leader will keep evaluating and asking about efforts in every territory instead of just waiting for someone to ask for help. The proactive leader feels her responsibility is to help all salespeople see all of the opportunities in their territory sooner than they would on their own and to help identify any problems or vulnerabilities earlier. Sooner and earlier are both actions that can help increase your competitive differentiation and customer satisfaction.

  To be a more proactive leader, you need to keep asking all of your salespeople for territory briefings, updates on specific accounts, and progress reports on already developed customer selling plans. Your goal is to help them discover issues or opportunities they haven't yet discovered on their own.

  Conduct a strategy session a minimum of once a week with each sales team member. This meeting can either be face to face or by phone. Some weeks your meeting might last several hours while other times it might only be a 15-minute update. The goals of these sessions are for you to (1) understand what has happened and what is planned for their account, (2) help identify what the best new business selling goals and plans are to win or keep this business, and (3) help identify all of the customer's decision makers, influencers, or observers your rep needs to be selling to that could affect the political outcome of the final buying decision.

  Your best role as a proactive coach is to keep asking questions. "What if . . . what about . . . have you considered? . . . Who else?" are the kinds of coaching questions you need to keep asking. The goal of these strategy sessions is for you to help your salespeople identify, consider, plan out, or predict more about what is happening in their territory than they currently realize.

- *Look for skill or awareness transfer opportunities in your sales team.* In Chapter 1 Coaching Question #5 asked "Are you managing a team of mountain men/women or are you leading a SWAT team?"

  Most sales teams function as mountain men/women where each sales rep focuses only on themselves. If one of your reps has a great idea of how to shorten their selling process, how is that idea being shared with the rest of your team? As a proactive leader you need to be looking to see if any of your sales team members have discovered (sometimes without their awareness) any new skills or awareness that might help the rest of your team increase their success. Then your job is to make sure the rest of the team benefits from this newly discovered awareness.

Consider conducting group strategy sessions where all members of your team get together to review what has been working and what selling ideas didn't work in the past few months. Remember your goal is to run your sales team with the SWAT team mentality that "What one learns all benefit." (Chapter 1).

- *Keep asking questions.* The best proactive leaders are the ones who are able to ask the questions they don't even know the answers to. What can you do to ask your sales team members questions neither you nor they have thought of? Your providing a different awareness might help them also identify different opportunities within their territory. By asking unique questions of your salespeople, you will be able to help them achieve more than they would be able to on their own.

Thinking Multiple Moves Ahead, the Second Critical Component of Being a Visionary Leader

How many moves ahead do you think and plan as a leader of your sales team? Chapter 1 discussed how most salespeople utilize only a next best move strategy to managing their territory. Most salespeople are functioning as the three-foot "Hellarewe" bird living in four-foot grass, also mentioned in Chapter 1. One of the most critical aides you can provide a sales team is to help them see "over the four-foot grass" and think more moves ahead than they are thinking now.

In addition to being more proactive, a visionary leader also needs to be constantly future focused in their thinking and planning. Most reactive managers tend only to be today and history focused in their coaching and leading efforts. History focused is anything that has happened in the past. Today focused is anything that has occurred within a 48-hour period with right now being in the middle.

Being a leader of a sales team means you want to help them achieve more, but achieving more will not happen if you (and your sales team) focus only on the history and today focused issues. You can't change the past as a manager, but you can help impact the future as a leader.

One of your sales reps, Laura, comes into your office saying there is a problem with the Johnson account and she needs your help. What questions do you most want to ask her? A reactive sales manager would ask only two questions. Their first question would be, "What happened?" followed by "So what do you need to do to fix it?"

These are fine questions for a sales leader to ask, but there is one additional view or perspective that needs to be discussed. After you have learned "what happened" and have discussed "what needs to be done to fix it" there is still a third set of questions based on the future.

"And Then What?"

You are still talking in your office with Laura. She has briefed you on what happened at the Johnson account and you have both offered ideas of what needs to be done to fix it. But now the critical coaching questions need to kick in. Just because Laura might be able to straighten out the problem doesn't automatically mean the Johnson account is still 100 percent happy with her, you, and your company. You need to talk about more than just what will fix this problem for now. You need to be asking future-focused questions to see what else can be done to either stabilize the Johnson account or to even begin efforts to grow their business.

Questions like, "How will you be able to tell if your Johnson contact is still angry over the problem or if everything is okay now?" You might also ask "What extra efforts can you do for the Johnson account that might help repair this last problem?"

But the best future-focused question is to ask, "And then what?" These are the three magic words of sales leadership. "And then what" is the universal truth of coaching a team. After Laura finishes telling you how she plans to straighten out the Johnson account, you could ask her, "And then what?" Just by asking this simple question you cause Laura to extend her vision and planning at her account and to start thinking about what else she can do at her account to help improve her selling situation.

Next time you are coaching a member of your team, try using this simple future-focused phrase. After they have told you all they think you need to know ask them, "And then what?" and see how the conversation continues into more idea generation and coaching opportunities.

What other future-focused questions can you ask anyone on your sales team? The natural reaction of most sales professionals will be to stay in the history and today arenas. It's your job as their coach/leader to help stretch them to also move forward in their planning. Only by thinking more moves ahead than either your customer or your competitors can you ever hope to increase your competitive advantage and to win more business.

This fourth of the five central leadership values of being a visionary leader needs to remain a central focus in all of your coaching and leading efforts to help your people achieve more than they can achieve alone. What can you do to increase your proactive and future-focused efforts with your sales team? How much proactive philosophy and "next several stepped" selling structures thinking can you help your salespeople see and achieve?

10

Mastering Your Fifth Central Leadership Value—Believing in the Structures of Selling

The fifth and final of the five Central Leadership Values critical to your success is your belief in the structures of selling. The vast majority of sales people are intuitive by nature. They see selling as an art instead of a science and believe that because each customer personality and buying situation is unique, so should every sales call also be unique.

How structured and consistent are the members of your sales team? Helping your people understand and apply the steps and structures of selling can significantly increase their consistency of selling and also improve their competitive advantage and selling success. Helping them utilize these structures is also one of the most important foundations of sales coaching leadership.

The Three Structures of Selling

There are three structures or sets of skills of selling: operational, tactical, and strategic.

1. *Operational selling skills* involve the fundamental skills of day-to-day selling. Some refer to operational skills as the foundations

or blocking and tackling skills of selling. Operational selling skills include:

- Steps of a sales call (Test #2 from Chapter 1).
- Personality flexibility awareness skills (understanding why people buy and understanding how to adjust your selling to best fit their personality type).
- Product and industry knowledge.

In learning the game of golf, the operational golf skills include understanding the proper grip of your club, the position of your feet and head as you swing, and how to adjust all of these functions for each of the different clubs in your bag.

2. *Tactical selling skills* involve the process or structures of selling. Tactical selling skills are the multiple-stepped plans that are necessary when you chain together a series of operational sales calls. Tactical selling skills include

- Understanding and controlling your identify to close selling process for new business.
- Understanding and controlling your January 1 to December 31 selling and support processes for maintaining your existing accounts.
- How to call higher, wider, and deeper within a customer's organization.
- How to utilize the rest of your team in your selling process.
- Your time and territory management skills.

In the game of golf, your tactical golf skills include understanding how to play the course, knowing which club to use under which conditions, and when to hit the ball short on your next shot to better position your second shot.

3. *Strategic selling skills* involve your ability to communicate your company's philosophy and competitive market positioning. Strategic selling skills include:

- Being able to answer a customer or prospect when they ask you, *"Why, based on all of the competitive alternatives available to me, do I want to buy from you?"*
- Understanding how your message and positioning are different or similar to your toughest competition.

- Understanding which market segments or market types are best served by your unique offerings and which customer types are better served buying from your competitors.

- Identifying and then applying your understanding of each of your customer's political environments to increase your selling effectiveness.

- Understanding how to maximize your personal selling philosophy and the way you want to be positioned in front of your customers.

In the game of golf, your strategic golf skills include understanding the philosophy of playing and how to handle the pressures of competition.

Coaching Question #38   How balanced are your operational, tactical, and strategic selling skills?

Though all three skill sets are critical to your success in selling, most salespeople and their leadership are out of balance. Observing salespeople, I consistently see the majority of sales people (and their managers) spend more than 90 percent of their time on operational issues or tasks, 10 percent on tactical processes, and little or no time on strategic issues.

Consider your last few sales meetings. What did you spend the most time on? Did you discuss with your team how they can best be positioning your company and products/services versus your competition (strategic)? Did you spend any time discussing how best your team can move a prospect more efficiently through your "identify to close" selling process (tactical)? How much time did you spend talking about your sales reps' current contacts within their important accounts and how they need to be calling on additional positions so they can get higher, wider, and deeper within these accounts (tactical)?

Or, like most other sales teams, did you spend all of your time in your last sales meetings discussing reports, deadlines, order entry concerns, order shipping problems, and who is forgetting to clean out the refrigerator every Friday afternoon (operational)? Most salespeople spend all day reactively responding to the operational demands of their territory, do little longer range planning for either their prospects or existing customers, and all have a different answer when asked why their company is unique.

In selling it is almost impossible to gain a competitive advantage based only on operational selling excellence. Competitive advantages are gained and maintained based on awareness and skills at the tactical and strategic levels—levels most salespeople are weakest in both understanding and applying.

What is the balance of your sales team's operational, tactical, and strategic selling skills? And what are you doing as their sales leader to help strengthen their awareness and skills in each of these three areas? Going back to the first four steps of *ISO 9000* covered in Chapter 4, as their sales leader you need to (1) evaluate where your people's skills and awareness are now, (2) identify and educate your people as to the best practices of selling and then (3) coach, lead, teach, and yell, if necessary, to help your people move from where they are today to where they need to be with their best practices in order to increase their competitive advantage. And finally, (4) When your team gets closer to the best practices you've set, you want to consider raising the bar to move to an even higher level to continue to improve your quality as well as your selling success.

The rest of this book expands upon the definitions of the operational, tactical, and strategic skills of selling. Your job as a sales leader is to first understand these skills and structures yourself so you can then teach and coach your sales team.

Your ability to coach and lead your salespeople requires you to become a student of selling. How can you teach your salespeople to improve a skill if you do not, as their coach, first understand all of the "best practice" steps and structures of that skill? The best tennis or golf coaches are the ones who understand all of the steps and structures of a successful swing, can evaluate the stepped details of how you are currently hitting the ball, and then offer tips and suggestions to help move you closer to the defined "best practices" of a proper swing.

The bottom line of sales leadership is that the only way to effectively coach an experienced and successful sales professional is to understand more about the skills and structures of selling than he does. You don't have to be a better salesperson than your people in order to help them, but you do need to understand all of the steps, structures, and philosophies of how selling works so you can coach even your best people to become better than they are now. This is why I love the concept of "I know you're good . . . but are you good enough to get better?"

Remember that increasing your awareness and ability to use the structures and processes of selling will increase your consistency and efficiency as a sales professional. And if we can increase your consistency and efficiency, you will also increase both your perceived professionalism and overall selling success.

> How many of the five central leadership values can you strengthen to increase your success as a sales leader?

This section has been devoted to discussing the five Central Leadership Values and how these five values can help increase your ability to lead your sales team. How many of these five values can you improve?

1. Being a leader instead of just the lead doer.
2. Being balanced as a coach, disciplinarian, and number cruncher.
3. Having empathy, loyalty, and trust in your sales team.
4. Being proactive and future-focused.
5. Believing in the structures of selling.

Chapter 5 discussed Jill's situation as the new VP of Sales for her father's company. You might remember Jill had never sold before and was now in charge of a team of five salespeople, all older than she was.

What can Jill do to become an effective leader of her sales team? Her first and most critical investment in her future as a sales leader is to understand and implement each of the five central leadership values into her daily efforts. She needs to also become a student of selling.

She needs to gain the attention and respect of her experienced sales team by working to understand more about the steps, structures, and philosophies of selling than any of her people. With her lack of selling experience it would be expected that the majority of her sales team will be much better with their operational blocking and tackling selling skills. But Jill has an opportunity to focus her learning and coaching efforts on the more impactful tactical and strategic aspects of selling. These are probably the weaker skills for most of her people and are also areas that can most contribute to the successful completion of a sale.

The next section, Section III, provides you with a 20-question breakdown of the best practice skills of sales leadership. Section IV provides a 20-question breakdown of the best practice skills of selling. The rest of this book centers on helping you apply each of these five central leadership values as a foundation to your ability to successfully lead your sales team.

Section

How to Improve Your Personal Sales Leadership Skills

Section Overview

CHAPTER 11 **Using the *Sales Leadership Evaluation* to Evaluate, Prioritize, and Develop Your Sales Leadership Abilities**

The 20-question *Sales Leadership Evaluation* in this chapter is a comprehensive analysis tool designed to help increase your awareness of your strongest leadership skills as well as the skills that, if improved, could most help you increase your ability to lead a sales team.

This is a subjective evaluation. There are no right or wrong answers. You are evaluating either your own or someone else's sales leadership skills based on how well you feel they are accomplishing each skill area/question. A free online version of this 20-question *Sales Leadership Evaluation* is also available at www.GreatSalesSkills.com.

The 20 questions in this evaluation are divided among the following four chapters (Chapters 11 to 15) and include additional copy with each question to help increase your awareness of the identified skill and to offer suggestions of how to improve.

For each question of the evaluation you will evaluate or score yourself (or the person you are evaluating) on a five-point scale of 1: Unaware, 2: Weak, 3: Just Average, 4: Leading, or 5: Best Practice.

CHAPTER 12   Evaluating Your Sales Leadership Abilities as an Administrator, Problem Solver, and Disciplinarian

This first leadership area being evaluated focuses on your ability to handle the business side of sales leadership and identifies your strength as an administrator, problem solver, and disciplinarian.

> *Sales Leadership Question #1*   Your skills as an organized administrator are _____?

> *Sales Leadership Question #2*   Your skills coaching your sales reps through problem solving are _____?

> *Sales Leadership Question #3*   Your skills managing and coaching the pricing and profitability decisions of your team are _____?

CHAPTER 13   Evaluating Your Sales Leadership Ability to Build And Retain a Sales Team

This second leadership area being evaluated focuses on your ability to build and retain a sales team. This leadership area includes both your ability to find and hire good people as well as your ability to train and improve your sales team.

> *Sales Leadership Question #4*   Your *new sales person* searching and interviewing skills are _____?

> *Sales Leadership Question #5*   Your *new hire* sales training program is _____?

> *Sales Leadership Question #6*   Your Performance Plan program in place for each member of your team is _____?

Sales Leadership Question #7   Your ongoing experienced sales team training process is _____?

Sales Leadership Question #8   Your accessibility to your sales force is _____?

CHAPTER 14   Evaluating Your Sales Leadership Ability to Lead

This third leadership area being evaluated focuses on your ability to successfully lead a sales team. This leadership area includes your ability to motivate and energize your team to help them get excited about achieving more than they could if you just left them alone.

Sales Leadership Question #9   Your sales team would rate their satisfaction working for you as _____?

Sales Leadership Question #10   Your amount of positive focused communications with your sales team is _____?

Sales Leadership Question #11   Your ability to initiate new ideas and account planning conversations with your team is _____?

Sales Leadership Question #12   Your ability to delegate to your sales team is _____?

CHAPTER 15   Evaluating Your Sales Leadership Ability to Be a Coach and Strategist of Your Selling Process

This fourth and final leadership area being evaluated focuses on your ability to be a successful coach and strategist to your sales team. This leadership area includes your ability to strategize and lead your salespeople through a more proactively controlled, structured, and competitively focused selling process.

Sales Leadership Question #13   Your ability to organize and lead your sales team as a single market force is _____?

Sales Leadership Question #14   Your sales team's ability to communicate a single message of competitive uniqueness and market leadership is _____?

Sales Leadership Question #15 Your ongoing new business prospecting process currently in place is _____?

Sales Leadership Question #16 Your marketing and promotional skills are _____?

Sales Leadership Question #17 Your ability to commit time to individually coach and strategize with each of your sales reps is _____?

Sales Leadership Question #18 The percentage of time you spend talking future-focused with your reps is _____?

Sales Leadership Question #19 Your ability and time committed to talking *tactical and strategic focused* with your sales reps is _____?

Sales Leadership Question #20 Your ability to communicate with customers to help your sales reps get higher, wider, and deeper is _____?

CHAPTER 16 Suggestions to Improve Your Sales Leadership Skills and Effectiveness

Completing this detailed assessment of your leadership skills is meant to help you identify both where your leadership skills are today as well as what you can do to strengthen these skills in the future. This is based on Step 1 of the *ISO 9000* process—to quantify where you are. Now that you know where you are, the next question is do you want to now get better?

It is important you complete your evaluation and improvement planning of your leadership skills prior to working with your sales team on their selling skills. Before you strengthen a team, you need to first strengthen the leadership.

This *Sales Leadership Evaluation* is the first step to helping you strengthen your ability to lead your sales team to achieving a better understanding and control of the skills, structures, and philosophies of selling.

CHAPTER

11

Using the *Sales Leadership Evaluation* to Evaluate, Prioritize, and Develop Your Sales Leadership Abilities

Goal of the *Sales Leadership Evaluation*

The goal of the 20-question *Sales Leadership Evaluation* is to help improve your ability to lead a sales team. By answering these evaluation questions, you can learn specific skills that could improve your leadership success. When your evaluation is complete, you can then select the specific skill areas that, if improved, could generate the fastest payback. With specific skills selected you can then develop and implement a skill development action plan.

Participation in this evaluation is meant to help you identify potential opportunities for improvement and increased success leading your team. It is not intended to determine fault or to focus on any leadership flaws you might have.

This is a subjective evaluation. There are no right or wrong answers. You are evaluating either your own, or someone else's sales leadership skills based on how well you feel they are accomplishing each skill area.

Go to www.GreatSalesSkills.com for a free online version of this 20-question Sales Leadership Evaluation.

You can also go online and complete both the interactive 20-question sales leadership and 20-question *Sales Evaluations* explained in this book. These are free evaluations that also include a detailed multiple page customized report offering feedback and improvement suggestions. This report is immediately available upon completion of your online evaluation.

www.GreatSalesSkills.com has been developed specifically to support the 20-question evaluations explained in this book. It is also a great source for books and training products that can help you expand the selling or sales management skills highlighted in each question.

How to Best *Evaluate* Your Current Sales Leadership Abilities

There are a number of ways to complete the *Sales Leadership Evaluation* process. Your first option is to conduct a detailed evaluation of your own leadership skills by personally answering all of the questions.

A second option is to use this evaluation to receive feedback and suggestions from your sales team. Have each member of your team complete this *Sales Leadership Evaluation*, filling it out based on how they perceive you and your leadership skills. Meet with your entire team after completing your own evaluation and discuss everyone's answers to each question and what they feel could be done to help you improve a specific area.

The goal of this exercise is to help you understand how your team feels you are doing as their leader and to identify areas they believe could be strengthened. As stated earlier this is not meant to be a *let's hammer on our boss* game but a positive forward looking opportunity for you to receive feedback and ideas of the areas your team feels could best improve their overall success.

To make the process more confidential, you might consider keeping the team responses anonymous by asking a third party to collect all evaluations and provide a detailed breakdown on your team's answers to each question. Numbers of evaluation scores given for each answer would be listed but no one individual's answers would be identified to you as their manager. This extra confidentiality step might help your team feel their answers won't be used against them later.

A third option is for you to ask your boss to complete an evaluation on your skills, then meet with him or her to compare answers to see if you both are in agreement about which are your strongest skill areas and which areas you both feel could be improved.

How to *Prioritize* the Leadership Skills That Can Provide You the Strongest Improvement Opportunities

This *Sales Leadership Evaluation* has been developed as a comprehensive analysis tool to help identify the areas most critical to a sales leader's success. No one who openly and honestly evaluates themselves will have a perfect score. The goal is not to get the highest score possible but to use this evaluation as a way to sort out and quantify as many specific leadership areas as possible.

All sales leadership skills are not created equal. After completing your detailed leadership evaluation, your next step is to prioritize your answers. You want to select the specific areas, that if improved, could generate the most profound leadership skill improvements and benefits to your team.

You will receive stronger long-term, sustainable improvement if you select only two or three areas to work on first. Once you feel you are achieving some level of improvement, you can then add additional learning opportunities.

How to *Develop* Your Personalized Sales Leadership Skill Improvement Plan

Once you have selected the skill areas you most want to improve, it is time to begin developing an action plan to help you enhance your leadership performance. The best way to develop an action plan is to first understand how adults learn and improve. Adult learning is based on a simple six-step process:

1. *Step 1: Increase your awareness.*   Awareness can be achieved by reading a book, attending a seminar, being coached, talking to someone, or observing others' behaviors.

2. *Step 2: Increase your understanding.*   This is the step where you realize we are really talking about *you* being the one to change. With this new awareness you now need to apply the idea or awareness to yourself to make sure it fits who you are and what you want to accomplish.

3. *Step 3: Raw implementation.*   This is the step where you work to do something—anything—differently. Your initial attempts to implement this new idea may be difficult or ineffective since few of us are polished or effective the first few times we try anything, but the important factor is you are now doing something new.

4. *Step 4: Refinement.*   Now that you are actually trying to develop this new awareness or skill it is time for you to work to get better. It is time for you to consciously work to improve and polish your new skill set.

5. *Step 5: Permanence.*   As you continue to hone this new awareness or skill, the goal now is to become so good and effective at it that you no longer need to think about doing it anymore. This skill then becomes a habit you consistently implement without applying any conscious effort.

6. *Step 6: Start over to the next level.*   Now that you have developed a permanent skill or awareness, you now want to go back to Step 1—Increasing Your Awareness by starting the entire process over again focusing on another area, skill, or awareness you can begin to improve.

114

How to Successfully Complete Your Personal *Sales Leadership Evaluation*

You will evaluate your sales leadership skills in the following four areas:

1. Your role as an administrator, problem solver, and disciplinarian.
2. Your ability to build and retain a sales team.
3. Your ability to lead.
4. Your ability to be a coach and strategist of your selling process.

There is a complete *Sales Leadership Evaluation* page in the Appendix. Making a photocopy will provide you a way to record your responses and still maintain a clean master for future use.

You will be asked to evaluate yourself (or the person you are evaluating) on 20 different skill areas. Analyze your current skill level for each question by circling a number between 1 and 5 based on the following ratings:

1 = Unaware. You don't even know or realize what you need in this skill area. You are also not aware of the negative impact to your team caused by this gap in your leadership skills.

2 = Weak. You have some skills in this area but are still either underdeveloped or weak in your implementation. You are most likely missing opportunities on a regular basis because of this underdeveloped skill. You may already acknowledge a lack of skill in this area but are not doing enough to fix or improve it on your own.

3 = Just Average. In business and in selling just average is not a good place to be. You are no better or worse in this skill than your competition. You can win in a competitive situation performing at this skill level as long as your competitors are also just average. You are performing at an acceptable level but are most likely having as many ineffective outcomes as you are successes. You are also missing a number of business and leadership opportunities because of your just average skills.

4 = Leading. You are advanced in this skill and are ahead of your competitors. There is still room for improvement, but you are better than most. You generate more successes than problems with this level of leadership performance.

5 = *Best Practice.* This evaluation score identifies you as one of the best at this skill compared to others in your industry, including your competition. Because of this advanced skill you are also most likely generating a consistent level of leadership success.

Coaching Question #39 How can you get the most value from your sales leadership evaluation?

Complete this evaluation based on how you honestly see yourself today, not how you would like to be evaluated by others or how you want to be in the future. Think of a normal week or your average involvement with a sales team member as you think about each question.

The 20 question evaluation is listed over the next four chapters. There are additional questions listed for each evaluation question, along with paragraphs explaining how a low or high answer to this question might translate into daily efforts. This additional information is meant to help you clarify and more accurately evaluate your current performance level.

Coaching Question #40 How can you get the most value evaluating someone else's sales leadership skills?

If you are evaluating another individual, you want to focus on how you honestly see them performing this questioned skill in their current leadership position. Be sure to evaluate them based on how they actually are today, not how you think they should be or how you hope they perform in the future. Also be sure to consider the overall performance or efforts of the person being evaluated. One instance, either positive or negative, should not be the only relevant determinant of their performance in this questioned skill area.

Before You Get Started

You will receive the best value from this evaluation if you approach this effort as a forward-focused positive skill improvement process meant to generate positive change and long-term improvements in your sales leadership skills. The more pressure you are under to complete this evaluation the less accurate, or valuable, your results will be. Remember there are no right or wrong answers to this evaluation. This is only your subjective opinion of the person being evaluated. The quality and validity of your complete evaluation will be directly tied to the honesty and accuracy of your answers.

12

Evaluating Your Sales Leadership Abilities as an Administrator, Problem Solver, and Disciplinarian

This first leadership area being evaluated centers on your ability to handle the business side of sales leadership. How strong are you as an administrator, problem solver, or disciplinarian?

Sales Leadership Question #1 **Your skills as an organized administrator are _____?**

1	2	3	4	5
Unaware	Weak	Just Average	Leading	Best Practice

Additional Clarifying Questions

- Are you effectively managing the financials and budgets of your department? Are all your reports current and accurate?

- Are you fighting unreasonable or disruptive demands made of the sales force by other departments?
- How consistently do you follow through on what you promise you will do?

A Low Organized Administrator Skills evaluation score means you have weak to nonexistent number crunching or paper handling skills. Your office is most likely a mess, you have a hard time locating papers you need, and your reports tend to be late, inaccurate, and disorganized. The paperwork part of the job is the area you are least interested in completing. You are also possibly not very comfortable or skilled with computers and your company's information tracking systems. Your upper management rarely gets informed of actions unless they directly ask you for an update or if your answers will make you or your team look good.

A High Organized Administrator Skills evaluation score means you have strong number crunching and paper handling skills. You run a well organized, disciplined office environment where needed information is readily and easily available. You have worked out systems or reports to keep your upper management updated on your team's selling progress. You pride yourself on your computer skills and are probably looking for ways to improve your sales team's client tracking systems.

You are excited about the opportunities and controls a CRM (Customer Relationship Management) computer software system could offer both your company and your sales team. Your overall strength in this area means your office and team are running with a high degree of efficiency and effectiveness.

Ideas to Help Improve Your Organized Administrator Skills This is the skill area most sales managers enjoy the least. Most sales leaders feel that completing all of the efforts necessary to be an effective and organized administrator will be done at the sacrifice of time spent helping the sales team (or their own territories) sell something.

But in all areas of business, information is power. The more and better the information you have, the more of a competitive advantage you gain. Maintaining effective information controls for your sales team is also a way to increase your ability to identify and track each team member's performance levels.

Idea #1   Evaluate your computer skills. Do you know how to efficiently retrieve information and reports from your company's systems? How effectively are you utilizing e-mail and the Internet to communicate with your sales team, the rest of your company, and your customers?

Idea #2   Evaluate your paper handling and time management skills. Is your desk organized? How efficient are you at handling the paper and information that goes with being a leader of a sales team?

Consider interviewing or spending time with the person in your organization who most impresses you with their organizational and information handling skills. Ask to spend some time observing how they organize and run their office and ask them for suggestions to improve your current systems and processes. Most of the best organized administrators are not recognized for these skills so they are usually flattered and impressed when someone asks for their help.

Idea #3   Evaluate all of the information and reporting demands being made of your sales team as explained in Chapter 7. You need to decide if these informational demands from others are reasonable or excessive.

Idea #4   Acknowledge that executives love information and organization. You need to accept the informational demands of your job. If upper management considers this one of your weak areas, you will likely hurt your long-term career potential by being so underdeveloped in such an important leadership area.

These demands are not going to disappear and will likely only continue to increase. Apply the most basic time management principles: schedule blocks of time each day to handle paperwork; don't let paperwork back up to the point it is unmanageable; touch a piece of paper or e-mail only once and look for ways to delegate. Attend a class or read some books on how to improve your time, paper, and computer management skills.

Sales Leadership Question #2 Your skills used to coach your sales reps in problem solving methods are _____?

1	2	3	4	5
Unaware	Weak	Just Average	Leading	Best Practice

Additional Clarifying Questions

- ◆ Do all members of your team know when to call for help with a problem, or are they holding onto problems too long before they ask for assistance?

- ◆ What kind of problem best practices have you identified and developed for your team so everyone understands how problems are to be solved and/or resolved?

- ◆ How often are you and your sales team solving the same type of problems? Do you evaluate all major problems, the solutions that were required, and then proactively adjust how your systems need to handle this type of problem in the future?

A Low Problem Solving Skills evaluation score means solving problems is an ongoing challenge taking more time and energy than it should. Your weak skills in this area mean you are either (1) ignoring problems in their early stages hoping your sales reps (or others) will eventually solve them without your help, (2) weak at coaching and delegation so you try to personally handle all problems your team encounters, or (3) you have intimidated your sales team in the past so they now delay bringing you problems until they absolutely have to.

A High Problem Solving Skills evaluation score means you are a strong, quick, and effective problem solver. You have trained your sales reps and support personnel to spot problems early and immediately identify resolution action plans. You also have effective communications and tracking systems to keep your customers and others in your company informed of any solution progress. You continually debrief after major problems to see what could be changed or improved within your company and team.

Ideas to Help Improve Your Problem Solving Skills   Problem solving tends to burn up the most sales leadership time. It is also an area that, if not managed properly, can easily get out of hand, taking over most of the available selling and sales leadership time. Ineffective problem solving is also one of the easiest ways to lose a long-term customer.

Idea #1   Evaluate past problems to see if there are any lessons to be learned. Too many sales leaders keep solving the same problems but with different customers each time. Your job as a leader is to constantly look at the bigger picture to see if the same types of problems are being repeated. Your job is also to evaluate what the real problems are. Most customer problems brought to sales leaders tend to only really be symptoms. Constantly missed delivery times could be a symptom of too small a delivery fleet, inefficient route assignments, or weak delivery management controls.

Idea #2   Get involved as a coach—not a doer. As discussed in Chapter 6, you need to be functioning more as a coach and leader than as the lead doer. If you continue to solve problems for your team, they will never learn to handle situations on their own forcing them to have to keep coming back to you for help. You need to view every customer problem as a learning and coaching opportunity. Occasionally, you may need to get directly involved in a customer problem, but get involved as a manager wanting to help, not as the head sales rep.

Idea #3   Get others involved. What other departments within your company could help resolve a recurring problem or help identify how to avoid problems in the future? Too many sales teams are afraid, for any number of reasons, to get other employees and/or departments from their company involved in customer problem resolution.

Idea #4   Take decisive action now. For most customers, the first solution offered will be the one your performance will be evaluated on. Too many times leaders try going cheap by throwing less than solutions at a dissatisfied customer. When the first pass at a solution is refused it just makes it tougher to resolve the problem later. Remember these are not problems you are dealing with but long-term customer relationships.

Idea #5   Follow up after a problem is solved to decide how (or if) anything within your company systems need to be modified, improved, or retrained to reduce the potential of this problem occurring again (or at least with this frequency). Could this problem have been brought to your attention sooner? Is there a way the sales rep (or others) could have identified the growing problem and gotten involved earlier? Could your team have been more proactive in how they identified, managed, or resolved the problem with the customer?

Also follow up with the client to make sure they are satisfied with both your problem resolution and your overall relationship. Just because a problem is solved does not mean you still have a loyal, satisfied customer. What can you and your sales team do to follow up with customers to assess their satisfaction level and to do something to help improve the account's satisfaction with you, your rep, and your company?

Sales Leadership Question #3   Your skills managing the pricing and profitability decisions of your team are _____?

1	2	3	4	5
Unaware	Weak	Just Average	Leading	Best Practice

Additional Clarifying Questions

◆ Are you able to predict a competitors' pricing when you are writing up a customer bid or proposal?

◆ Do you accurately track the past pricing wins and losses so you can identify and predict your competitors' pricing strategies? How often are you surprised by a lower than expected price from a competitor?

◆ Are you able to maintain a stable profitability range for all accounts sold?

A Low Pricing and Profitability Decision Making Skills evaluation score means you are weak predicting your competitors' prices and maintaining your profit margins. You tend to get surprised often by your competitors' actions and customer demands. It's likely your pricing philosophy is based on a "shoot from the hip" style of quoting with little planning. You probably have weak pricing and bid reporting systems that prevent you from being able to track and predict your competitors' actions. Your pricing decisions have caused you to lose a lot of proposals or to wind up giving away too much profitability to win a sale. Your lack of any kind of pricing consistency is also likely confusing and frustrating your sales team.

A High Pricing and Profitability Decision Making Skills evaluation score means you are an effective manager and leader of your team's pricing and profitability decisions. You tend to generate higher average margins than others in your company. You have established effective competitive pricing tracking systems to help you better prepare for future bidding. You have directed your sales team members to conduct pricing research to effectively debrief any major competitive wins or losses. You are rarely surprised by a low price or unusual proposal from your competitors.

Ideas to Help Improve Your Pricing And Profitability Decision Making Skills A lack of effective competitive pricing skills can significantly strip away your team's (and company's) profits. Knowing when you can safely quote a strong profit margin and also predict when you have to offer lower prices/margins is a critical role of a sales leader.

Idea #1   Set up some type of pricing tracking system so you can track past wins and losses. Work to identify competitors' prices and final concessions. The only way you can lower your future pricing decision making risk is to improve your pricing tracking systems and efforts.

Idea #2   Work with your team to communicate your competitive value differential. Your customer is not buying a lower price from a competitor, they are buying a product or service that has not had its value differential communicated. Customers will pay a higher price if they see a stronger value being offered compared to your

125

competitors'. What can you do to lead your team in a stronger communications of your added value and uniqueness?

Idea #3   Walk your senior management through your understanding of the pricing and profitability strategies of your company. Make sure everyone agrees with the pricing and margin strategies you are implementing.

13

Evaluating Your Sales Leadership Ability to Build and Retain a Sales Team

This second leadership area being evaluated centers on your ability to build and retain a sales team. This includes both your ability to find and hire good people as well as your ability to train and improve your sales team. How strong a team builder are you?

Sales Leadership Question #4 Your new salesperson searching and interviewing skills are _____?

1	2	3	4	5
Unaware	Weak	Just Average	Leading	Best Practice

Additional Clarifying Questions

♦ Have you established solid sources to provide or help you identify good sales candidates? Are you satisfied with the quality and quantity of your candidates recently interviewed?

- Do you have multiple individuals interview all sales candidates?
- Do you always drug test, check the background references and resume facts of a candidate before making an offer?

A Low New Salesperson Searching and Interviewing Skills evaluation score means you have weak to nonexistent searching, interviewing, and hiring skills. You do not have an organized system to find and evaluate potential new hires. You have only one person (probably you) interview candidates, and don't have a set of preidentified interviewing questions you ask. You don't perform background checks, but tend to immediately hire the first person who seems like a good fit. You also likely have higher turnover of your sales staff due to the ineffectiveness of your hiring processes. Many companies spend only a few minutes interviewing and selecting a new hire but then spend years trying to mold them into what they wanted them to be when they first interviewed them.

A High New Salesperson Searching and Interviewing Skills evaluation score means you have a solid new hire system in place. You have multiple sources helping to identify solid candidates to consider and a team of individuals to help conduct multiple interviews of a candidate of interest following a set of predefined and agreed upon interviewing questions. You also perform background checks of candidates of interest and encourage them to spend a day with one of your salespeople to help insure they are really interested in working for your company. With this solid a hiring process you tend to have a strong retention rate with your sales team.

Ideas to Help Improve Your New Salesperson Searching and Interviewing Skills The majority of sales managers agree this is an important skill even if no one in their company has ever taken the time or energy to organize it.

> Idea #1   Develop multiple sources to identify potential sales candidates. What are you doing to build your new hire candidate network? Do you inform others when you are hiring salespeople? Informing your current sales team of when you are hiring can be a good source of candidates. The Internet has also now become a solid source of new sales candidates.

Idea #2   Establish a consistent interviewing process: If you develop structure and consistency within your interviewing process you will improve your hiring results. Develop a new hire system that includes identifying who will interview a candidate, determining what needs to be accomplished in each interview, and who will coordinate the background, drug testing, and resume checks on all job finalists. Consider having numerous individuals interview a candidate to help you gain a more accurate read on the individual and their personality.

Without a solid set of interviewing "best practices" you are likely to have little consistency in your interviewing, making it more difficult to compare candidates of interest. Without solid interviewing "best practices" to follow, your interviewers are also likely to do more of the talking than the person being interviewed. Even if you hire a new rep only once every few years, you still need to develop a solid hiring and interviewing process so it is ready when you need it.

Idea #3   Help candidates be sure they want to work for you. Just because you like them doesn't mean they have enough knowledge about you and your company to know they are going to like working for you. The last step before extending a job offer needs to be inviting the candidate to spend a day in the field with one of your sales reps. The goal of this process is for candidates to have any final questions answered and to get a clear understanding of exactly what the job involves. Too often candidates are so anxious to get a job they never really consider if a company is the best fit for them. Look how expensive it would be for you to hire a candidate, but only after joining your company they realize they do not like their new job. Now you wind up only financing them for months as they look for a new job.

Sales Leadership Question #5   Your *new hire* sales training program is _____?

1	2	3	4	5
Unaware	Weak	Just Average	Leading	Best Practice

Additional Clarifying Questions

- ◆ Do you and your team believe new hire training is not needed because experienced = trained?
- ◆ Do you have a written, organized, and structured *new hire* sales training program currently in place?
- ◆ Do you have a way to track and measure a *new hire's* progress through their training process?

A Low New Hire Sales Training Skills evaluation score means you probably have a weak to nonexistent new hire training program beyond teaching them the technical aspects of your products/services. You are following the invalid assumption experienced = trained so the only training in place tends to be of a technical and/or pricing nature. Your salespeople learn to sell the way my father learned how to swim. You throw them into the deep end of their territory and assume they will figure it out and learn to survive on their own. You view new hire sales training as an expense you cannot afford to spend.

A High New Hire Sales Training Skills evaluation score means you have a solid, organized, and effective training process in place. During this training you help new hires understand the products/services, company philosophy and history, competitive uniqueness selling messages, and expected selling "best practices" already embraced by other team members. You understand how newly hired sales rep training can help them become more productive, sooner in their territory. You view your new hire sales training as an investment in your team's competitive advantage.

Ideas to Help Improve Your New Hire Sales Training Skills

Idea #1   Establish a new hire entry level training process. Even if you have only one new hire at a time you need to have an established training program and learning process identified. Create a three ring binder that identifies the skills to be learned in the first few weeks on the job. Promise each new hire an incentive bonus at the end of their initial training based on how they improved the training book you gave them. Ask them to insert any instructions or forms they are given to help make the training process easier for the next new hire. Even though they might be selling full time in

130

their territory after the first or second week on the job they can still be talking to others and working to learn all of the skills they will need to be successful.

Idea #2   Identify the benchmarks you will use to evaluate the progress of newly hired salespeople. Identify any weak habits or concerns as early as possible in their employment so you can work to correct and improve their behaviors. Tracking their progress through training also provides a great way to identify when someone is really excelling in their new job and also gives you a way to evaluate how to improve your training process.

Idea #3   In addition to an organized new hire training process you also need someone to be assigned as their coach or mentor. The job of this mentor is to help answer questions and assist as a new hire eases into your organization. In many cases the new hire's sales manager is so overworked with other responsibilities that they have little time to invest in coaching and training a new hire. If this describes your environment then consider asking another salesperson on your team to coach and mentor your new hire until they are stable in their new job and territory.

Sales Leadership Question #6   Your Performance Plan program in place for each member of your team is _____?

1	2	3	4	5
Unaware	Weak	Just Average	Leading	Best Practice

Additional Clarifying Questions

- ◆ Do you have an annual performance plan in place where you evaluate and work to improve all aspects of your sales team's selling efforts?

- ◆ Do you discuss each rep's current performance plan several times throughout the year to provide informal feedback and progress updates?

- ◆ As part of their performance plan evaluation do you also ask each person to evaluate and provide feedback on how you are performing as their sales manager/leader?

A Low Performance Plan evaluation score means you probably don't even have one. You do assign salespeople quotas at the beginning of the year but nothing else. You view performance plans as just more paperwork that doesn't provide any long-term value to either you or your team. You assume a sales rep's earnings will give them a good indication of how they are doing in their job.

A High Performance Plan evaluation score means you have an organized and structured annual written performance plan in place for each team member. You seek their involvement in their plan design at the beginning of the year, provide ongoing informal feedback throughout the year, and get them involved in their end of year review and planning for the next year. You also believe that performance plans for both your new and senior reps are one of the most significant contributors to their ongoing long-term growth. You understand you cannot expect long-term success and growth in an individual if they don't first have a long-term improvement plan in place.

Ideas to Help Improve Your Performance Plan Skills

Idea #1   Start a performance plan as soon as possible following the guidelines and suggestions offered in Chapter 24. A performance plan gives you an ongoing structure you can use to coach and improve a salesperson. A performance plan is also a great way to quantify your salespeople's selling best practices.

Idea #2   Make sure your performance plans are full year plans. Too often sales teams have performance plans that are quickly written at the beginning of the year and then ignored until it's time to review the salesperson's efforts for the year. You want to have several one-on-one informal conversations throughout the year discussing a team member's progress and growth.

Idea #3   Be sure to separate your performance plan process from your pay raise system. You do not want a salesperson walking into their annual performance review expecting to learn what their raise will be for the year. You want them to see their performance plan as a coaching guide and opportunity to improve their future. Salary raises or bonuses are to be regarded as feedback for how well they have already done their job.

Sales Leadership Question #7 Your ongoing experienced sales team training process is _____?

1	2	3	4	5
Unaware	Weak	Just Average	Leading	Best Practice

Additional Clarifying Questions

♦ How much training have you conducted for your sales team in the past 12 months?

♦ How much of your sales training in the past year focused only on product knowledge training?

A Low Experienced Sales Training Awareness evaluation score means the only sales training your company conducts is on product knowledge. You believe in the invalid assumption experience = trained and view training as an unnecessary expense due to your only hiring experienced people.

A High Experienced Sales Training Awareness evaluation score means you see sales training as a component of your team's competitive advantage. You believe no matter how good (and successful) a salesperson is, they can always be better. You understand sales training incorporates a number of different topics and skill categories. You also believe the long-term skill development and growth of your sales team will produce long-term productivity increases.

Ideas to Help Improve Your Experienced Sales Training

Idea #1 Don't just throw sales training at your team. Research the sales training skills each team member needs to develop to help increase their competitive advantage and selling success. Following the processes outlined in this book, first evaluate and work toward improving your sales leadership skills, next follow the processes outlined in Section V—Developing a Successful Sales Improvement Strategy. You need to first *evaluate* where your salespeople are right now (Chapter 21), *design* an effective skill improvement process (Chapter 22), implement your training process for each team member (Chapter 23), track the progress and successes of each team member (Chapter 24), and finally lead them to success by working to strengthen your leadership and sales skills (Chapter 25).

Idea #2   Make sure your sales training is a process instead of just a series of independent events. Successful sales training includes sharing new ideas and discussing and practicing new skills. But it also includes the ongoing coaching and tracking of your team's progress implementing their new skills and awareness. You don't want to just *train* your team: you want to *change* your team.

Idea #3   Sales training can be conducted by individual study and coaching. Sales training doesn't need to be just classroom teaching. For smaller teams you may be better served leading your team through a series of discussions about a book, audio, or video on selling.

Sales Leadership Question #8   Your accessibility to your sales force is _____?

1	2	3	4	5
Unaware	Weak	Just Average	Leading	Best Practice

Additional Clarifying Questions

◆ How accessible are you? How easy is it for your sales reps to get in touch with you when they need something?

◆ Do your sales team members feel they can bring you bad news without getting yelled at? Can they bring you a problem, asking for help, without already feeling they have to have identified the solution?

◆ Do you initiate discussions with your sales team members when you suspect they are struggling with a problem or challenge?

A Low Sales Force Accessibility evaluation score means you are hard to get in touch with and receive help from when team members need guidance or assistance. Part of the problem could be you are so involved as a doing sales manager that you have little time to devote to coaching and helping your team members. By now most of your team members have probably given up on your being available, or interested, in helping them with their problems so they tend to try solving them on their own (not always a successful strategy).

A High Sales Force Accessibility evaluation score means you are open and available to your team. They know and trust that you are there to help them and understand your loyalty and commitment to helping each of them be more successful. You have set aside specific times they know you will be available. They are also comfortable going to you for help with a problem knowing you will be supportive and involved.

Ideas to Help Improve Your Sales Force Accessibility

Idea #1   Remind your team of your commitment to help them be more successful. Most salespeople will not ask for help if they feel they will be talked down to or harassed. Your sales team needs to feel you are on their side before they can be open enough to trust asking for help.

Idea #2   Define times each day or week when you will be available to offer help and advice to your team. One VP of Sales decided his one hour commute to and from the office each day was a good opportunity for extra time to coach and communicate with his team. He encouraged his team to contact him on his cell phone during these times.

One of my first sales managers made it known he was always available Saturday mornings as he worked on paperwork and straightened up his office. He continually reminded us that if we joined him on Saturday mornings, he could devote extra time to discussing and strategizing how to handle our customers and/or problems. Although he was available throughout the week, these Saturday meeting times became a valuable coaching opportunity for all of his team members.

Idea #3   Don't shoot the messenger. One of the easiest ways to turn off a team coming to you for help is to blast anyone bringing you a problem. Remember to be more balanced in your positive to negative communications as discussed in Chapter 8.

14

Evaluating Your
Sales Leadership Abilities

The third leadership area being evaluated centers on your ability to successfully lead a sales team. This leadership skill set includes your ability to motivate and energize your team.

Sales Leadership Question #9   Your sales team would rate their satisfaction working for you as _____?

1	2	3	4	5
Unaware	Weak	Just Average	Leading	Best Practice

Additional Clarifying Questions

♦ Do your sales reps feel you listen and understand their concerns and challenges?

♦ Do your sales team members feel you are helping them achieve more than they would be achieving if just left alone?

A Low Sales Team Satisfaction evaluation score means your team is probably not supportive of your efforts. They do not feel you are on their side, that they can trust you, or that they are important to you. A team that expresses low satisfaction with their manager/leader is likely not working as hard or as effectively as they could be.

A High Sales Team Satisfaction evaluation score means you are perceived as a effective leader who is on their side, offering full support and trust, and energized by their success. Your team feels you are helping them achieve much more than they ever could on their own. They feel they are learning, growing, and advancing because of your coaching and guidance. You are one of the main reasons they enjoy their job.

Ideas to Help Improve Your Sales Team Satisfaction   The second key to generating long-term success within a sales force covered in Chapter 3 included the ability to make your team members want to follow your leadership.

Idea #1   Apply the coaching ideas outlined in Chapter 3 to help identify how you can increase your power (positional, personal, and informational) and ability to be an effective leader.

Idea #2   Focus on your team and not on yourself. Use terms like "we" instead of "me" when describing what your team needs to be accomplishing. Make sure your language communicates that you realize no one works *for* you but they all work *with* you. Your team will be more willing to follow your leadership if they feel you respect them and are committed to their success.

Idea #3   Ask your team how you are doing as their leader and for the suggestions on what you could be doing to do an even better job. If you are coaching and helping them improve, don't you think it would help your team environment if they also had a chance to give you feedback and ideas? Ask your team to complete this *Sales Leadership Evaluation* on you and discuss as a team how they feel you are doing and what they feel would help them achieve more and increase their success. Just asking for their feedback and opinion on your performance will help increase their loyalty and commitment to you and their team even if you don't agree to everything they say or want changed.

It is, however, important to put at least some of their suggestions into practice even if you begin small and move slowly. If you ask for their suggestions and then do nothing about their ideas, you will do more harm than good.

Idea #4   Apply the central leadership values outlined in Section II (Chapters 5 to 10). Your success as a leader and their satisfaction following you will be directly related to your ability to communicate these personal leadership traits.

Sales Leadership Question #10   The amount of positive communication you have with your sales team is _____?

1	2	3	4	5
Unaware	Weak	Just Average	Leading	Best Practice

Additional Clarifying Questions

◆ How much of your communications language with your team is positive versus negative?

◆ Are you working to catch your people doing something right or are you focused on looking to see if your people are doing something wrong?

◆ How positive is your personal energy and attitude? Is your personal life in balance? Are you positive and excited about your job?

A Low Positive Communications evaluation score means you are probably not a very positive person to be around. The majority of communication with your team tends to focus on negatives. Your people know they will hear from you immediately if they do something wrong but also expect to hear nothing from you if they do something right. You communicate a level of stress and concern about your team's sales and future because of your "glass is half empty—and probably ready to break" attitude. You are also likely to not be very happy with your work or personal life and do not communicate a high degree of positive energy.

A High Positive Communications evaluation score means you project a positive energy to the people around you. You appear truly positive and excited about your team and their potential. You deal with problems that occur, but with a positive attitude that communicates things can be fixed and improved. You are an energizer to your team. Because of you and your shared energy they want to work harder increasing their success levels and spending time with you.

Ideas to Help Improve Your Positive Communications

Idea #1   Understand that an important part of your job as a leader is to motivate and energize your team (and others). Your positive attitude combined with the affirming communications of encouragement discussed in this book will help strengthen your ability to successfully lead a team. People want to be inspired and to believe they are following a positive cause. Your role as a leader is to help them see the positives, the potential, and the excitement that is possible.

Idea #2   Your car battery has to be fully charged before you can help jump someone else's car. Check to see that your personal life is in balance. Being the leader of a sales team takes a lot of energy. If any major part of your life is not in balance, you will not have as much energy to successfully energize and grow a team. What can you do to improve or stabilize any energy or attitude zappers in your life?

Idea #3   The best way to generate positive energy in someone is to make them feel valued and important. Focus your energy and language on them and their experiences. Make sure you spend social time with your team encouraging them to talk and share what is important to them. If you increase their positive energy, their positive selling efforts and success will also increase.

Sales Leadership Question #11   Your ability to initiate new ideas and account planning conversations with your team is _____?

1	2	3	4	5
Unaware	Weak	Just Average	Leading	Best Practice

Additional Clarifying Questions

♦ Are you an initiator or a reactor to new ideas and account planning? Do you initiate discussions with your team or do you wait for things to be brought to you?

♦ Are you able to help your people see more moves ahead than they would on their own?

♦ Do your team members feel spending an hour with you planning and strategizing for one of their accounts is a positive investment of their time?

A Low Ability to Initiate New Ideas and Account Planning evaluation score means you are reactive as a leader and coach of your sales team. You wait for someone to ask for help or to bring you a problem. You tend to focus on the today and history issues of a problem, spending little time discussing and planning for future efforts or initiatives. You are functioning as more of a manager and administrator than a leader. You spend most of your time helping solve problems instead of working to make new ideas happen.

A High Ability to Initiate New Ideas and Account Planning evaluation score means you are a positive leader helping your people increase their awareness and future planning. You realize that competitive advantages and opportunities are hidden in your team's future actions, not in their past. You are a positive addition to any brainstorming session, helping add unique insights and offering new, fresh ideas to help increase your sales team's success.

Ideas to Help Improve Your Ability to Initiate New Ideas and Account Planning Skills

Idea #1   Ask questions—don't tell. Your job as a leader is not to tell your team all of the answers but to help them discover what you already know. Ask more questions to generate original and creative thinking within your team.

Idea #2   Get team members to think outside the box. You are most effective when you can help a team member see things from a different perspective or with a new, increased awareness. If your team can't figure out a solution, change their perspective or the

141

angle of observation. It is often easier to see more clearly from the outside looking in than from the inside looking out.

Idea #3   Don't take credit for ideas you provided during planning and strategy sessions. You want your team members to be the heroes. Make your group feel the positive ideas they generated were the team's ideas—not yours. Your job as a leader is to empower people, not make them better followers.

Idea #4   Take time to plan and strategize. Creative thinking rarely occurs under pressure and stress. Hold strategy planning sessions or account discussions away from the office where stress and distractions are reduced.

Sales Leadership Question #12   Your ability to delegate to your sales team is _____?

1	2	3	4	5
Unaware	Weak	Just Average	Leading	Best Practice

Additional Clarifying Questions

◆ Are you able to delegate as a sales leader or do you feel as though you have to do everything yourself?

◆ Are you constantly looking for things you can delegate to members of your team?

A Low Ability to Delegate evaluation score means you are a one man band wanting to do everything yourself. You are the "super doer" discussed in Chapter 6. You feel you get things done faster and better when you do them yourself. Instead of delegating to share the work with others, you are more likely to try taking things away from members of your team. You don't play well with others, instead demanding to always be holding the ball.

A High Ability to Delegate evaluation score means you are exhibiting the positive traits of a true leader. You realize your job is to help others get better through delegation combined with coaching so your team members can learn and grow. You understand you are building skills in your team for the future. Even if you could handle a responsibility yourself, you realize in the future you might need others to do these roles. Only by learning now will they be prepared for the performance pressures you and your team will require in the future.

Ideas to Help Improve Your Ability to Delegate Skills

Idea #1 Evaluate the most critical skills each salesperson needs to improve. Consider delegating tasks that require your salespeople to strengthen or work on the weak skills you have identified.

Idea #2 Take a chance but still protect yourself. The only way someone can learn and grow is through trying something new. As a leader you need to give your people the opportunity to fail. Only by having the opportunity to fail will they ever be able to prove to themselves and to you that they have the ability to succeed. You also need to protect them, your customers, and your company. At the same time you empower someone to take a risk, you also need to build in some type of observation or monitoring so you can quickly identify if things are not going in a positive way.

Idea #3 Work to increase your trust and comfort in yourself. The only way you can delegate and empower others is when you first feel empowered yourself. Successful delegation, combined with effective coaching can occur only when you feel empowered and comfortable with your skills and environment.

15

Evaluating Your Sales Leadership Ability to Be a Coach and Strategist of Your Selling Process

This fourth and final leadership area centers on your ability to be a successful coach and strategist to your sales team. This leadership area includes your ability to strategize and lead your sales people through a more proactively controlled, structured, and competitively focused selling process.

Sales Leadership Question #13 **Your ability to organize and lead your sales team as a single market force is _____?**

1	2	3	4	5
Unaware	Weak	Just Average	Leading	Best Practice

Additional Clarifying Questions

◆ When was the last time a tough prospect or account was presented to your sales team to see if others could offer any insight or direction?

◆ How much debriefing do you do with your entire sales team about what worked to win accounts or didn't work causing you to lose business?

◆ When was the last time you led your entire sales team in a discussion and coaching session on how you could improve your selling processes, shorten your selling cycle, increase your prospect qualifying efforts, or increase your competitive advantage?

A Low Leading Your Team as a Single Force evaluation score means your sales team is probably a collection of independent, isolated salespeople each worried only about their own performance and not doing much to contribute to the success of others on your team. You do little to get them working as a team, instead managing them like they were a group of independent Old West gunfighters instead of as an army or SWAT team. Each member of your team has a different definition of who your best customers are and even why your company's offerings are unique. You also provide little skill coaching or account strategy assistance, assuming they can do all of this planning on their own.

A High Leading Your Team as a Single Force evaluation score means your sales team is functioning effectively as a single SWAT team. The SWAT team philosophy of "What one learns benefits all" is being applied by your team on a regular basis. You have team sessions to help identify selling strategies and selling processes for specific accounts on the assumption that what is happening at one account is probably also occurring at others. All of your sales reps share a common belief of who their best customers are and why they buy from them. You have built a team sprit where all members feel connected and interested in helping others be successful.

Ideas to Help Improve Your Ability to Lead Your Team as a Single Force
The majority of sales managers are being pulled in so many operational and administrative directions that they have little time left to act as a coach or strategist. Each team member functions independently from

146

the others and almost never gets involved in discussions of how to sell better, how to move through selling processes more consistently and effectively, or how the rest of the team could learn from one person's successes or problems. As a leader you need to work to bring your team closer together.

Idea #1   Make sure your people feel comfortable and safe sharing with the rest of their team. Your salespeople should not feel they are in competition with each other. Your competitors need to be the competition—not the other members of your team.

Most salespeople work in an environment of isolation feeling treated as an independent individual. Their egos are so wrapped up in their job description that asking another sales rep for help on an account is perceived as an admission of weakness. Your job as team leader is to help them minimize these ego issues or negative feelings and understand the benefits of trusting others on their team. Your communications and approach to team focused efforts is the key to building this trust among all team members.

Idea #2   Hold regular sales team meetings where the sales reps are asked to share the toughest selling situations they currently face and discuss suggestions to help with this problem.

Be aware it might take awhile for your team to gain enough confidence in their peers so they become comfortable sharing their sales challenges with the group.

Idea #3   Meet with your entire sales team and begin defining what attributes describe a *best customer*. The lack of a clear and agreed upon definition of who your best customers are is one of the most common sales exposures in business today. A lack of a clear agreement within your sales team as to who your best customers are is also a management problem. If you haven't worked with your people on this critical issue how can you assume they all have the same definitions?

Ask each member of your team to write down the attributes of your best or core customers. After everyone has written down their answers, build a list of your team's answers on a flip chart. The majority of sales teams have completely different definitions of what makes a *Best* or *Core* account.

A *best customer* is defined as one who sees the most value differential in your company and products. Typically, you have the strongest ability to prove your competitive uniqueness to these customers. They are the center or core of your best accounts, and appreciate the quality, value, and added services you offer. Even under increased competitive pressures, you will tend to win the business of this *best customer*. Having a clear definition of your best customer attributes gives a clear direction to your team's new business prospecting efforts, and helps clarify which new company services or customer offerings will have the greatest potential impact on your most important customers. A clear best customer definition also becomes a significant contributor to your developing and communicating an effective strategic message of competitive uniqueness (Sales Leadership Question #14).

Idea #4   Conduct planning sessions with your entire team to clarify and define your team's selling best practices or procedural guidelines. A better definition of your selling structures and philosophies, agreed to by the entire team can help each sales team member improve their selling processes, shorten their selling cycles, increase their prospect qualifying efforts, and even increase their competitive advantage.

Once your definition is clarified and agreed upon, you then need to be sure you keep reminding your team of this new definition. To retain this message, you need to be constantly referencing and reminding your team of this new messaging and how to use it.

Idea #5   Hold Win-Loss reviews for major accounts. The goal of these Win-Loss debriefing meetings is to discuss how your selling processes or strategies can be improved in the future. It is not meant to be an inquisition to assign fault and blame or torture the responsible rep. Make sure to keep the discussion focused on what every team member could be doing in their own territory to either avoid the problem(s) that caused the loss or to insure they are able to consistently replicate the actions that caused the win.

Conducting Win-Loss reviews is one way you get your sales team functioning as an actual team. Discussing account problems, selling strategies, and successes helps the members of your team feel connected to one another, improves your account planning by providing better ideas from a wider range of individuals, and helps train your team on the selling best practices you expect all team members to be following.

Idea #6   Conduct a sales team meeting where they each complete the 20-question *Sales Evaluation* presented in Section IV. Have each rep complete their evaluation and then have the group discuss their collected answers and what they could be doing to increase their evaluation score (and your competitive advantage). Also ask the team to help define the next best selling skills to be worked on that could generate the most team success.

Sales Leadership Question #14   Your sales team's ability to communicate a single message of competitive uniqueness and market leadership is _____?

1	2	3	4	5
Unaware	Weak	Just Average	Leading	Best Practice

Additional Clarifying Questions

♦ How are your sales team members answering a customer who asks, *"You're the fifth vendor I've talked to this week about this stuff. Why, based on all of the competitive alternatives available to me, do I want to buy from you?"*

♦ How many different answers to this question are your sales team members taking to your markets?

♦ How much of a competitive advantage are your best salespeople gaining by their answer to this question?

A Low Single Message of Competitive Uniqueness evaluation score means each member of your team is presenting a different answer when your customer or prospect asks them why they are better than their competition. You and your team have never met to discuss and debate the best set of answers and are not even sure what each other is saying when asked this question. If you have discussed each other's responses to this question you are not impressed with any of your team members' answers.

A High Single Message of Competitive Uniqueness evaluation score means you are a strategic focused leader of your team. You realize the critical importance of having a polished and consistent team answer to this "Why buy" question from a customer or prospect. You constantly remind your team of the best answers to this question and also push your team to uncover the answers your competitors are giving when asked.

Ideas to Help Improve Your Single Message of Competitive Uniqueness Skills
Like the definition of a best customer, a lack of clarity or consistency to your strategic message of competitive uniqueness is also one of the most common sales exposures in business today. This "Why buy" question is also the toughest question in selling to answer.

Idea #1   In a team meeting ask them the "Why buy" question and ask each rep to write down the bulleted answers they would tell a prospect or customer. After everyone has completed their answers write down all your team's responses on a flip chart. You will most likely find your sales team generated a wide range of responses as well as a large percentage of answers that are competitively generic. The problem with having a variety of responses is that this is a symptom that you and your company are not communicating any kind of consistency of competitive message.

How many members of your company communicate with your prospects and customers? Look at the exposure you have if several members of your team communicate with a prospect/customer and each provides a completely different answer to this question. How many different messages about your overall philosophy, competitive uniqueness, or strategic company positioning are you and your company taking to your markets?

Idea #2   Meet with your team to begin developing a consistent and competitively unique answer to this "Why buy" question. Once you discover how varied and weak everyone's answers are, the next step is to improve your team's best answers to this "Why buy" question.

Follow this stepped process if you and your team want to improve your answers to *"Why, based on all of the competitive alternatives available to me, do I want to buy from you?"*

Step 1:   List all of their team's responses to the "Why buy" question on flip charts.

Step 2:   Identify your toughest competitors listing their strengths and weaknesses.

Step 3:   Cross out all of the items on your Step 1 list that are already being said by your toughest competitors.

Step 4:   Prioritize what is left of your Step 3 list by assigning a value to each item.

A—The strongest uniqueness against your competition.

B—A fairly strong uniqueness against your competition.

C—Weak uniqueness against your competition.

Step 5:   Package your message of uniqueness utilizing the strongest A points from Step 4.

Step 6:   Test your new message of uniqueness by trying it on a couple of your most loyal customers. A strong message will be visual, simple, will include your toughest competition, and can be stated in two minutes or less.

Your message needs to be visual, or sketched out on paper to help your prospect follow your major points and to give you control in case of an interruption in the conversation. It needs to be simple so your team and customer can actually remember your message. It needs to include your toughest competition to help you position your company for your customer/prospect to understand, and it needs to be able to be restated in less than two minutes so it can be repeated multiple times to the same customer over a period of weeks or months to help train them on your messaging.

Step 7:   Continue testing your new message by presenting it to a selection of customers and prospects.

Step 8:   With your message now proven, teach your new message to all employees that communicate with your customers.

Step 9:   Continually coach your team to insure they continue to deliver your strategic message of uniqueness on an ongoing basis. Also continue to retest your message to confirm it is still current and accurately reflects the reality of your current competitive environment.

Do not publish your final message on any of your printed literature or website. While you want your sales team presenting your message on a regular basis, you do not want to put it into print, on the Internet, or on your trade show booth. Putting your message into that type of formal "hard copy" is the easiest and fastest way for your competitors to gain access to your message.

Sales Leadership Question #15   Your ongoing new business prospecting process currently in place is _____?

1	2	3	4	5
Unaware	Weak	Just Average	Leading	Best Practice

Additional Clarifying Questions

♦ How consistent are the new business (finding new companies to sell) prospecting efforts of your sales team?

♦ How consistent are the existing customer prospecting (finding new business opportunities to sell within existing accounts) efforts of your sales team?

♦ Do you have a defined stepped prospecting process for both your new company prospecting as well as new business from existing customers prospecting that is being consistently followed by all members of your team?

A Low New Business Prospecting Skills evaluation score means you and your team have no formal new business prospecting program in place so your new business generation is haphazard and inconsistent. It is likely a reactive process of new company prospects calling in asking for help combined with your existing customers identifying additional areas they feel you can bring value. Everyone is happy when someone brings in a new account but no one is consistently going out to find these new customers. You likely have a few team members actually generating success from their prospecting efforts but you also have others doing nothing to find any new accounts (or new business from existing accounts) unless the lead is handed to them for follow-up.

A High New Business Prospecting Skills evaluation score means you and your team have a clearly defined, stepped process identified and being followed to help generate both new business from existing customers and new customer business. The new business tracking systems you have in place allow you to monitor and coach your team's process. You view new business prospecting from both new and existing companies as a critical growth effort that needs to be proactively implemented, tracked, and coached to maintain its long-term success.

Ideas to Help Improve Your New Business Prospecting Skills   New business prospecting (calling on new companies as well as looking for more from existing accounts) is a critical component of your sales team's long-term growth and success. But most sales teams approach new business prospecting in a disorganized, unplanned, and inefficient way.

Idea #1   Implement the *ISO 9000* four-step process (Chapter 4) for your new business prospecting efforts.

> *Step One:* Assess what each member of your sales team is currently doing to consistently generate new company business. Identify how much of their prospecting is proactive (initiated by them) compared to reactive (someone gave them a lead or the customer called you). Most new business prospecting is completely reactive. Also track how much of their new business being generated came from new customers versus new business from existing accounts.

> *Step Two:* Meet with your entire team to identify and design the best practices of new business prospecting. You need to define this process for both existing and new companies. You need to define the steps from the time you identify a prospect opportunity until you close the sale. You also want to identify the best job titles to initially contact, suggested telephone or

face-to-face selling scripts, suggested voice mail scripts, and sample letters.

Step Three: Start training and coaching your team on their new business process. You need to track their efforts as well as their results. Meet with your team on a regular basis to discuss their successes and frustrations. See if you need to modify or improve any of your defined new business best practices.

Step Four: Lead your team to ensure your new business prospecting efforts remain a part of your team's ongoing selling efforts.

Idea #2   Commit to making new business prospecting an ongoing high priority process. Most sales people dislike prospecting due to its high percentage of negative responses and difficulty getting heard by new prospects. Establish a set of minimum expectations for finding the best prospects to contact, the best methodologies to use to contact these prospects, and the expected frequency of calls. If you don't actively monitor and coach your team, they will stop prospecting. If you don't pay attention to your team's ongoing prospecting efforts, new business development will likely disappear from your sales reps' radar screens.

Idea #3   Track your team's prospecting progress. Ask them to track how many voice mails they leave before the average prospect calls back, how many companies they contact on average before one talks to them, how many sales calls (both telephone and face-to-face) and how many proposals are issued before making one sale. By collecting this data from your team, you can begin identifying which team members are generating the strongest levels of success. By identifying your best prospectors, you can compare their performance numbers (phone calls made to get a call back, etc.) against the lesser performing reps and identify why one gets better results than the others.

Sales Leadership Question #16   Your marketing and promotional skills are _____?

1	2	3	4	5
Unaware	Weak	Just Average	Leading	Best Practice

Additional Clarifying Questions

- ◆ Is your company's Marketing Department helping your salespeople achieve more than they would have achieved if just left alone?
- ◆ Are your sales tools increasing or decreasing your sales team's efficiency and effectiveness? How do your sales tools compare to the tools being used by your competition?
- ◆ Does your Marketing Department effectively communicate with your sales reps? Do they attend your sales meetings or go on sales calls? Are they helping to identify new opportunities and/or markets?

A Low Marketing and Promotional Skills evaluation score means there are no marketing and promotional efforts initiated by you, your team, or your company. Materials like websites, printed literature, and trade show displays are designed without your input and are not effective sales tools. A number of reps do not even use some of the printed materials Marketing developed (without your input). Marketing is a different department that has little to do with sales and since you as the sales leader are also probably not trained in effective marketing and promotion, little is done to improve these efforts.

A High Marketing and Promotional Skills evaluation score means you and your company have a strong commitment to the integration and partnering of sales and marketing. Both departments work as a team with the results being more effective sales tools that are more focused and aligned with your selling messages and more consistently utilized by your sales team.

Ideas to Help Improve Your "Marketing and Promotional" Skills   Marketing, Promotions, and website development are areas most managers are weakest in and subsequently devote little attention to strengthening. But they are also areas that can significantly increase both your sales team's selling efficiency as well as help communicate your added value and competitive uniqueness to prospects and customers.

Idea #1   For most businesses the Internet and website have become the most critical, and powerful, components of marketing. Work with your Marketing Department to strengthen your website.

155

If you do not have a website or a marketing department that can help, include Internet consultants and website developers in the re-design. Be sure to research your competitor's websites on a regular basis and check where your company comes up on various search engines to insure you are in the top few listings for your company and products.

Idea #2   Work to insure your sales team and website are commu-nicating one coordinated message to your markets.

What is the job of an outside sales rep? Most define that a salesper-son's job is to:

- Find new prospects.
- Communicate your uniqueness and value of buying from you and your company.
- Close business and take orders.
- Provide *after-sale* support.

What is the purpose of a company website? To accomplish the same four tasks as your sales team. How integrated and coordinated is your company website to your outside sales team's efforts? Consider asking each rep (and managers) the following questions:

- How often do you reference your website when talking to prospects or customers?
- How are you using our website and Internet presence as a sales aid to your selling efforts?

You will probably learn that your website and Internet presence (e-mail updates and marketing, etc.) are having little usage and impact by your sales team.

Next, ask a selection of newer customers the following questions:

- How much impact did our website have on your buying decision?
- What reference information did you utilize?
- How much time or attention did our sales team give to our website?

The majority of salespeople don't understand or utilize their company's website. They view it as an independent marketing component that doesn't affect them or their selling efforts.

Want to learn how comfortable your team really is with your company website? Write a 5- to 10-question test about your website asking basic questions like what color it is, what is listed on the site, is there a letter from your president? Do you have satisfied customer testimonials? Don't be surprised if a number of team members fail this test. If they are not using your site to help their selling efforts, why would they know what is on it? Also consider testing them on your competitor's websites. They will probably know even less about their competitors' sites than they do about their own.

In many companies salespeople dismiss websites because they are not sales focused. Most websites present the company history or technical product issues and devote little space to your competitive uniqueness selling messages. As was stated in Idea #2 from Sales Leadership Question #14, you do not want to publish your strategic message of competitive uniqueness. But your printed literature and website can both dance around your message by communicating the impact you can have without actually listing the exact marketing message being verbally delivered by your sales force.

Idea #3   Train your entire team how to use the Internet, e-mails, online search engines, and your company website. Most salespeople know little about the Internet or how to maximize their presence in online search engines. Most have also never received any training or coaching on proper e-mail etiquette.

Discuss with your team how the Internet and your website can be effective sales tools. Discuss how your website compares to your toughest competition. Discuss what additional functions or ideas could give your website a competitive advantage.

Idea #4   Evaluate how effective and sales focused your printed literature, advertising, sales aids, and trade show booths are to your selling efforts. Are they supporting your selling messaging and positioning? Are they enhancing your selling capabilities? Are they even being used by your sales team?

There is a theory of marketing that states printed materials are not meant to sell your product or service but to affirm your quality and pricing to your customer. Could you imagine going into a Lexus or BMW car dealership and their giving you a black and white brochure generated off their office computer? Is your printed literature communicating and maintaining your professionalism and pricing strategy? The simple rule is if you are higher priced than your competition, you also need to have a higher quality brochure compared to theirs.

Sales Leadership Question #17   Your ability to commit time to individually coach and strategize with each of your sales reps is _____?

1	2	3	4	5
Unaware	Weak	Just Average	Leading	Best Practice

Additional Clarifying Questions

- How much ongoing coaching help and guidance are your people receiving—especially your best people? Do you coach and plan with each rep?

- What percentage of your time do you spend on administrative, special pricing, and reactive problem solving? And what percentage do you spend proactively coaching and leading your sales team?

A Low Ability to Commit Coaching and Strategy Time with Your Reps evaluation score means you most likely feel you are too busy or overworked to devote much time to coaching your team. You are probably carrying your own accounts as a doing sales manager and feel buried with all the reporting, paperwork, special pricing, and problem solving you are doing. Your salespeople feel more like abandoned orphans than family members. You define your job as a sales manager as making sure your people perform above minimum. If someone is doing okay and generating solid numbers, you just don't have time to get actively involved in helping them increase their success.

A High Ability to Commit Coaching and Strategy Time with Your Reps evaluation score means you realize the only way you can help your salespeople achieve more is by your investing more coaching time and energy. You have reduced your time demands from others, have delegated the less critical stuff you used to handle, and have improved your time management skills to free up time to actually function as a coach and leader of your team.

Ideas to Help Improve Your Ability to Commit Coaching and Strategy Time with Your Reps   Question #8 of this *Sales Leadership Evaluation* asked about your accessibility to your sales force. That question centered on your availability and attitude of wanting to help your sales team. This question is now asking if you are actually investing time each week coaching and leading your sales team. Most managers are so bogged down in the internal administrative, report preparation, data analysis, pricing research, and technical product issues that they have no time left to actually do their job of leading their sales team. How much time are you able to devote each week to coaching and leading your team?

Idea #1   Keep track of your schedule to see how much time you are able to actually invest each week in coaching. List these seven areas of responsibility of a sales manager. Ask each of your people to list what percentage of your time (on average) they feel you spend each week on these activities:

1. Administrative.

2. Report generation.

3. E-mails.

4. Special pricing issues and questions.

5. Customer problem solving (shipping and technical product issues).

6. Selling in your own accounts.

7. Coaching and strategy time with your sales reps.

Be prepared for your sales team to rate you worse than you rate yourself feeling you spend much less time on coaching than on administrative and report issues. Just as in the other *ISO 9000* instances you are starting off by evaluating where you currently are before designing a plan to improve your coaching time.

Idea #2   Evaluate your time management skills. Effective time management is based on increasing both your efficiency and effectiveness. Are there areas you could improve to free up more time to then be able to devote to your sales team?

Idea #3   The majority of sales managers are overworked. Before any sales manager can become a more effective coach and strategist, they will likely need help rearranging their priorities and time commitments to be able to actually spend time proactively coaching their people. Ask your management to help you reprioritize and realign your responsibilities to free up more time to coach.

Idea #4   Delegate the less revenue critical responsibilities. What are you doing each week that either could be done by someone else or that is not necessary? Too many times we focus our energy on what we want to do instead of what is best to be completed. The only way you will free up more time to coach will be by reducing or eliminating other, less revenue critical tasks.

Idea #5   Start by working to increase your coaching time on the more critical accounts. If you have not been devoting time to coaching, then consider performing triage on your customers and sales teams. Just as in the medical profession, "triage" means you have to assess, and then prioritize for treatment, the relative severity and opportunities present in each account. Start by investing your newfound time on the accounts that could generate the fastest and largest increases in sales or profitability. Also consider identifying problems that are being experienced by a number of your sales team so you can coach them all at once on this problem or opportunity.

Idea #6   Acknowledge that every sales manager or leader believes they don't have enough time to be a coach and are always being pulled into less productive areas. Other leaders of their sales teams are overworked but still find ways to coach—why can't you?

Sales Leadership Question #18   **The percentage of time you spend talking future-focused with your reps is _____?**

1	2	3	4	5
Unaware	**Weak**	**Just Average**	**Leading**	**Best Practice**

Additional Clarifying Questions

- ◆ When talking to a team member about an account and/or problem, what percentage of your time and questions are devoted to talking future-focused, identifying how to move forward instead of just dissecting the past?
- ◆ Reviewing the files and documentation on each sales team member, what percentage of the information they maintain on an account is history, today, or future-focused?

A Low Future-Focused Skill evaluation score means you spend your time dealing with "what happened" and "so what will it take to fix" type of conversations. You are probably spending the majority of your time as a transactional sales manager just dealing with the problems and paperwork of your job. The majority of your coaching and thinking are based only on a "next best" effort mentality. You devote little time or attention to thinking and planning multiple moves ahead. This type of leadership mentality works better for maintaining a team than growing one.

A High Future-Focused Skill evaluation score means you are functioning more as a leader than as a manager. You devote time to history and today focused issues but try to push all coaching conversations into a future-focused mode. You are helping your people see "over the four-foot grass" (the "Hellarewe" bird from Chapter 1). You believe you are more value as a coach and strategist if you help your reps focus on where they are trying to take their accounts instead of dealing only with what is currently happening. You continually ask your team members "and then what?" when talking about their accounts.

Ideas to Help Improve Your Future-Focused Skills

Idea #1   Go over the ideas covered in Chapter 9 that discussed how you could master the fourth Central Leadership Value of being more of a visionary leader by being more proactive and future focused in your sales leadership efforts.

Idea #2   Ask your sales team to evaluate the amount of time you spend with them on history, today, and future-focused discussions. Ask their help to keep the team focused more on future-focused issues.

Sales Leadership Question #19   Your ability and time committed to talking tactical and strategic focused with your sales reps is _____?

1	2	3	4	5
Unaware	Weak	Just Average	Leading	Best Practice

Additional Clarifying Questions

♦ How often do you talk about the multiple steps involved in your tactical selling processes?

♦ How much time do you spend talking to your team about how to get higher, wider, and deeper in their accounts?

♦ When was the last time you worked with your sales team to develop ways to increase their strategic positioning and competitive differential?

A Low Tactical and Strategic Focused Skill evaluation score means you spend little time as a leader coaching your team on the process, structures, and strategies of selling. You are likely more of a transactional focused coach dealing with the stuff going on right now. You don't see much of a vision or direction of where your team's selling needs to be going. You assume improving the operational excellence of your team's blocking and tackling skills are all that is necessary for selling success. You and your team will likely be outsold on a regular basis by your competition. They are thinking more moves ahead than you are and are applying a stronger political awareness to their account plans.

A High Tactical and Strategic Focused Skill evaluation score means you are effectively leading your team by helping them see more than they could see on their own. You are constantly pushing all members of your sales team to think and plan multiple moves ahead, to think through a stepped selling process, to increase their political presence at their accounts by working to get higher, wider, and deeper and to be more organized and focused when communicating their strategic message of competitive uniqueness. You are helping your team members achieve more than they would have achieved without your vision and understanding of the selling components that really do increase your selling success—the tactics and strategies of selling.

Ideas to Help Improve Your Tactical and Strategic Focused Skills

Idea #1   Review the ideas covered in Chapter 10 discussing how you could master the fifth Central Leadership Value of committing to defined structures of selling. Also work your people through the *Sales Evaluation* in Section IV, which discusses the components of effective tactical and strategic selling.

Idea #2   Continually remind your team that operational excellence is critical to any salesperson's success, but will do little to help increase your competitive advantage. The tactical and strategic areas of selling are the main drivers to your increasing your multiple stepped thinking and planning of your accounts combined with a stronger positioning of strategic value differential.

Idea #3   Ask your sales team to evaluate the amount of time you spend discussing operational, tactical, and strategic issues in their accounts and territory. Also ask their help to keep the entire team more focused on the tactical and strategic aspects of selling.

Sales Leadership Question #20   Your ability to communicate with customers to help your sales reps get higher, wider, and deeper is _____?

1	2	3	4	5
Unaware	Weak	Just Average	Leading	Best Practice

Additional Clarifying Questions

- How often do you go on sales calls to your sales reps accounts?
- How often are your sales reps able to use you to get higher, wider, or deeper within their accounts?

A Low Ability to Communicate with Customers evaluation score means you are not being effectively used by your sales team. You don't see how you, as their sales manager, play an important role in helping each of your people grow and expand their contacts within their accounts. Because you lack awareness of this skill you are also not pushing your sales reps to take you on calls. Your presence as a sales manager in your reps' accounts is not being used to increase their selling effectiveness and competitive advantage.

A High Ability to Communicate with Customers evaluation score means you have become an effective sales tool to your sales team. You know with your assistance, your sales reps can achieve higher levels of customer executives, call wider in their accounts with your help opening doors into other customer departments, and help them get deeper into the departments they are already in. You also understand how to ask the tougher or more sensitive questions of a customer your reps are not able to ask. Your goal by going on customer calls is to be a booster rocket to your reps helping them get higher and further than they would without your help.

Ideas to Help Improve Your Ability to Communicate with Customers Skills As a sales leader you are a great sales tool to help improve your team members' understanding and ability to sell within the political environment of their accounts by your ability to help them get higher, wider, and deeper.

Idea #1   Set a goal that every time you visit an account with a rep, you will somehow try to get higher, wider, or deeper. You can be an effective tool to get to new people at an account or to be asking the tougher or more sensitive questions your sales reps have not been able to ask.

Idea #2   Strategize with your reps about the key prospects or accounts where you, as a sales tool, can help them increase their competitive advantage, shorten their selling process or improve their account loyalty. Most sales reps are either unaware or afraid to use their managers as effective sales tools. You will need to push them to think of more and better ways to use you to improve or open up an account.

Idea #3   Discuss with your team how they can use other members of your company to also get higher, wider, and deeper. As discussed in Chapter 6, most sales reps function as Super Doers and tend to either downplay the effectiveness of using team members to help sell or are afraid that bringing others into a call will actually hurt their selling efforts. Part of your coaching and planning needs to be identifying who in your company you need to keep away from customers, who can be the most persuasive when taken on a sales call, and how to properly set up the customer and brief your company employee to properly prepare for their call. Using other company people on sales calls can be a positive value added addition to your selling efforts—but it does need to be properly set up and managed.

16

Suggestions to Improve Your Sales Leadership Skills and Effectiveness

The goal of the *Sales Leadership Evaluation* outlined in this section is to help you increase your awareness of your strongest sales leadership skills as well as the skills that, if improved, could most help you increase your ability to lead a sales team.

Completing this detailed assessment of your leadership skills is meant to help you begin strengthening your ability to lead a sales team. Your completion of this evaluation is also meant to help you identify the best opportunities for improvement and increased success to help you identify both where your leadership skills are today as well as what you can do to strengthen these skills in the future. This is only Step One of the *ISO 9000* process—to quantify where you are. Now that you know where you are, the next question is—do you want to get better?

www.GreatSalesSkills.com

If you want more information and a free multipage report offering additional suggestions to improve your leadership skills visit www.GreatSalesSkills.com, the companion website to this book, for a free online version of this 20-question *Sales Leadership Evaluation* and the *Sales Evaluation* explained in Section IV. These are free evaluations and both include a detailed, multiple page, customized report offering personalized feedback and improvement suggestions. Either report is immediately available upon completion of your online evaluations.

Now That You Have Completed Your Sales Leadership Evaluation

The first suggestion is to re-read Chapter 11—Using the *Sales Leadership Evaluation* to Evaluate, Prioritize, and Develop Your Sales Leadership Abilities.

Next, consider going back and reading all of the supporting information provided with each of the leadership questions covered in this section. Consider how many of the Additional Clarifying Questions as well as the low (or high) evaluation score descriptions, fit your current leadership style. Start to build a list of the "best practices" skills, attitudes, or philosophies you would most like to strengthen to best help you move to a more effective level of leadership.

It is also important that you complete your evaluation and improvement planning of your leadership skills prior to working with your sales team on their selling skills. Before you strengthen a team, you need to first strengthen their leadership.

In Section V—Developing a Successful Sales Team Improvement Strategy you will also learn more about how to apply a stepped process of growth and change to your sales force upon their completion of the *Sales Evaluation*.

We have been talking about the definition of a sales manger—to help each of your people achieve more than they would have achieved if just left alone. This *Sales Leadership Evaluation* is the first step to helping you strengthen your ability to lead your sales team to achieving a better understanding and control of the skills, structures, and philosophies of selling.

Now, are you ready to start evaluating your sales team?

Section

IV

How to Improve a Salesperson's Selling Skills and Abilities

Section Overview

CHAPTER 17   **Evaluating a Salesperson's *Operational Selling Skills and Abilities***

This 20-question *Sales Evaluation* is a comprehensive analysis tool designed to help you and your sales reps increase awareness of your strongest selling skills, as well as the skills that, if improved, could most help you increase your selling abilities.

This is a subjective evaluation and like the *Sales Leadership Evaluation* there are no right or wrong answers. You are evaluating either your own, or your sales reps' selling skills based on how well you feel they are accomplishing each skill set. A free online version of this 20-question *Sales Evaluation* is also available at www.GreatSalesSkills.com.

The following 20 questions in this evaluation are divided among the following three chapters (Chapters 17 to 19) and includes additional copy with each question to help increase your awareness of the identified skill and to offer suggestions to improve.

For each question of the evaluation you will evaluate or score yourself (or the person you are evaluating) on a five-point scale of 1 = Unaware, 2 = Weak, 3 = Just Average, 4 = Leading, or 5 = Best Practice.

The first six questions focus on *operational* selling skills and abilities. The lack of strong operational selling skills is a major missing piece in most, otherwise experienced and successful, sales reps' abilities.

The major operational areas to be evaluated are your understanding of the technical side of your business, your understanding of the fundamentals of selling, and understanding how to manage your time and information.

Sales Question #1   Your technical knowledge of your products/services and how they relate to your industry is _____?

Sales Question #2   Your knowledge of your competitors' products and their customer success stories is _____?

Sales Question #3   Your knowledge and daily usage of the steps of a sales call are _____?

Sales Question #4   Your understanding of personalities and ability to identify, and then mirror, your customers' communications style is _____?

Sales Question #5   Your personal *time and territory* organizational skills are _____?

Sales Question #6   Your ability to utilize technology to increase your productivity and effectiveness is _____?

CHAPTER 18   Evaluating a Salesperson's *Tactical Selling Skills and Abilities*

The next eight questions focus on your *tactical* skills and abilities related to selling. Increasing your tactical skills is one of the critical *drivers* (along with strategic skills) to increasing your competitive advantage.

The major tactical areas to be evaluated are your understanding of how to maintain and grow your business, how to manage your selling process, and how to maintain and control your customer.

Sales Question #7   Your ability to proactively manage, control, and resolve customers' problems is _____?

Sales Question #8   Your ability to keep your existing accounts stable and under control is _____?

Sales Question #9   Your ongoing new business prospecting process is _____?

Sales Question #10   Your ability to think and plan multiple moves ahead in each of your customers and prospects is _____?

Sales Question #11   Your knowledge and understanding of your competitors' pricing practices are _____?

Sales Question #12   Your ability to utilize company support resources in your territory is_____?

Sales Question #13   Your ability to communicate what your customers want to buy instead of just what you have to sell is _____?

Sales Question #14   Your understanding of the political environment and decision process of each of your accounts is _____?

CHAPTER 19   Evaluating a Salesperson's *Strategic Positioning Selling Skills and Abilities*

The final six questions focus on your *strategic* skills and ability to communicate your company's philosophy and competitive market positioning. Your strategic skills also involve your personal philosophy and commitment to ongoing training and desire to want to get better. Increasing your strategic skills is the second of two critical *drivers* (along with your tactical skills) to increasing your competitive advantage.

The major strategic areas to be evaluated are your ability to manage the strategic aspects of your selling process and your commitment to a philosophy of ongoing personal development and improvement.

Sales Question #15   Your ability to communicate your competitive uniqueness and value is _____?

Sales Question #16   Your knowledge of your competitors' strongest *value points* they use to sell against you is _____?

Sales Question #17   Your ability to win business at a higher price/margin by communicating your stronger value is _____?

Sales Question #18   Your ability to represent yourself in a professional, truthful, and ethical manner is _____?

Sales Question #19   Your ongoing commitment and efforts to grow and improve your selling skills and awareness is _____?

Sales Question #20   Your ongoing use of one or more coaches or mentors to help you get better is _____?

CHAPTER 20   Suggestions to Improve a Salesperson's Selling Skills and Effectiveness

The goal of this 20-question *Sales Evaluation* is to help you analyze your team's current skill level and increased your awareness of their strongest skills as well as the skills that, if improved, could most help them increase their selling abilities.

The key to your team advancing beyond their current selling level is to help them understand where they are today (the first step of the *ISO 9000* process) and then to help them identify where they need to grow and improve in the future. Now that you know the skill levels of all members of your sales team, it is time to get to work identifying the selling "best practices" they should be working toward and leading them as they work to improve their selling abilities, focus, and success.

Additional information and a free multipage report offering suggestions to improve the selling skills of your team is available at www.GreatSalesSkills.com, the companion website to this book.

CHAPTER

17

Evaluating a Salesperson's *Operational Selling Skills and Abilities*

This 20-question *Sales Evaluation* is a comprehensive analysis tool meant to be administered to help salespeople increase the awareness of their strongest selling skills, as well as the skills that, if improved, could most help them increase their selling abilities.

This section has been written from the perspective of a salesperson evaluating their personal selling skills. You might consider asking each of your salespeople to read this complete section as they evaluate their own selling skills. You can also send your salespeople to www.GreatSalesSkills.com where this 20-question evaluation is also available free online and includes a detailed customized report offering improvement suggestions. Your team will receive the most value from this *Sales Evaluation* if you, as their manager, also complete an evaluation on each salesperson.

This evaluation is meant as a positive looking forward coaching opportunity and is not meant as an inquisition on your past. Your involvement in this evaluation is meant to help you improve your skills and success.

As a sales leader, when you meet with each team member to compare and discuss their evaluation, begin by noting some positive attributes to help keep the meeting constructive and productive. You want to discuss improvement opportunities, rather than hammering them for what they haven't done.

1. One question at a time, ask the rep where he graded himself on each question and why. Share how you evaluated each skill discussing any inconsistencies between your two scores.

2. Help build a list of next best skill areas that could provide the greatest payback if improved.

3. Develop detailed action items for the salesperson to be working on. Include specific completion dates to ensure their plan will be implemented. Each sales rep needs to agree with the scope and focus of any implementation plan to insure their buy-in and acceptance.

4. Discuss possible resources to help them accelerate learning and growth.

The completed evaluation and action items for each salesperson become an effective performance plan to be worked on for the next six months to a year. A copy of past evaluation responses needs to be saved to evaluate whether progress is being made. Saving these responses is also a great way to demonstrate that improvements have indeed occurred.

Evaluating Operational Selling Skills and Abilities

Focusing on your personal selling skills: Are your personal selling skills improving or impairing your success?

The first of your skill areas to evaluate is your *operational* or foundation selling skills and abilities. In Chapter 10 operational selling skills were defined as the skills involved in the fundamentals of day-to-day selling. Some refer to operational skills as the foundation or blocking and tackling skills of selling. Operational skills also refer to the ability of your team to be consistent.

A lack of strong operational selling skills is a major weakness in most, otherwise experienced and successful, salespeople. The majority of sales professionals learn to sell by trial and error—no training, no coaching, no direction, just raw experience trying to figure out how to sell and succeed on their own.

After several years, sales professionals who survive are able to build a strong enough experience base and establish their territory. However, the lack of training and structure leads to selling practices based on hunches and intuition. Intuitive salespeople can be successful, but they tend to lack consistency in their skills. On some calls they are brilliant, but on others they are ineffective or do not accomplish all they could. A way to profoundly increase overall selling success is to build operational selling skills by adding more structure and consistency to daily selling efforts.

The major operational areas to be evaluated are your understanding of the technical side of your business, the fundamentals of selling, and managing your time and information. How much in-depth skill building sales training and coaching have you had over your selling career?

Consequences of Your Operational Skills and Abilities Being Underdeveloped

- A lack of consistency in selling efforts. On one call you do great but then *crash and burn* on the next.
- A difficulty developing and maintaining long-term customer relationships due to inconsistent and ineffective communications skills.
- Customers sometimes mistake your weak operational skills and abilities as a lack of ethics and/or professionalism.

The Positive Results and Benefits of Your Having Competitively Advanced Operational Skills and Abilities

- Customers and prospects perceive you as being more professional and ethical than your competition.
- You make fewer mistakes and erroneous statements so you spend much less time correcting problems.

Your Understanding of the Technical Side Of Your Business

Salesperson Question #1 **Your technical knowledge of your products/services and how they relate to your industry is _____?**

1	2	3	4	5
Unaware	Weak	Just Average	Leading	Best Practice

Additional Clarifying Questions

- Do you know more than your customers about how your products/services can benefit their business?

- Do you understand, and can you intelligently discuss, the major technical trends happening within your industry?

- Do you understand your customers' businesses and how they utilize your products/services? Can you answer or solve the majority of your customers' technical questions?

A Low Product/Service Technical Knowledge evaluation score means you receive little respect from either your customers or your own internal support people. You also tend to burn up support resources helping you solve problems you should have been able to solve on your own. You consistently miss new business opportunities by wasting time going after business that is not the best fit for your products/services.

A High Product/Service Technical Knowledge evaluation score means customers see the value your relationship adds to their business. They appreciate your technical problem-solving abilities and knowledge of how your products/services can improve their business. You are able to keep your competitors from getting your customer's attention. You also have the respect and support of your company's internal technical support team, which means you receive positive and faster assistance when faced with a customer problem.

Ideas to Help Improve Your Product/Service Technical Knowledge Your product and technical knowledge is the most important component of your operational selling skills. It all starts or stops here. A sales call will grind to a halt, and all credibility will leave if the customer realizes you don't know your products or services.

Idea #1   Talk to your company's technical experts. Your internal support team can provide technical or product training and can help you increase your competitive product knowledge.

Idea #2   (for sales leaders) Do you want to find out how technically competent your sales team really is? Have your technical people prepare a written test of 10 to 20 questions asking about the technical, or performance, aspects of your products. You don't need long or complex answers, just enough to show if they have a solid understanding of what you sell. Consider questions like "Our #5250 model is acceptable but is never to be used with a plastic compound base." Have each team member complete this technical test to help you determine if additional technical training is required and beneficial.

Though your product and technical skills are the most important foundation of selling, don't feel you are in a crisis if some salespeople don't do well on your test. For the majority of businesses, technical knowledge is the easiest skill to teach someone new to sales and your company. Just as in all of our *ISO 9000* examples, the first step to improving the technical competency of your sales team is to first find out where your people are right now.

Salesperson Question #2   Your knowledge of your competitors' products and their customer success stories are _____?

1	2	3	4	5
Unaware	Weak	Just Average	Leading	Best Practice

Additional Clarifying Questions

- Can you identify each of your competitors' top *Showcase* accounts? (A "showcase" account is one of the best current satisfied customers, who provides testimonials and tours of their facilities to show your prospects how good a company you are to do business with.)

♦ Do you know more about each of your competitors' products or services than they know about yours?

♦ Can you identify the specific conditions or environments where you can outperform each of your competitors' products or services? Can you also identify under what conditions each of your competitors' products or services is a better fit for a customer than yours?

A Low Knowledge of Your Competitors' Products and Their Success Stories evaluation score will likely mean you get surprised on a regular basis by what your competitors have proposed. You are also consistently surprised by how positively your customer or prospect reacts to your competitors' proposals. You tend to waste a lot of time explaining how unique your products are even though your customer or prospect believes they are the same as your competition. You miss opportunities to take business away from your competition because you are not aware of their gaps or exposures.

A High Knowledge of Your Competitors' Products and Their Success Stories evaluation score means you have the ability to anticipate your competitors' strategies and be more proactive in your selling efforts. This allows you to pursue their current customers by discussing ways to improve their usage and service beyond what your competition currently supplies. You ask tougher, more focused usage questions of prospects and differentiate your competitive value by focusing on the key competitive differences between your products or services and ignoring the areas or components where you are evenly matched.

Ideas to Help Improve Your Knowledge of Your Competitors' Products and Their Success Stories Like your product and technical knowledge, having a solid understanding of your competitors' products is an important component of your operational selling skills. A lack of solid competitive product or service knowledge means you miss opportunities to prove you are a better competitive choice and hinders you from successfully pursuing prospects when they tell you they are having problems with your competitors' products or services.

Idea #1   (for sales leaders) Ask your company's technical experts for help. Ask them to work with your sales team to better understand how the competitors' products or services outperform yours.

Idea #2   One of the best (and legal as well as ethical) ways to learn about your competitors' satisfied customers is to start calling on them. Make sales calls on your competitors' showcase accounts. The odds of your winning their business is low, but the goal of calling on a few of these competitive showcase accounts is to conduct competitive research.

Start to build a relationship with these competitive showcase accounts by asking questions like, "What do you like most about their products?" "What most impresses you about how they support and service your account?" and "Why do you feel they are the best in our industry?" You want these prospects to just think you are trying to win away their business. If they believe you are trying to persuade them to switch they will likely tell you the most positive attributes and values they have been taught to say about your competitors' products. It is likely the positive comments a prospect tells you about your competitor are the same comments they tell your competitions' other prospects when they are brought to them for a positive reference. A tour of their facilities can also reveal the kinds of things your competitions' prospects see when brought through this showcase account by your competitor.

One final side benefit of your calling on these competitive showcase accounts is it will stress out your competition. You can count on the showcase prospect telling your competitor you are calling on them now. This will likely cause your competitor to invest additional time in this account to make sure they are still loyal and safe to use in their selling efforts. Now isn't that fun!

Idea #3   (for sales leaders) To find out how well your team understands your competitors' products or services and how they perform against your offerings, ask your technical people to prepare a written test of 10 to 20 questions about the technical, or performance, aspects of each of your toughest competitor's products. Just as with the technical test, you do not need long, complex answers,just enough to determine if they have a solid understanding of what they are selling against. Consider questions like "Their low-end model has a ___% weaker induction suction than our #2550 model." Have each team member complete this test to see if additional technical training is needed.

Your Understanding of the Fundamentals Of Selling

How well do you understand, and consistently utilize, the basic steps and structures of selling?

Salesperson Question #3   Your knowledge and daily usage of the steps of a sales call is _____?

1	2	3	4	5
Unaware	Weak	Just Average	Leading	Best Practice

Additional Clarifying Questions

- Do you know the steps of a sales call well enough to be able to write them down in less than a minute?
- Do you plan out your sales calls in advance based on these steps?
- Do you have consistently persuasive sales calls with customers where you maintain a calm control of your call even when you are pressed for time or dealing with challenging situations or problems?

A Low Knowledge and Daily Usage of the Steps of a Sales Call evaluation score means your sales calls are wildly inconsistent. On one call you are persuasively brilliant and on the next you crash and burn. You are most ineffective when you are either not given enough time in a call or are dealing with a resistant prospect. You miss selling opportunities (especially with new prospects) because of your lack of consistent selling skills.

A High Knowledge and Daily Usage of the Steps of a Sales Call evaluation score means you perform consistently even under pressure. Short time frames or difficult situations do not faze you and you are able to generate positive outcomes to these calls. You come across as more customer-focused because you have productive sales calls where you ask more questions and listen more than you talk. Your customers tend to give you more time because they are confident you will be both efficient and effective in your communication.

Ideas to Help Improve Your Knowledge and Usage of the Steps of a Sales Call
This is a critical operational foundation skill for all salespeople. The most successful reps also tend to be the most consistent salespeople. Your consistency is directly tied to your understanding and usage of the structures of selling and persuasion. A strong understanding and consistent usage of the steps of a sales call lead to positive sales calls.

Idea #1   Can you write down the steps of a sales call? Try it. As simple as this sounds the vast majority of experienced salespeople cannot complete this exercise in less than a minute. Why a minute? If it takes you longer than 60 seconds, you are not using these steps to guide you through a sales call. If it takes you longer than a minute to write down the steps this is an academic exercise rather than a process you are implementing on every sales call. You probably don't know the steps, have never been through "steps of a sales call" training, or feel intuitively that each sales call is completely different so you don't need any kind of standard steps and just sell with a "go in and wing it" selling style. None of these reasons will generate any kind of consistent results in a sales territory!

What if you are a sales manager? As a sales manager you also need to be able to write down the steps. How can you coach a salesperson on how to improve their selling skills if you don't know what the steps are yourself?

In case you were wondering, most sales training defines the steps of a sales call as (1) lower resistance, (2) ask questions to learn and qualify, (3) present your solutions, (4) close, ask for the order, and (5) agree to your next contact.

Idea #2   (for sales leaders) Watch for the steps of a sales call when you go on sales calls with your team. As a manager you need to observe how proficient your team members are in their utilization of these steps. Did they sail through the steps in their call maintaining control and a persuasive dialogue with their customer or did they bounce around on their call missing important selling opportunities?

Salesperson Question #4 **Your understanding of personalities and ability to identify, then mirror, your customer's communications style is _____?**

1	2	3	4	5
Unaware	Weak	Just Average	Leading	Best Practice

Additional Clarifying Questions

◆ Can you identify two or three of the most significant personality traits of each of your customers?

◆ Do you quickly adjust your selling style to better mirror your customer's personality on every sales call?

◆ Is your personality awareness and flexibility based on your intuitive reactive skills (you just eventually know what to do)? Or is your personality flexibility based on your proactive awareness of a defined structure that allows you to identify and bend within the first two minutes of a sales call?

A Low Personality Awareness and Ability to Bend Your Communications Style evaluation score means you demonstrate very little flexibility in your communication style. You tend to sell to one personality—your own. You do well in selling situations unless your prospect communicates in a different way than you do. You are missing tremendous selling opportunities in your territory due to your inability to communicate, and relate to those different from you.

A High Personality Awareness and Ability to Bend Your Communications Style evaluation score likely means you have the ability to be persuasive with a wide range of customers. You can persuasively communicate with both detailed technical people as well as *big picture* senior management. You are able to assess and then adjust your communication style within the first minute or two of a sales call so you rarely have an unsuccessful or ineffective meeting. Your customers feel you really understand their concerns and they appreciate your ability to talk in their language—not yours.

Ideas to Help Improve Your "Personality Awareness and Ability to Bend Your Communications Style" Skills A flexible communication style is one of the key elements of persuasive selling. This requires utilizing some type of personality structure to insure a consistent flexibility in your client communications. Many sales professionals believe they exhibit effective "personality awareness" but are only utilizing an intuitive approach feeling they can eventually figure their customer or prospect out and will know what to say.

The most popular "customer personality flexibility" training structure taught by a number of training organizations is referred to as *The Four Quadrants of Personality*. It evaluates and helps identify anyone's personality based on two measurements. The first measurement evaluates which side of your people skills you communicate. Are you more *task* oriented, wanting to talk about work and sports, or are you more *people* oriented wanting to talk about hobbies, vacations, and family?

The second measurement of someone's personality evaluates which side of your communications skills you communicate. Are you more *big picture* oriented, more of a risk taker and talker, or are you more *detail* oriented, more of a risk avoider who would rather listen than talk? Each of these personality types requires a vastly different style of persuasive selling to be effective.

Combining those two axes identifies four major personality types. There are numerous training programs currently available but most describe the four personality types as:

1. *Driver Personality Type.* Someone who focuses on the big picture in their communications, preferring the discussion of major points rather than details, loves to talk, and is very task oriented. These are the in control types who prefer communications to be brief, to the point, and without fluff and emotion.

2. *Expressive Personality Type.* Also a big picture communicator (like the Driver type), loves to talk, tell jokes, and is very people or emotionally focused, wanting to be your friend. Their communication style is to be in charge, keep things brief and to the point but (unlike the Driver) uses lots of impressive flash, fluff, and emotion to make their points.

3. *Analytical Personality Type.* Someone who is very detailed in their communication (wanting lots of details and supporting information) and is also very task oriented (like the Driver

type not wanting a lot of emotion). These are the number cruncher types who want things organized and broken down into detailed spreadsheets based on accurate data without any fluff and emotion.

4. *Amiable Personality Type.*   Also very detailed (like the Analytical type) in their communication but are also very people oriented (like the Expressive type). These are the nurturer types who want to first know you as a person before talking business. They are also easy to push around and to force into a decision—but a decision they will reverse after you leave.

Though people are a blend of all four personality types there are one or two that are the dominant personality styles in each of us. Successful understanding of personality styles requires you have a clear understanding of your own personality and communication style. You also need to understand how to identify in the first few minutes of a sales call your prospect's personality and communication style. With this awareness you can then adjust your communication style to blend with your customer's personality. How flexible are you in utilizing some type of personality structure as part of your daily selling efforts?

Other personality structures include understanding *Neuro-Linguistic Programming (NLP)*. One component of NLP is that we all have one of three styles of best receiving new information. You learn best through "auditory" "visual" or "kinesthetic" (touching or feeling) methods.

Idea #1   Personality Awareness and Flexibility is a complex topic that needs to be researched and practiced to be mastered. You can learn more about the various detailed training materials available to help you increase your personality flexibility skills at www.GreatSalesSkills.com.

Idea #2   (for sales leaders) Most sales reps believe they have a clear understanding of how to utilize flexible communications with a customer. Consider testing these beliefs. If a sales rep says they have been through personality training before, ask them to name the four personality types. Then ask them what your personality style is using that structure. Does your team need more training and coaching in customer personality flexibility?

Your Understanding of How to Manage Your Time and Information

How organized, efficient, and effective are you at managing your time and the information flows of your job?

Salesperson Question #5 **Your personal "time and territory" organizational skills are _____?**

1	2	3	4	5
Unaware	Weak	Just Average	Leading	Best Practice

Additional Clarifying Questions

◆ Are your personal time management or organizational skills contributing to or inhibiting your control of your territory?

◆ Do you use some type of paper or electronic calendar system to efficiently keep track of your *To Dos*, appointments and action items? Do you ever miss appointments or requests for information because you forgot to write down and keep track of the times and dates?

◆ Do you begin your week by preparing a complete five-day plan or do you go into work on Monday and just start responding to messages and complaints?

A Low Time and Territory Organizational Skills evaluation score means you tend to be disorganized, distracted, and ineffective in getting things done. You lose things and forget to follow through on promises you make. Your work areas are stacked high with unfinished and unknown *stuff.* Your pockets and calendar are filled with little pieces of paper listing urgent reminders and promises made. You waste a tremendous amount of time just trying to find things, and you do little planning or organizing. Your territory information tracking tools are out of control. You have no idea where your clients' records are, and you have no records of important customer conversations. Despite all this, you still tell people in your office, "Don't touch anything. I know exactly where it is" even when you really don't.

A High Time and Territory Organizational Skills evaluation score means you are both efficient and effective in your territory management. You are in control and are highly organized. You maintain a computerized calendar and prioritized To Do list. Your desk is clean and organized. There are no piles of unfinished work on your desk or the floor of your workspace. You waste little time looking for misplaced documents or files and can easily get your hands on any needed item. You have detailed and accurate records that are well organized and easy to access. You have bailed yourself out of a number of customer crises by having the records to show you did everything timely and properly. You also spend a lot of your time focusing on the future of what you want to do.

Ideas to Help Improve Your Time and Territory Organizational Skills

Idea #1   (for sales leaders) Conduct an inspection of a salesperson's desk, calendar, car, and briefcase. Are these critical sales areas organized or do they look like a paper bomb just went off? The more disorganized these work areas are, the more likely a critical customer request or document will be misplaced or lost.

Idea #2   (for sales leaders) Most salespeople have a disorganized and inefficient customer information organization and tracking system and are overwhelmed with customer requests, paperwork, and To Do lists. Evaluate your sales team's ability to organize their customer and order tracking information. Ask a few detailed questions about one of their important accounts to see how efficient they are in retrieving the information requested.

Idea #3   (for sales leaders) Lead your team in a discussion of the best practices of time and territory management. Ask each to write down three time and territory management habits they use effectively and three habits that are wasteful, inefficient, or ineffective. Lead them through a group discussion of how they can improve their efforts.

Salesperson Question #6   **Your ability to utilize technology to increase your productivity and effectiveness is _____?**

1	2	3	4	5
Unaware	Weak	Just Average	Leading	Best Practice

Additional Clarifying Questions

- ◆ Do you have a solid understanding of your company's internal computer systems? How effective are you at using products like Microsoft Word, Excel, and PowerPoint?

- ◆ Are you utilizing a client tracking or Customer Relationship Management (CRM) software package like ACT, Goldmine, Maximizer, or one of the other 100+ software programs available, or does your company have its own customized package to electronically track your territory and all activities?

- ◆ How efficient are your online information researching skills using search engines like "Google?"

A Low Technology Skills and Usage evaluation score means you do not understand or are struggling with the technology of your business. Computers and advanced electronics make you uncomfortable. You lack computer skills and can barely send e-mails. You do little research on your industry, customers, prospects, or competitors on the Internet. You use your computer only as a glorified typewriter and are still struggling with your company's internal software systems. You do all of your planning and territory tracking on paper (if at all).

A High Technology Skills and Usage evaluation score means you are one of the most connected and efficient members of the sales team. You take advantage of all the electronic productivity tools available to you. Your customers are impressed with how easy it is to always be in contact with you and how quickly you respond to their e-mails and phone calls. You prefer communicating via e-mail rather than telephone because of the increased efficiency and productivity it provides you. You live on the Internet and find it a great resource for information on customers, prospects, and your competition.

Ideas to Help Improve Your "Technology" Skills and Usage Strong technology skills will only continue to become more critical to the job of selling. What can you do to make sure you have the technology skills and education you need to be both efficient and effective in fulfilling your information requirements?

Idea #1   Check out your local community college, university, or large computer store. Most offer some type of ongoing seminars and classes in various software and computer tools.

Idea #2   (for sales leaders) Put together a test or set of exercises for your salespeople to determine their technology skills and understanding.

18

Evaluating a Salesperson's
Tactical Selling Skills and Abilities

Are you spending all of your time trying to do things right or are you spending your time working to do the right things?
—Zig Ziglar

Are you managing and leading your sales territory on purpose? The second skill area to evaluate is the *Tactical* skills and abilities of selling. In Chapter 10 tactical selling skills were defined as "the ability to understand and control the steps and structures of the selling process." Tactical skills include the multiple stepped plan necessary when you chain together a series of operational sales calls.

Your major Tactical abilities to be evaluated are your understanding of how to maintain and grow your business, your knowledge of how to manage your selling process, and your effectiveness in maintaining and influencing your customer. Honing your tactical skills is one of the critical drivers (along with Strategic skills) capable of increasing your competitive advantage.

Consequences of Having Underdeveloped *Tactical Skills and Abilities*

- You waste a tremendous amount of time in your territory due to false starts and/or stalled selling efforts. You appear to be wandering around your territory without accomplishing anything.

- Your buyer controls the pace of your sales call, and leads you through the selling process, diminishing your ability to communicate a value proposition. The customer will be able to position their buying process toward lower prices and away from your value differentials.

- You have a difficult time predicting when a prospect will finally close the sale and agree to buy from you.

- Though you will likely be able to maintain your existing business, there will be little new business discovered or generated.

- Time will be spent pursuing and even supporting unprofitable or troublesome accounts that shouldn't have been sold in the first place.

- Your customers interpret your weak tactical skills and abilities as a lack of understanding about what your customers want and a lack of confidence in what you have to offer.

The Benefits of Having Competitively Advanced *Tactical Skills and Abilities*

- Customers or prospects perceive you as being more professional and ethical than your competition.

- You make fewer mistakes and erroneous statements so you spend less time correcting problems.

- You sell and maintain more business in your territory since you have mastered the steps of the selling processes, established strong customer contacts, and created better positioning against the competition.

- You produce higher profit margin business due to your strong leadership role within your accounts.
- You conduct more aggressive new business prospecting including new business from existing accounts.
- You require less management time to successfully run your territory.

Your Ability to Maintain and Grow Your Business

Salesperson Question #7 Your ability to proactively manage, control, and resolve customers' problems is _____?

1	2	3	4	5
Unaware	Weak	Just Average	Leading	Best Practice

Additional Clarifying Questions

- Can you predict and resolve customer problems before they even complain?
- Are you able to more than just fix your customers' problems? Do you also work to put plans in place to insure your customers' long-term satisfaction with you and your company?
- Are you talking on a regular basis to your customers' management to evaluate how you and your company are performing and to try to identify how you can do an even better job?

A Low Ability to Proactively Manage, Control, and Resolve Customer Problems evaluation score means customer problems are a major time burner for you. You allow problems to fester and your customers are normally not satisfied with how long it takes you to solve them. Your customers do not trust your ability to solve problems, so they either go around you to complain to someone else in your company, or they keep checking up on you to make sure you are working on their problem. Problems are usually not resolved to your client's satisfaction, and you

191

have lost customers because of your inability to positively and proactively solve their problems. Too often problems seem to control you rather than your controlling the problems.

A High Ability to Proactively Manage, Control, and Resolve Customer Problems evaluation score means your ability to proactively solve your customers' problems is a significant part of your competitive advantage. You are able to successfully manage your customers' complaints. You resolve problems quickly so they rarely are blown out of proportion. In a number of cases you have identified and resolved problems before your customers were even aware of them. Your customers trust your ability to resolve problems and don't feel the need to constantly check up on you. When you do learn about a problem you go into proactive mode, planning a quick resolution to your customers' problems.

Ideas to Help Improve Your Ability to Proactively Manage, Control, and Resolve Customer Problems Most sales reps are completely reactive in their selling and support efforts. Are you driving your territory, or are you just responding to the requests and demands of your existing customers?

Idea #1   Work to anticipate potential customer problems. Are you able to predict and react *before* even receiving a customer complaint? How many problems have you been able to identify and resolve before your customer realizes there is a problem? The sooner and faster you can react to these situations, the less stressed your customer will be and the more loyal they will be to you and your company. One way to increase your ability to predict potential problems is by increasing your communication with a wider number of individuals and departments. Talking to more individuals within important accounts can help you identify and fix problems more efficiently than you do now.

Idea #2   (for sales leaders) Meet with your entire sales team and define your "best practices" of proactively managing and supporting existing customers. Analyze scenarios when you have been successful and when you have failed in resolving a customer problem.

Salesperson Question #8 Your ability to keep your existing accounts stable and under control is _____?

1	2	3	4	5
Unaware	Weak	Just Average	Leading	Best Practice

Additional Clarifying Questions

- Do you have low account turnover in your territory? Do you have a low number of competitive losses in a year?

- Are your existing customers generally happy with you and your company?

- Are you able to keep surprising your existing accounts (in a positive way) by the way you keep improving your responsiveness and ability to continually increase your support and value positioning?

A Low Ability to Keep Existing Accounts Under Control evaluation score means you have high account turnover in your territory. You lose more than the average number of accounts in a year to your competition. You also spend a lot of your time working on low margin or smaller sales instead of focusing your attention on the greatest payoffs in your territory.

A High Ability to Keep Existing Accounts Under Control evaluation score indicates you have a very stable territory with low account turnover due to competitive losses. You are able to focus your attention on the business opportunities that generate the greatest return on your time. Your customers are impressed with your commitments to ongoing quality improvement and increased responsiveness to identified problems and feel they are important to both you and your company. You continually demonstrate to your existing accounts your strong added value differences.

Ideas to Help Improve Your Ability to Keep Existing Accounts Under Control Skills   The best way to increase your sales is to not lose the stuff you already have. How much account turnover are you experiencing in your territory?

Idea #1   Evaluate if your customers are getting the maximum effectiveness and cooperation from your entire sales team (administrative,

193

technical, and sales). The stability of your territory (i.e., low account turnover) is directly related to the ongoing proactive support you are able to offer. It is also directly related to how you maximize your use of your sales support team (senior management, technical support, etc.) when solving problems. How are you coordinating the resources and support issues within your accounts when something needs to be fixed or improved? What can be done to work as a team to improve your "best practices" of how you and your entire team respond to a customer's problem?

Idea #2   Prepare now for potential customer problems. You need to identify and establish relationships now with various people and departments within your existing accounts to prepare for any future problems. How often are you talking to your customer's management to evaluate how you and your company are performing and to identify how you can do an even better job? Continual quality (and service) improvement is one of the best ways to keep your competitors away from your accounts. Are there any more customer management people you can be talking to? What else can you do to increase the stability of your current accounts?

Idea #3   Are there ways you can proactively surprise your customers (in a good way) by providing extra support or affirming your commitment to their business? You cannot gain a competitive advantage if all you are doing is reacting and responding to customer requests. How many efforts did you initiate that your customer didn't already expect?

Salesperson Question #9   Your ongoing new business prospecting process is _____?

1	2	3	4	5
Unaware	Weak	Just Average	Leading	Best Practice

Additional Clarifying Questions

 ♦ Do you have an ongoing new business development process in place for additional or new applications within both your exiting and new customers? Do you devote time to proactively look for new opportunities within your existing accounts each month?

◆ Is your new business prospecting a planned and organized program covering your entire business year?

A Low New Business Prospecting Skills evaluation score means the only new business you generate is business handed to you by existing customers or company-provided new business sales leads. You never seem to be able to invest in new business development efforts. This is especially a problem with senior sales reps who have been in the same territory for years. You are a *farmer* working to maximize the returns on the territory you already own but are doing little to generate any new business *hunting*. Your territory is slowly shrinking and you are doing little to restock or to grow your business.

A High New Business Prospecting Skills evaluation score most likely means you are a *hunter* working to grow your territory at the same time you work to retain and maintain the business you already have. Your territory and sales volumes are expanding and growing. You are not afraid to call on new companies or new departments within existing accounts. You see any competitive installation as a new business opportunity and are constantly looking for new companies to call on that are currently buying from your competition.

Ideas to Help Improve Your New Business Prospecting Skills   As we briefly discussed in Chapter 1 are you a *rainmaker*, making things happen in your territory or are you just a *weather forecaster*, proud of how you can predict what is happening without any involvement from you? Most salespeople do very little rainmaking.

There are two acceptable definitions of new business prospecting. One definition is looking for additional business within an existing account by selling to other departments, locations, or selling additional business applications.

A second acceptable definition of "new business" prospecting involves your going out and finding new companies to sell. How many new account sales calls have you made in the past 30 days? Successful new company prospecting has to be an ongoing, proactive, and continual effort. You cannot just try to prospect once a year. Ongoing calling and follow-up are two of the ways to get new companies interested in you and your products or services. What is your new business plan for the next year?

Idea #1   Review the best attributes shared by your core customers (suggested in Chapter 3). Having a proactive Best Attributes of Our Core Customers list allows you to focus your new business efforts on the accounts with the highest probability of winning due to their ability to take maximum advantage of your company's unique value offerings.

Idea #2   Group your work when you start a new business telephone prospecting effort. Don't just sit down to call a new prospect; sit down and call 10 or 20 at a time. To insure an easier new business process, consider working your new business opportunities as a single multiaccount group rather than 15 new business opportunities to work and track separately.

Idea #3   (for sales leaders) Organize a New Business prospecting Best Practices plan for the year. Include both your plans to grow existing accounts as well as your strategy to find new customers. Focus on how your new business plan includes planning multiple moves ahead for new business prospects for the entire year ("What will I do different in January compared to April compared to September?"). Also include targeted industries or customer groups, sample voice mail message scripts, and identified best individuals to approach with new business ideas.

Your Ability to Manage Your Selling Process

Salesperson Question #10   Your ability to think and plan multiple moves ahead in each of your customers and prospects is _____?

1	2	3	4	5
Unaware	Weak	Just Average	Leading	Best Practice

Additional Clarifying Questions

 ◆ How often are you surprised by your customers and prospects?
 ◆ How many moves ahead are you thinking in your account management and territory selling efforts? This includes having plans in

place for all of your major accounts as well as a plan of action for all prospects.

A Low Ability to Think and Plan Multiple Moves Ahead evaluation score means you are not managing your customers, they are running you. You have no idea how you will make your sales numbers for the year or what you will be working on next month. You stay busy and are making sales but are not in control of what is happening in your territory. You are great at responding to customer requests and following up on sales leads but the vast majority of what you do is completely reactive.

You believe each customer selling situation needs to be managed and planned individually. You see no consistency in the selling and support processes you move an account through over a year. You can be outsold by competitors who are able to think more moves ahead in their selling process than you do. Your territory is exposed to competitive attacks due to your lack of long-range planning with your accounts.

A High Ability to Think and Plan Multiple Moves Ahead evaluation score means you are in control of your territory and customers. You think about and communicate with your accounts based on a *multiple calls ahead* thought process. You have your week, month, and year planned. You are always thinking about and have identified multiple applications or selling projects ahead for each of your major accounts. You are able to avoid wasted or useless projects.

You have a thought out and proven selling process identified for your new application sales. You have learned that, no matter how unique the selling situation appears, there are consistent *selling best practices that* can be applied through any selling situation. Understanding the *Identify to Close* selling process allows you to be more proactive and aggressive with your selling efforts. This more proactive, stepped approach increases your competitive selling advantage. Your ability to understand and communicate your entire buying/selling process allows your customer to put more trust and interest in you and your company.

Ideas to Help Improve Your Ability to Think and Plan Multiple Moves Ahead Skills Not thinking enough moves ahead in the selling process is a common problem for even the most experienced sales teams. Salespeople tend to get lulled into a comfort level of needing only to focus on their next sales call on an account.

Idea #1   Develop a multistep plan for the entire year for important existing accounts. Most reps only have a *next best sales call* mentality hoping their customer tells them what to do next. Are you thinking and planning the entire sales year to maximize your impact and competitive advantage? What do you plan to do to continue to earn their business throughout the year? What do you plan to do for them different in the first quarter compared to the second, third, and fourth?

What are the next three applications or business opportunities identified and available for you within each of your major accounts? What is your plan for the year as to when to bring in your senior management or technical support experts? Who are the next two management (or higher) levels you want to get to in each account? What kinds of customer training and demonstration sessions do you want to conduct?

Idea #2   (for sales leaders) Meet with your sales team to list the steps of your *ID to Close* selling process. Be sure to discuss what you can do to be more consistently proactive in your implementation of these steps. By identifying your steps your team will become more proactive thinking more moves ahead than they are now.

To learn if they currently have a solid understanding of your selling processes, give them this test: Draw a horizontal line on a piece of paper. On the left side of the line put Identify and on the right side put Close. Now ask each team member to write down the steps of the *ID to Close* selling process they currently utilize. When (or if) they have written down their steps, next identify which of their steps are proactive (initiated by the rep) and which steps are reactive (controlled or defined by the customer). The vast majority of selling steps completed tend to be reactive in nature.

The majority of experienced sales reps are vague in their explanation of the selling process some have been utilizing for years. Most salespeople just reactively wait for their customers to tell them what to do instead of proactively selling them on what needs to be done both now and in the future.

Idea #3   (for sales leaders) Make sure your team understands the competitive advantages of thinking more moves ahead than their competition. Getting salespeople to think multiple moves ahead requires extensive coaching and guidance from your sales management team.

The best way to get your entire sales team thinking multiple moves ahead with their accounts is for you as their leader to keep asking them questions. Extensive questioning is one of the best ways for salespeople to be guided into the *multiple steps ahead* selling philosophy. And one of the most effective questions for a manager to keep asking is *"And then what?"* as was discussed in Chapter 9.

Salesperson Question #11   Your knowledge and understanding of your competitors' pricing practices are _____?

1	2	3	4	5
Unaware	Weak	Just Average	Leading	Best Practice

Additional Clarifying Questions

- Can you accurately predict in a proposal or bidding situation where your competitor will price their offering compared to yours?
- How often are you surprised by a competitor's price?
- Competitive pricing awareness involves the ability to predict when and how much competitors will cut their prices to win business during final buying negotiations.

A Low Awareness of Your Competitors' Pricing Practices evaluation score means you are constantly surprised by your competitors' price quotes and pricing strategies. You are not able to predict where their pricing will finalize so you are not able to effectively sell against them.

A High Awareness of Your Competitors' Pricing Practices evaluation means you are able to better control your selling process. You are able to predict your competitors' pricing and negotiating strategies so you can start talking early about how your final customer proposal will look.

You are also able to win against the competition even when you have a higher price.

Ideas to Help Improve Your Awareness of Your Competitors' Pricing Practices Skills

Idea   (for sales leaders) Establish a central tracking system to track all competitive pricing you identify. You need to have a central tracking system that monitors your competitors, pricing strategies, and processes. This includes keeping track of competitive "pricing and negotiating game plans." Can you predict how much of a last minute price concession they will offer a prospect based on past proposal tracking? As the leader of your sales team, you need to insure there is an efficient and effective way for this information to be collected and made available for your entire sales team.

Salesperson Question #12   Your ability to utilize company support resources in your territory is _____?

1	2	3	4	5
Unaware	Weak	Just Average	Leading	Best Practice

Additional Clarifying Questions

♦ How are you utilizing your entire sales team (sales manager, senior executives, and technical support) to positively impact your prospects and existing customers and to help strengthen long-term account relationships?

♦ How are you using your support resources to get higher, wider, and deeper within your accounts?

♦ Can you identify in advance where and when members of your sales team can help improve your selling efforts?

A Low Ability to Utilize Company Support Resources evaluation score means you rarely use other members of your company to help you sell new business or keep the business you have. You are missing major opportunities to get higher, wider, and deeper within your accounts and are also missing significant opportunities to communicate a stronger added value and competitive differential through the presence of additional support within your accounts. You probably feel uncomfortable or untrusting introducing other employees from your company into your accounts. The only time you take others on calls is when either the customer or your sales team members demand that they go.

A High Ability to Utilize Company Support Resources evaluation score means you take full advantage of all support resources available in your company. You most likely have more members of your sales team present in your accounts compared to others in your company. You understand how senior members of your management team and technical experts are positive contributions to your ongoing selling efforts and competitive advantage positioning. You are able to utilize them to get higher, wider, and deeper within both your prospects and established accounts. You are also able to plan these types of visits in advance and use them as part of your master selling plan. You are very effective at briefing these sales team visitors as to what to expect and how to maximize their time with your customers.

Ideas to Help Improve Your Ability to Utilize Company Support Resources Skills   In most businesses there are two problems with getting sales reps to better utilize company support resources. The first problem is with the reps who would, as the Super Doers we have discussed, rather do everything themselves. But the second problem will probably be with your company's support people. Most support people have not been effectively trained or coached on how to positively contribute as a team player to the selling process.

Idea #1   (for sales leaders) Combine your team's discussion about better utilizing your company resources with the discussions of your *ID to Close* selling process suggested in Sales Question #10. Discuss how utilizing more of your company's support resources (sales manager, senior executives, and technical support) could help your sales team improve their competitive advantages by more effectively getting higher, wider, and deeper in their accounts.

Most sales reps bring their support team (managers and technical experts) in way too early in their selling process. There are several ways to analyze your *ID to Close* selling/buying process. One way is to divide the *ID to Close* selling process into three distinct phases buyers go through to select a final vendor.

Phase 1:   The Discovery Phase   This is the buying phase where the customer considers a wide variety of solution alternatives. "Should I add a computer, outsource the function, or just hire another clerk" are discovery focused evaluations. This is a selling phase most sales reps can handle on their own since customers are still asking only big picture types of questions. A technical expert or sales manager involved in this phase would probably not contribute anything to the selling efforts.

Phase 2:   The Evaluation Phase   This is the buying phase where the customer has selected the finalist solutions they feel will best solve their problems and are now considering several competitors to decide who can best solve their problems/needs. This is normally where they ask the most technically focused questions. This is also the phase where the buyer issues a request for price (RFP) or a Request for quote (RFQ).

This is the ideal time to bring in any of your technical experts since this is when customers will be asking the most technically focused questions.

Phase 3:   The Selection Phase   This is the time when your customer will do the most negotiating and "playing one vendor off another." This is when the customer will say to you, "The Johnson Company has offered to do this at no charge; Will you?" or "They have proposed charging $10,000 per unit; Can you match it?"

The beginning of the Selection phase is the best time to bring in a manager. This is after a formal proposal has been issued to your buyer but before they have made a final vendor of choice selection. This is the time where your customer/buyer is looking for the vendor company to validate and confirm what has already been promised by you, the sales rep.

There is also a rule of using a sales team that most sales people violate. The simple rule is that you should always use a new sales team member to help you get either higher, wider, or deeper within an account. Having a technical expert or member of your management team only call on the people you have already been talking to is a waste of a sales call. The new members of your selling team should be helping you get either higher, wider, or deeper at the account than you have been able to get on your own. How have you been using the various members of your sales team to get higher, wider, and deeper?

Idea #2 (for sales leaders) Meet with the various players who would be part of your company's sales support resources to insure they understand their role on these sales calls, understand the major messages and philosophies your team is working to promote, and are clear in what you expect them to do (and not do) in front of a customer on a call. Be sure to continue coaching these support people after their sales calls. Remember you want to catch these support people doing something right instead of looking for calls where they caused your salespeople problems.

Your Ability to Maintain and Control Your Customer

Salesperson Question #13 **Your ability to communicate what your customers want to buy instead of just what you have to sell is _____?**

1	2	3	4	5
Unaware	Weak	Just Average	Leading	Best Practice

Additional Clarifying Questions

- Do you spend the majority of your sales calls asking questions and listening (the better way) compared to doing all the talking and presenting (the less effective way)?

- How much time do you spend talking to customers and prospects about what you want to sell them instead of talking about what they really want to buy? How much time do you spend talking about your customer, their problems, and requirements/needs compared to just talking about your products/services and what they can do for your customer?

- Do your sales letters, presentations, and sales literature focus more on how your customers can receive benefits from your products/services, or do they focus only on how great your products/services are?

A Low Ability to Communicate What Your Customers Want to Buy evaluation score means you are excessively *me* focused in your selling. You spend the majority of your sales calls talking and *pitching* the features and advantages of your products. You ask only enough questions on a call to be able to identify what and how you want to sell. You are so busy selling you spend little time actually understanding what your customers want and why they might be interested in buying from you.

A High Ability to Communicate What Your Customers Want to Buy evaluation score means you come across as more professional, empathetic, and persuasive than your competition. You spend a lot of time asking questions and listening to what your customers and prospects are saying. You realize most customers or prospects tell you only their symptoms, and that it is up to you to understand enough about their business to be able to identify what the real problems and solutions are.

Ideas to Help Improve Your Ability to Communicate What Your Customers Want to Buy Skills   The majority of all salespeople, no matter what their experience level, tend to focus their efforts on themselves and their products or services. They ask questions only as a way to break into their presentation about how their products or services will solve a customer's problems.

Most salespeople spend the majority of their *listening time* (when the customer is talking) planning what they will say when it is their turn to talk. What percentage of your sales calls do you spend talking versus listening? And of greater importance (and more positive reactions from your customers) how many questions do you ask them about their business environments that are not directly related to selling your products?

Learning and understanding more about your customer's environment and challenges than your competitors know can help you gain a competitive advantage. Do you know who your customer's toughest competitors are? What their most significant challenges and frustrations are? Increasing your listening and questioning skills as well as letting your customers talk more can make them feel important and more comfortable with you and your company.

Idea #1 The first and most important suggestion is to find out if this "talking about me and my stuff" is a problem for you and your selling efforts. Consider recording some of your phone conversations so you can go back and listen to your calls to see how much you actually spoke. Ask your sales manager when they ride with you to observe how much time you spend talking versus listening to your customers. Set a goal of asking more questions on each sales call. Consider asking your closest or friendliest customers how they would describe your listening and questioning skills.

As a sales consultant I spend time riding with experienced and successful sales professionals. I have timed a number of these sales calls with a stopwatch and have observed that the average sales rep spends more than 90 percent of their time on a sales call speaking. The calls are interactive but the customer asks brief questions taking less than a minute to ask (*"Why are you so expensive?"*) that generate multiple minute answers from you, their rep. What percent of a sales call do you spend talking versus listening to your customer?

Idea #2 (for sales leaders) Conduct an *X*s and *O*s test of any of your letters, proposals, brochures, or trade show booth copy to see if you are truly customer focused.

Step 1. Circle any words in your document referring to your customer (their name or words like *you* and *your*).

Step 2. Place an *X* through any words in your document that refer to you or your company (your name, your company name, or words like *I, me, us, my, we,* or *our*).

Step 3. Count the total number of *X*s and *O*s and identify what percentage of this document is customer focused (greater percent of *O*s) versus "you and your company" focused (greater percent of *X*s).

A persuasive letter will have more *O*s than *X*s, but the reality is that more than 90 percent of the words marked will likely have *X*s through them. What percentage of your written materials centers on your customer (the ones with the money) compared to you and your company's internal issues?

Make the *X*s and *O*s test a standard evaluator of any letter or proposal written by you or your team before you even spell-check your document.

Idea #3   (for sales leaders) Incorporate the *four core values* into every sales call. One of the most critical components that blends being more customer focused with more strategic positioning of your selling message is to utilize the four core values of how and why customers buy.

There are only four reasons (or core values) a customer will select a vendor in a competitive environment: They choose you because (1) you did more than anyone else to *lower their risk*; (2) you were able to prove you could do more than anyone else to *make their life or work easier*; (3) you did more than anyone else to prove you were either the *lowest total cost or could increase their profitability*; or (4) you did more than anyone else to prove you could help *increase their competitive advantage*. These are the only four reasons people buy. All other reasons are subcategories of these four core values of buying.

Want to test this four core values concept with your sales team? In your next team meeting ask your reps to compile a list of all the reasons their best customers buy from them.

Next, explain the four core values and how these are the only four reasons people buy in a competitive environment. Now compare the two lists, and ask your salespeople how many items on their Why Our Best Customers Buy list fit into at least one of the four core values. It will be a 100 percent fit: "*Lower my risk*," "*Make my life, or work easier*," "*Increase my profitability*," or "*increase my competitive advantage*" are all at the center of helping customers and prospects to understand your value proposition.

Next apply this Xs and Os test to your team's answers to why your best customers buy from you and the four core values. Notice all four of the core values are customer focused Os What percentage of your Why Our Best Customers Buy list is framed in customer or O-focused language? Most lists will be more than 90 percent X or "me and my company" focused.

The profound strength of the four core values is that they are 100 percent customer focused. Utilizing these core values throughout the selling process immediately changes your selling focus and language to be more customer focused dealing with the fundamental reasons they buy in a competitive environment.

What to test the four core values? Have your sales team agree to use the four core value terms on all sales calls, both phone and face-to-face meetings for the next week. Then meet again and discuss if any of your sales team members actually saw or received a noticeable reaction when they used these four core values.

Be aware that increasing your listening and questioning skills starts with your being aware this is an area that can be improved. Then the tougher part is to actually start improving your customer focus. What can you do to increase your competitive edge by being more listener and customer focused compared to your competition?

Salesperson Question #14   Your understanding of the political environment and decision process of each of your accounts is _____?

1	2	3	4	5
Unaware	Weak	Just Average	Leading	Best Practice

Additional Clarifying Questions

- Do you understand how decisions are really made within each of your accounts? Do you understand how they politically evaluate and make decisions?

- Can you identify all of the *behind the scenes* major influencers and decision makers at each of your accounts?

- How effective are you at getting higher, wider, and deeper within your customer's organizations? Are there any more customer management people you can be talking to? Are you using other members of your company to help you get higher, wider, and deeper within your accounts?

A Low Political Environment and Decision Process evaluation score means you actually believe all of your customers' buying decisions are based on whose product/service is technically best (or cheapest) for their company. You do not understand how decisions are made at your accounts and are constantly surprised when your competitors with no apparent competitive product, service, or price advantage, keep winning the business. Because of your lack of political awareness you are happy to focus only on your established contacts and do little to get higher, wider, or deeper within their organizations. You are probably not even aware how exposed your accounts are to competitors calling on other departments or contacts to propose alternative solutions.

A High Political Environment and Decision Process evaluation score means you have solid control over your territory. You understand how your customers make decisions and how their political decision processes work. You have worked to get higher, wider, and deeper within your key accounts and know that these varied contacts are one of the reasons you have so few competitive losses. Your understanding of your customers' political environments makes it easier for you to utilize senior management on important customer sales calls and allows for few surprises in your territory, since you are usually able to see major problems coming in advance of any complaints.

Ideas to Help Improve Your Political Environment and Decision Process Skills

Idea #1   (for sales leaders) Lead your team in a discussion analyzing your customer's political environments and how your sales people can better understand and even participate in how their customers really make decisions.

Does your team really understand how your larger customers make decisions? What have you and your team been doing to get higher, wider, and deeper within your important accounts? You cannot understand nor have an impact on the decision-making processes of your customers if you only have one or two *front line production level* contacts. You need to be talking to upper management, other departments, and the front line of the departments you have contacts in now. The higher, wider, and deeper you get within an account has a direct impact on your understanding of their political decision-making processes.

Idea #2   What can you do to get more connected within your more important accounts? Consider asking some of your stronger contacts to explain how their decision making process really works. A great time to broach this is after they have completed a major evaluation and buying effort. Debriefing to better understand how they made their decision can give you significant insights into their political and decision-making environment.

Idea #3   Encourage your reps to bring you, their leader, on sales calls. Getting your sales leader in front of your main contact's managers is a way for you to get higher within your customer organization. You as a manager can also ask questions about the customer's decision making and political environment your rep would likely never be able to ask.

19

Evaluating a Salesperson's
Strategic Positioning Selling Skills and Abilities

The third and final skill area to evaluate is your *strategic* skills and abilities of selling. In Chapter 10 strategic selling skills are defined as your ability to communicate your company's philosophy and competitive market positioning. Strategic selling skills also involve your philosophy and commitment to ongoing training and your desire to want to get better.

Increasing your strategic selling skills, along with your tactical skills, is one of the critical *drivers* to increasing your competitive advantage. How strategically focused are your selling efforts and messaging?

Consequences of Having Underdeveloped
Strategic Skills and Abilities

- Lower profit margins on business won due to your inability to communicate a strong differentiation in value and support.

- Fewer competitive wins due to your inability to differentiate your company and product/services compared to your competition.
- More frequent losses of existing accounts to your competition due to your inability to communicate any type of value and support differentiation.
- A lack of interest in improving your skills and working to increase your personal competitive selling advantage.

Benefits of Having Competitively Advanced
Strategic Skills and Abilities

- More frequent competitive wins even when your customer/prospect perceives little difference in your product/services.
- Higher profit margins and less price sensitive buyers.
- More loyal and supportive customers.
- Less time spent getting the attention of new customers/prospects to the value of moving their business over to you.
- The interest and commitment to working with a coach to help you get better.

Your Ability to Manage the
Strategic Aspects of Your Selling Process

Salesperson Question #15   **Your ability to communicate your competitive uniqueness and value is _____?**

1	2	3	4	5
Unaware	Weak	Just Average	Leading	Best Practice

Additional Clarifying Questions

- Have you identified the *value drivers* of most importance to your customers?
- Can you identify the strongest attributes your best, largest, and/or most profitable customers have in common?

◆ How are you answering customers or prospects who asks you, "Why, based on all the competitive alternatives available to me, would I want to buy from you?" (Your *elevator* speech)

A Low Ability to Communicate Your Competitive Uniqueness and Value evaluation score means you have a difficult time differentiating your products or services to customers and prospects and are under significant pricing pressures. If your customer does not understand your competitive differences, they are going to buy based on lowest price. When a customer does ask you why they should buy from you rather than the competition, your answers are very product and technically focused.

A High Ability to Communicate Your Competitive Uniqueness and Value evaluation score means you are functioning at the most advanced and successful levels of selling. The ability to communicate a brief, yet focused strategic message of competitive uniqueness is the foundation of your ability to differentiate and prove value to your customer/prospect. You understand that your strategic message needs to focus on the positive impact you can provide your customer/prospect, not on how your product/service functions. You also understand how a stronger message of competitive uniqueness allows you to successfully sell to higher levels within your customer's political environment.

Ideas to Help Improve Your Ability to Communicate Your Competitive Uniqueness and Value   The lack of a strong strategic message of uniqueness is one of the most common sales exposures in business today. Successful strategic or philosophy selling is based on your ability to communicate a brief, consistent, and organized customer focused message of how and why you offer more long-term value than your competitors. Though the most critical component of selling, it is also the area least developed or understood by the majority of salespeople.

How developed and effective are your strategic message of competitive uniqueness skills? For most salespeople the answer to this question is neither consistent when compared to the rest of your sales team nor effective at communicating your market uniqueness when compared to the messages of your competition.

Idea   (for sales leaders) To improve your team's strategic selling abilities, you need to begin by identifying their current awareness and skill levels (Step One of *ISO 9000*). Begin this three-step team exercise by asking each rep to write down their answer to a customer or prospect asking, "Why, based on all of the competitive alternatives available to me do I want to buy from you?" This is one of the most critical exercises to walk a sales team through and can be performed either one-on-one or with your entire team.

1. *Set up the scenario.* Say you were recently talking to a prospect and, as you began your presentation the prospect said, "You are the fifth vendor I've talked to this week. Why, based on all the competitive alternatives available to me do I want to buy from you?"

2. *Have each team member write down the three or four strongest reasons they would cite to answer this prospect's question.* It is critical that each member write down their own answers before discussing all answers as a team. You need to understand what each team member is saying before comparing answers.

3. *Write everyone's answers on a flip chart or white board to evaluate your team's responses.* Notice any problems with your team's list? When I walk a sales team through this exercise, there are consistently four problems with the responses to this "Why buy from you?" question. How many of these four problems does your team have with this question?

The First Problem: Everyone Has Different Answers

It is normal for each member to communicate profoundly different answers to this question. Why do so many groups have such wildly different answers to this question? When was the last time you as their leader led them in a discussion of why you and your company are competitively unique in your market? Most sales teams have never had this type of discussion.

When most reps join a company they immediately start asking co-workers, "Why do prospects and customers buy from us?" They also ask, "Why we are unique compared to our competition?"

The problem starts when you, as the new sales rep (1) get completely different answers from each team member you ask and (2) aren't really impressed with any of the answers you do receive. At this point most sales reps simply start formulating their own message, one they think will give them the best competitive selling opportunity. But this evolutionary message process also means each team member is selling with a different message.

Even worse, all the other members of your sales team are also communicating their own uniqueness message. Look at the problem that occurs: The customer likes the message and approach the sales rep presents. One of your technical support people next talks to the prospect, but that technical person delivers a completely different message compared to what the rep said. And finally your sales manager visits the account and delivers a completely different message.

What would you believe if you were the prospect and have now heard three completely different messages from three different individuals from the same company? Most prospects just discount everything they heard thinking you are all lying or just making it up as you go telling the buyer only what you think they want to hear.

Consider also completing this exercise with the technical and other support members of your company to see how different all of their messages are that are also being communicated to your prospects and customers. How many different messages are you and your entire sales team presenting to your markets? How do you plan to make the messages being delivered more consistent?

The Second Problem: The Same Four Answers Are on Everyone's List

When there are similarities in the answers, they tend to be the same four responses to "Why should I buy from you?"

1. My high quality products (or services).
2. My strong level of support.
3. My competitive prices (I'm not the lowest price, but I am competitive).
4. You get me!

What's wrong with these four answers? Nothing except they are said by every sales rep selling anything. Look at the problem. A prospect or customer asks you, "Why, based on all the competitive alternatives available to me do I want to buy from you?" If you answer with the same generic responses "high quality products, strong level of support, competitive prices, and you get me" then you are only affirming to your customer/prospect there are no differences between you and your competitors. The less differentiation they see, the more likely they will then decide to just buy based on price. Go through your team's answers and see how many of their responses fit into these four generic statements.

The Third Problem: The Majority of Answers Are Sterile

A "sterile" answer is one that does nothing to compare yourself to your competitive alternatives. Answers such as "quality," "service," "satisfied customers," or "our years in business" are all sterile answers since they are not being compared to anything or anybody.

A "competitive," or "nonsterile" answer would be to say, "We have the highest quality," "We offer the most consistent service," "We have the highest ratings for satisfied customers," or "We have the most years in business." Remember your customer has asked you why they want to buy from you *compared to your competition*. You cannot effectively answer a competitive question with a sterile or noncompetitive answer. Look at the answers from your team. How many of their responses are sterile and do nothing to compare themselves to your competitors?

The Fourth Problem: Your Answers Are Focused Only on Yourself instead of on Your Customer/Prospect

Conduct the Xs and Os test on your salespeople's responses, (discussed in Salesperson Question #13) going through their answers to the "Why buy from you?" exercise. Were the majority of your answers Xs or "Me and my company" focused?

At this point you have now completed your inventory of your sales team's current strategic messaging skills and are likely not very happy with their responses. You also probably agree you need to help your team improve their answers to this "Why buy" question. If you have completed the other best practices tests, you also see the need to improve other selling processes and structures.

The key to helping your team improve from where they are is to help them identify where they need to be by working as a team to define their selling best practices they need to be working toward.

Idea (for sales leaders) Lead your team through the exercise of redefining your team's best answer to the question "Why buy?" and follow the 10 steps of redefining your sales message outlined in Chapter 15 "Sales Leadership," Question 14.

Work through your groups "Why buy" list attacking each of these four problems one at a time. Cross off any answer that fails the test. Before moving on, see if you and your team can brainstorm ways any crossed off term can be reworked so it will pass the problem area being discussed.

Salesperson Question #16   Your knowledge of your competitors' strongest *value points* they use to sell against you is _____?

1	2	3	4	5
Unaware	Weak	Just Average	Leading	Best Practice

Additional Clarifying Questions

♦ How strong is your awareness of the message being delivered by your competitors when your customer asks them, "Why buy?"

♦ What are the strongest messaging and positioning statements your competitors use to differentiate themselves versus their competitors?

A Low Knowledge of Your Competitors' Strongest Value Points evaluation score means you have no idea how your competitors are explaining their competitive advantage over you and your products/services. You might know their products and pricing but not what they say when a prospect asks them why they should buy from them instead of you. Because you have no idea how your competitors are communicating their uniqueness, any message you deliver is likely to just be a generic match to what everyone else is already saying. If that happens, then your customer will conclude there is no significant value differentiation between you and your competitors encouraging them to buy based only on price.

A High Knowledge of Your Competitors' Strongest Value Points evaluation score means you are selling at the most advanced levels. By understanding the messaging and positioning of your competitors, you are able to focus on your own message that can zero in on your true competitive differential. You understand that the only way you can develop your own message of competitive uniqueness is by first understanding what everyone else is already saying.

Ideas to Help Improve Your Knowledge of Your Competitors' Strongest Value Points Skills   How can you develop and communicate a message of uniqueness unless you already know what all of your competitors are already saying?

A strong strategic message of competitive positioning is based on your ability to explain your value differential as a relative, competitive message of uniqueness. That means you first have to know what all the others are saying before you can even begin to define what your message is or needs to be.

Idea #1   Ask your customers! You do not have to be sneaky or unethical about this. Just ask them. Questions like, *"What did you like most about Competitor A?"* or *"What do you wish we were doing more of that Competitor B is already doing?"*

A number of sales reps will try implementing this idea but will make a major mistake of not keeping their questions about their competition positive. Remember you are asking these questions of your customers to learn about your competition, not to win the competitive uniqueness argument. The more negative your questions (*"What do you see are the gaps or problems with my competitors"*), the less value you will receive from their answers. You want the customer to feel positive and comfortable with your questions so they give you honest, accurate, and helpful insights.

Idea #2   Continually research the Internet and marketing communications of your competition. What does their website say about their uniqueness and value? Can you identify their messaging from any of their literature or advertising?

218

Idea #3   Follow the suggestions outlined in Chapter 17 "Sales Question 2" and make sales calls on your competitors' best showcase accounts to conduct competitive research. This is one of the best (and legal as well as ethical) ways to learn about your competitors satisfied customers.

Idea #4   (for sales leaders) Institute a program of ongoing competitive awareness. Assign at least one of your toughest competitors to each of your reps so they can become the "team expert" on that competitor. They are responsible for visiting that competitor's website on a regular basis and are to become the central resource for the rest of your team keeping everyone informed of any changes in the competitor's products, prices, market positioning, or messaging.

   The only way to maintain an accurate understanding of each of your competitors is to maintain an ongoing, proactive effort to monitor their promotional materials and to continue to interview their current and past "best" customers. Just as your team's messages were all over the place when you began evaluating your team, you can assume your competitors are no better organized with their messaging than you were.

Salesperson Question #17   Your ability to win business at a higher price/margin by communicating your stronger value is _____?

1	2	3	4	5
Unaware	Weak	Just Average	Leading	Best Practice

Additional Clarifying Questions

- What percentage of your proposals do you win even though you are higher in price than the competitors also going after that business?

- Are you able to proactively position at the beginning of your selling process to a new prospect that you won't be the lowest price but that you can show them how you are their lowest total cost alternative? And then can you back that statement up?

A Low Ability to Win Business at a Higher Price/Margin evaluation score means you focus only on selling the technical aspects of your products or services and believe your customers buy only from the lowest priced vendor. You spend a lot of time asking prospects to allow you to bid and you get excited when a prospect tells you that you will need to "sharpen your pencil" in order to win their business. You experience many competitive losses and when you ask, are told you lost the business because *"Your price was too high."*

A High Ability to Win Business at a Higher Price/Margin evaluation score means you have moved beyond just selling the product and now work to communicate the impact your products/services can have on your customers' business. You consistently maintain higher prices and stronger margins on just about all you sell because your customers understand and see the added value you bring to their business. You prove to your customers that even though your competitors might offer lower prices, you are able to prove a lower total cost of usage.

Ideas to Help Improve Your Ability to Win Business at a Higher Price/Margin Skills Understanding how to sell a value focused message so you can win business at a higher margin is really the summarization and implementation of all the earlier questions combined.

You cannot sell a stronger valued product or service unless your personal selling skills are consistently being implemented. You need to have strong tactical selling structures and processes that allow you to be more proactive in your selling efforts and a strong, clearly defined strategic philosophy and message of competitive uniqueness that you deliver on a consistent basis.

Idea Strengthen and improve the consistency of your selling efforts by learning more about the skills, structures, and philosophies of selling. The ability to win business at a higher price or margin occurs only when you are able to outsell, outmaneuver and outposition your competition. This boils down to one simple concept: Are you working to improve your skills and abilities so your personal selling skills actually become an important component of your overall message of competitive uniqueness?

Your Philosophy toward Ongoing Personal Development and Improvement

Salesperson Question #18   Your ability to represent yourself in a professional, truthful, and ethical manner is _____?

1	2	3	4	5
Unaware	Weak	Just Average	Leading	Best Practice

Additional Clarifying Questions

◆ Do you consistently avoid saying negative things about your competition? Can you effectively sell your competitive advantage without being negative or derogatory about your competitors?

◆ Are you always honest and accurate in the reports you provide to your company including expense accounts and costs of doing business? Have you ever padded your company expense accounts by adding false or exaggerated charges?

◆ Have you always honored the trust your customers (and company) place in you by always maintaining the confidentiality of sensitive customer (and company) information?

A Low Ability to Present Yourself in a Professional, Truthful, and Ethical Manner evaluation score means you are not being completely open, honest, and professional with your customers or others in your company. Even though your customers are friendly to you, they sense a lack of openness or truthfulness in your interactions so they do not really trust you. You cannot seem to get close enough to your customers to learn what is really going on because they just don't know if they can put their trust and confidence in you. You occasionally submit expense reports listing larger expense amounts than you actually spent but figure everyone else does it so it must be okay.

A High Ability to Present Yourself in a Professional, Truthful, and Ethical Manner evaluation score means you are perceived by your customers and fellow team members as being ethical, honest, and trustworthy. They know you will honor their trust by keeping any appropriate information confidential. You are able to learn more about the inner workings and decision-making process within your accounts because they trust you enough to tell you what is really going on. Everyone you deal with knows your word is as good as a contract, and they can count on you always standing behind everything you say and promise.

Ideas to Help Improve Your Ability to Present Yourself in a Professional, Truthful, and Ethical Manner Skills Trust and honesty are two attributes you can never acquire. They have to be earned. The reality though is that all salespeople, even the most unethical and immoral ones, feel they *are* professional, truthful, and ethical. These are not things you can just do occasionally but have to be an ongoing and focused effort if you want to continue to earn the respect and trust of those with whom you deal.

> Idea This issue is not whether you are "usually" or "mostly" truthful and ethical. It can only be a 100 percent committed process and philosophy. Consider working on your professionalism, truthfulness, and ethics by daily implementation of these values in a purer and more consistent fashion than anyone else in your market. It takes time to prove you are truthful and ethical, but when you constantly maintain these standards of behavior, they becomes a significant component of the quality and standards of your company.

Salesperson Question #19 Your ongoing commitment and efforts to grow and improve your selling skills and awareness are _____?

1	2	3	4	5
Unaware	Weak	Just Average	Leading	Best Practice

Additional Clarifying Questions

- How many books on selling have you read in the past 12 months? How many articles have you read? How many seminars have you attended?
- What selling skills or awareness have you changed/improved in the past 12 months?

A Low Commitment to Grow and Improve evaluation score means you are stagnant in your growth and skill development. You might be one of the most senior and successful members of your sales team, but you are not investing in yourself. You are not personally growing or working to increase your competitive advantage. You are also not really interested in getting coaching help that might push you into changing and/or growing in your job. You like things just the way they are and see significant change as either not relevant to you and your superior skills, too stressful, or just too much extra work.

A High Commitment to Grow and Improve evaluation score means you are excited about the lifelong opportunities in selling and are working to become better in your job every year. You read books on business, marketing, and selling and attend classes at your local college or university. You are constantly looking for ways to increase your skills and awareness as a way to increase your competitive selling advantage and are indeed good enough to continue to get better.

Ideas to Help Strengthen Your Commitment to Grow and Improve Skills   A personal commitment to want to get better is something that needs to come from within and is really part of your values system. You cannot just assign someone to grow and improve; they have to be interested and willing to work to change and improve.

Many older or more experienced sales reps get lulled into feeling they are senior enough, or successful enough to not need to invest in any type of learning or growth. A person with a very large ego tends to make a very weak and disinterested student. How much work and effort have you been investing in your personal growth and learning?

Idea #1   Do something, anything, to improve your skills. Inertia tends to be the greatest inhibitor to growth and learning. You don't have to make major steps to change. Just take any kind of step to get started and then keep going.

Congratulations that you are more than halfway through this book. Just getting this far in your reading is a significant accomplishment. I have heard a number of different experts reference the statistic that more than 90 percent of the population has not finished reading a book in the past 12 months.

Idea #2   Get help. Exercise programs, weight loss, all of these topics are similar to improving your sales skills. It has been proven you can stay committed longer and will work harder if you have a friend or partner also committed to your skill or awareness improvement. Who else can you recruit to join you in your growth intuitive?

Salesperson Question #20   Your ongoing use of one or more coaches or mentors to help you get better is _____?

1	2	3	4	5
Unaware	Weak	Just Average	Leading	Best Practice

Additional Clarifying Questions

- How coachable are you? Do you have a coach/mentor? How often do you two talk?
- How open are you to new ideas and suggestions, especially ones that require changing the way you have always done things?
- How open are you to coaching and guidance from your sales manager and senior company management?

A Low Ongoing Use of a Coach to Help You Get Better evaluation score means you are on your own and are not getting any coaching or guidance to help you get better. There is no one pushing or encouraging you, and you have no one to *bounce ideas off* with your account planning and strategizing. Your lack of awareness of the benefits of coaching also mean you most likely brag to others about not having a coach and see the lack of a coach in your life as an affirmation of your seniority and success.

A High Ongoing Use of a Coach to Help You Get Better evaluation score means you have someone helping you stretch and improve to get better. You realize that, no matter how good you are, you can always get better. You use your coach to help you think more moves ahead and to identify new strategies to help increase your competitive advantage and selling success. You are open to ideas and suggestions from others to help you get better.

Ideas to Help Improve Your Ongoing Use of a Coach to Help You Get Better Skills   There is an assumed rule of management and coaching: The more senior the salesperson, the less likely they are being coached and helped. Where is your seniority? And how open and interested are you to being coached and helped to get better?

Idea #1　Decide if you are really coachable. How open and interested are you to getting help, advice, and increased awareness? Whom can you identify who can help you through your thought processes and analysis?

Consider the differences between selling and professional sports. Professional athletes spend more than 90 percent of their time in planning, preparation, and practice and only 10 percent of their time in actual implementation. How much time do you spend in planning, preparation, and practice?

Another significant difference is that almost all professional athletes have at least one coach to help them get better and more competitive. How many senior sales people do you know who actually brag about not having, or needing a coach. Can you name any professional athletes currently competing who do not have at least one coach?

If you want to get better . . . if you want to increase your competitive advantage you need an outsider's view and perspective to help . . . especially if you are already a senior and successful professional.

Understand what top athletes have already learned. Your coach doesn't have to be a better "player" than you are, they just need to understand how to help you be a better "player" than you are today.

Idea #2　What do you do if you do not have anyone at your company who can effectively help you to get better? Form your own coaching or support group. Ask one or two other reps at your skill and awareness levels if they want to be part of your "coaching group." The idea is that everyone in the group acts as both a coach and someone who wants to be coached. If you are not getting any effective or helpful coaching help at work, then consider looking elsewhere to get help and guidance.

We know you are good. Now are you good enough to get involved with a coach to help you get better?

20

Suggestions to Improve a Salesperson's *Selling Skills and Effectiveness*

By this point you have hopefully completed your inventory of the current selling skills of your team. You are also likely not very happy with your team's responses.

The goal of this 20-question *Sales Evaluation* is to help you evaluate your sales team's current sales skills. Hopefully, you have increased your awareness of their strongest sales skill areas as well as the skills that, if improved, could most help them increase their selling abilities.

The key to helping your team improve from where they are today (the first step of the *ISO 9000* process) is to help them identify where they need to grow and improve in the future. You need to identify the selling "best practices" they should be working toward, and to actively coach them on how to get there.

Once you have completed the *Sales Evaluation* on both you and each member of your sales team, you can begin identifying the best opportunities for improvement and increased success. Now that you know exactly where the skills are for all sales team members, it is time to get to work improving their abilities, focus, and success. Are you ready to help your team get better?

> For more information and a free report offering additional suggestions to improve your selling skills and the selling skills of your team, visit www.GreatSalesSkills.com, for a free online version of this 20-question *Sales Evaluation* and the *Sales Leadership Evaluation* explained in Section III. These are free evaluations and each includes a detailed multiple page customized report offering personalized feedback and improvement suggestions. This report is immediately available upon completion of your online evaluations.

Now That You Have Completed the Sales Evaluation for Your Entire Sales Team and for Yourself

You, as the leader of your sales team have hopefully also completed reading all of the chapters up to this point. You need to have a solid understanding and focus on strengthening your sales leadership skills before you begin working with your team to help them strengthen their selling skills.

Consider going back and reading all of the supporting information provided with each of the sales questions covered in this section. Consider how many of the Additional Clarifying Questions as well as the "A low (or high) evaluation score means . . ." paragraph descriptions fit your current selling style and the selling styles of the rest of your team. Try applying all of the "Idea" suggestions outlined at the end of each sales question. Build a list of the "best practices" skills, attitudes, or philosophies you would most like to strengthen to best help all the members of your team increase their selling success and profitability.

In the next section you will learn more about how to apply a stepped process of growth and change to your sales force. The evaluations are all now hopefully complete, so it's now time to actually get to work improving your sales team.

Section

V

Developing a Successful Sales Team Improvement Strategy

Section Overview

CHAPTER 21 *Evaluate* **Your Sales Force in an Open and Honest Environment**

You have been reading about all of the steps and components necessary to analyze and lead a sales team to a more proactive, structured, and focused selling process. It's now time to start employing the step-by-step processes you will train your entire sales organization in as you evaluate, design, implement, track, and lead their sales team to success.

Chapter 21 offers a detailed step-by-step process of working through these chapters (mostly in order) to help lead you through the successful redesigning, retraining, and refocusing of your sales team. There are no shortcuts in rebuilding a sales team. You need to work through all of the processes and components that make up the total leadership and sales culture of your company. The success of your sales processes and leadership will quickly disappear (or never actually appear) if only one of these processes or components are missing or out of alignment.

CHAPTER 22 *Design* Your Ongoing Sales Improvement Strategy

By now in your improvement process you should have a fairly comprehensive inventory and analysis of your team's skills, including their gaps and exposures.

Now is the time to finish defining and implementing your "best practices." By this point in your change process it is guaranteed you will have multiple times the amount of "best practices" projects you need for the time and funding you actually have available. You and your team need to determine which of the various next best "best practices" projects you can work on that will generate the most significant results or pay-offs to your team.

As you select your next "best practices" to work on, keep in mind that there are a number of things you have to do to be competitive but only a few that will actually increase your competitive advantage. Try to work on the big stuff first that will have the greatest impact on your quality, customer service, selling effectiveness, or competitive advantage.

Once you decide on the changes to focus on, it is time to get to work implementing the new skills, tools, structures, processes, and awareness with your sales team.

CHAPTER 23 *Implement* a Learning Growth Strategy for Each Sales Team Member

Improving a sales force requires you first to improve your sales leadership skills and awareness, then improve the sales tools available to your team to help communicate your competitive uniqueness and finally train your people on how to utilize all of the newly discovered and defined skills and awareness. This is the best and most consistently effective way to improve a sales team.

Although most sales leaders want their first step to be conducting a sales training class, conducting training without having leadership skills or sales tools and processes in place will only mean that any ideas taught will quickly be lost by your team.

When it is time to conduct training, you have a number of sales training alternatives or approaches that are outlined in Chapter 23 to select.

Now that you are implementing a solid sales training process and building of your team's skills, it is now time to discuss how you will keep them focused on their growth opportunities.

CHAPTER 24 *Track* **Sales Team Member's Improvements by Utilizing a Comprehensive Sales Performance Tracking System**

Now that you are starting to implement your training, you can begin tracking your sales team members' progress and improvement. Most sales organizations tend to only have "sales performance" tracking systems in place. They track only how much is sold and at what profitability. But to strengthen and improve a sales force, you need to track the sales skills of your team members as well as their progress through the outlined assignments and training. You need to track not just *what* your team has sold (the traditional model) but also *how* they are expected to perform their job. Though these two tracking systems will be integrated in the information and value they can provide you as a leader, we are still talking about two separate, yet complementary, tracking systems.

The reality is that if you don't measure and track it, it won't change.

CHAPTER 25 *Lead* **Your Sales Team by Ongoing Coaching of Your Defined *Selling Best Practices***

The goal of a sales leader is to help each of your people achieve more than they would have achieved if just left alone. The two most critical responsibilities of a sales leader are (1) leading and motivating your entire team and (2) leading your team's selling process as a coach and strategist. An old leadership concept states "You *manage* processes but you *lead* people."

Each sales rep requires a different amount and style of coaching help. Your job as their leader is to understand them well enough to be able to push them to change. You also need to proactively seek opportunities where your help and guidance can be of productive help. That can occur in informal discussions about an account, when you are out making sales calls with the rep, or during any regularly scheduled account briefings or planning sessions.

You know you and your team are good. Are you now good enough, and equipped with the right tools to help them get better?

CHAPTER

21

Evaluate Your Sales Force in an Open and Honest Environment

Kate had worked as a sales rep for a Chicago printing company for more than 10 years. It wasn't one of the large "national market" printers but was large enough to cover the Chicago area with her and eight other sales reps. Until nine months ago the sales force had reported to Tom, the VP of sales, who was also a "selling manager" carrying his own accounts. Tom was definitely not a good manager and tended just to leave the sales team on its own while he focused on selling his own accounts. Kyle, the third-generation owner and president, spent his time more on the office and production staff than on the sales team.

The sales team really needed a lot of help. Kate was the most senior sales rep, while the rest of the sales team was new or had weak selling habits. The problem was that her company kept hiring inexperienced junior sales reps to save money by not buying experienced sales talent, but then never coached or trained the new people once they were hired.

Nine months ago Kyle fired Tom. Kyle had been complaining for months that Tom was not doing his job as the VP and was only acting as the lead rep. Kate and the other eight sales reps were mostly left to figure things out on their own. When Kyle fired Tom

233

he announced he would also be taking over as the leader of the sales team. Kyle figured Tom was doing little to lead the sales force anyway, so he thought he could save some money and just leave the vacant sales VP position unfilled.

The company's sales plan was based largely on commissions with a very small base. After Tom's firing, Kyle hired two new sales reps, giving each of them half of Tom's old territory as a way to provide them with some immediate income.

But sales at the printing company continued to slowly yet consistently decline. The two new hires were not generating the additional revenue growth Kyle had been counting on. Kyle finally had enough and decided to make some changes. Since Kate was the most senior sales rep and seemed to be the only one who really understood what she was doing, Kyle promoted her to VP of sales.

Though Kate had never been a manager before, Kyle had noticed that the rest of the sales team always went to Kate when they had questions or needed help. Kyle also realized he didn't have the time or patience to look outside the company and go through a drawn-out interviewing, hiring, and training process.

Kyle needed his sales VP to also be producing his or her own sales to help cover the cost of having someone lead the sales team. Since Kate was already generating some solid sales revenues, he figured he could get by with only bumping her salary up a little while also offering her some bonus dollars if she could turn sales around.

Kate agreed to take on the new job responsibility as long as Kyle also stayed involved to help her figure out what best to do to turn around the sales team and revenues. They agreed Kate and Kyle would work together on identifying what needed to be done. Kate would be directly in charge of the sales team as well as implementing the ideas and processes Kate and Kyle developed. Kate also had one additional demand: She knew they needed to bring in some consulting expertise to show them what to do to improve sales.

Kate had heard me present at a printing conference and liked my ideas on advanced sales and sales leadership. During our first phone conversation Kate asked me, "So now what do I do? I don't even know where to start!"

I suggested Kate and Kyle work through the chapters of the new book I was writing to help them successfully redesign, retrain, and refocus their sales team. I explained that there were no shortcuts to rebuilding a sales team and that they needed to analyze and repair all of the processes and components that make up the total leadership and sales culture of their company. The success of one sales process or member will quickly disappear (or never reappear) if even one of these processes or components is missing or out of alignment.

Chapter 1   Why is it so hard to improve a sales force—and why do we tend to lose it once we change it?

I first evaluated Kate and Kyle's opinions of what it takes to make a sales team successful. Kate agreed that all four of the invalid leadership assumptions covered in Chapter 1 were indeed invalid, but Kyle had basically believed them and had really been following them all. He had assumed experience = trained (Invalid Leadership Assumption #1) and thought that was just the way selling and salespeople worked. Not only did he think people were "born for sales" he also assumed anyone who called themselves a salesperson knew how to sell (Invalid Leadership Assumption #2).

He also had assumed, even though he was not spending time with his sales team, that they would still be in their territories finding new opportunities to grow their sales (Invalid Leadership Assumption #3).

When we started talking about the fourth and final invalid leadership assumption ("You don't need to invest in a strong manager/leader if your team is already functioning as a solid team"), Kate started laughing and asked Kyle, "Is that why you gave me the VP job?"

Kyle agreed his belief in these four invalid leadership assumptions was a major contributor to the poor sales his company had been experiencing the past few years: "You got my attention," Kyle said, "so now what do we do?"

Coaching Tip #1.   As you work through these processes to improve your sales team, you need to start by making sure you and your organization's senior leadership do not believe any of these invalid notions about how selling and sales management function. You will experience profound surprises from senior management such as the sudden lack of support, the lack of funding, or the disruption of your planned change process if they believe any of these assumptions are true.

Coaching Tip #2. Start communicating with your sales team so they understand as soon as possible that you need their help and support to improve the sales organization. Lead them in a discussion of the kinds of positive improvements this redesign and refocusing could have on them. Explain the new sales tools and structures you want their help developing that can sell more and make their jobs easier.

It is critical you inform your sales team early about what you want to accomplish, how these changes directly benefit both the company and the sales reps, and that you are asking everyone to contribute to the planning and development required to achieve this newly defined success. If you say nothing to the sales team while you work with management "behind the scenes," you run the risk of having them possibly perceive the changes as detrimental to their careers.

Once a negative attitude about this type of change settles into a sales team, it is both time-consuming and difficult to reverse. Though some of your sales team might be suspicious or initially negative about your plans, you are still better off keeping them informed than risking their outright rejection and resistance.

Chapter 2 Is your senior management creating and supporting a positive *sales culture* that will allow your sales team to be successful?

Kate and Kyle agreed the first major challenge to address was the negative sales culture that currently existed (Chapter 2). We did some brainstorming and agreed Kyle and Kate would meet with the entire sales team to discuss the changes they were planning to implement and the expectations they had for all members of the team.

In their group meeting Kyle acknowledged the vital role the sales reps played in the success of the company. However, he also explained that the current revenue levels were not sufficient to keep the company in business long-term. He told them Kate was taking over as the VP of Sales and that she would be working with him and the consultant he hired (me) to redesign and refocus the entire sales organization. She would also be spending time working with each member of the sales team to help them increase their sales skills, their sales volumes, and their commissions. "Everybody in the lifeboat rows," Kyle announced as he identified that Kate would also spend time selling to her own accounts to help generate revenue.

The sales reps all agreed things definitely needed to improve to keep the company afloat, but all expressed concerns of not really knowing what to do to significantly increase sales or to win a lot of new customers' business.

With the initial meeting completed, I focused my efforts on Kate and Kyle. We discussed the need to change the sales and office culture immediately but agreed it needed to be done in a positive and affirming way. All agreed many of the reps would quit and go work elsewhere (taking many of their accounts with them) if Kyle did what he really wanted to do, which was yell to try to motivate the team.

Coaching Tip #3. Communication with senior management is essential to insure they are supportive of your efforts to redesign and refocus your sales organization. Explain the details of the changes you plan to implement with your sales team and review the concerns raised about senior management in Chapter 2. Also identify the potential benefits the changes will have on the company and how senior management's support can increase your chances of success.

It will take time for your sales team to notice a positive change in senior management if their interactions have been problematic in the past. Since believing that a positive change in management attitude is real and permanent and can take a long time for a sales force, allow time for your team to see that senior management has agreed to increase their contribution to the success of the sales force.

> **Chapter 3** The six commitments to generating long-term change and success within a sales force

Discussing the printing company's current selling environment showed Kate and Kyle they needed to improve all six of the commitments required to generate long-term change in their team

(Chapter 3). The problem though was that they needed to begin increasing sales now.

We discussed what both could do to informally talk to the team. To help align the first four commitments, they agreed to meet with each rep one-on-one to discuss what each thought about the values of the company and its three generation history (the first commitment), how communication could be improved (the third commitment), and what everyone's responsibilities and expectations needed to be (the fourth commitment).

Kyle felt he needed to handle the second commitment of making sure the reps supported Kate as the head of sales and that she was committed to helping the reps get better and earn higher commissions.

The fifth and six commitments were more of a challenge. Kyle decided to meet with some owners of other printing companies to learn about the compensation and commission programs they were using. The reps had been complaining that their compensation program was not competitive with other companies, and Kyle suspected they might be accurate in their concerns.

The sixth and final commitment involved the team agreeing to a single strategic selling message of uniqueness. Kate knew that each rep gave different reasons as to why their company was unique and that most of what they were telling prospects and customers were the same things being said by other printers in Chicago.

Coaching Tip #4. The six commitments outlined in Chapter 3 are the critical foundation components of an effective and successful sales team. You need to spend time understanding how each of your team feels about these six commitments. A lack of belief or commitment to any one will cause the collapse of your training plans and processes.

Sales reps will challenge or disregard anything you try to change or do if they do not agree with you on just one of these commitments.

Chapters 12 to 15   Taking the Sales Leadership Evaluation

Since we had already initiated extensive evaluations and assessments of the company's current conditions, it was a good time to also get an understanding of where Kate's and Kyle's current leadership skills really were.

To test the validity of the *Sales Leadership Evaluation*, I first asked them to describe what kind of sales leader they thought they were. Kate replied, "New. I am comfortable talking about how to sell, but leading a sales team is something I really don't know anything about, so the only way I can really describe my sales leadership skills is 'new.'"

Kyle said he felt he was a good leader due to his experience running the company but didn't see much difference between managing salespeople and the rest of his employees. He asked, "Keeping this place afloat for this many years has to count for something, doesn't it?"

The reality of evaluating someone's skills is if I ask you a vague and intuitive question I will most likely receive back a vague and intuitive response. Neither of their answers would help assess where they are and how to help them get better.

To make things more structured I gave them a copy of the 20-question *Sales Leadership Evaluation* and asked them to evaluate both themselves and each other.

What a difference in the feedback! Increasing the structure asking specific questions about their leadership skills immediately generated a more detailed and usable set of responses. More importantly, it generated a number of questions asking, "So how do you do that?" Just completing the leadership evaluation became the start of their sales management training.

Kate felt she really had nothing to compare sales leadership to. She had joined the printing company right out of college. Though she enjoyed working for the company she commented she never did have a sales manager there that was worth a damn as a leader. "They all just kind of shoved me out the door and told me I could do it, and when I returned with a few sales they said, 'See, you can do this. You don't need my help.'"

Kate gave herself mostly 1s (Unaware) and 2s (Weak). There were a few areas she felt were at least Just Average (scoring a 3) such as "Your skills as an organized administrator" (Leadership Question #1), "Your accessibility to your sales force" (Leadership Question #8), and "Your amount of 'positive focused' communications with your team" (Leadership Question #10).

She also felt she had at least developed some of the skills addressed in the evaluation from her informal coaching and helping out the reps who had come to her when she was in her own territory. "But helping a few reps does not make me feel like I know what I'm really doing."

Kyle gave himself a number of higher scores because he felt he had at least been doing a credible job as the head of sales for nine months. "But you were never around and rarely offered us any help!" Kate complained.

Most of his answers were Weak (scoring a 2) or Just Average (scoring a 3). He felt he was good at finding and hiring strong salespeople but really couldn't describe the steps he went through except to say, "I know talent and potential when I see it." The reality was that both of them were consistently Weak at best as sales leaders.

They both felt they had done poorly on the evaluation. I reminded them this was not a test but an evaluation of where they are today.

Coaching Tip #5. Anyone involved in leading your organization's sales team needs to complete an initial evaluation on their sales leadership skills to determine their starting "base line." How can you know you have improved if you don't know where you started? It is important, especially in these initial efforts, to remind everyone involved that these evaluations are not tests but subjective assessments to help guide the learning and growth processes of the team. This *Sales Leadership Evaluation* is one of the most advanced (i.e., detailed and complex) evaluations available today. Most sales managers are unhappy with their completed evaluations. You need to remind them that this is a "positive future-focused" activity and the first step in learning and improving occurs when you are at least able to identify what you don't know but want to learn. We are not as concerned with where you have been as we are with where you want to go.

> **Chapters 17 to 19** Giving the Sales Evaluation to all sales team members

Next Kyle and Kate filled out a *Sales Evaluation* on each of their 10 sales reps. They also completed a *Sales Evaluation* on themselves and each other. As expected, everyone evaluated did better on the first Operational Selling questions than they did on either the Tactical or Strategic

Selling questions. Though they disagreed on the individual question scores of a lot of the evaluations, they felt overall that they were in agreement as to where each of their sales reps were.

We decided it was too early to introduce these evaluations to the sales team. Giving them this evaluation now with their current weak selling skills was potentially too disruptive and/or depressing. Kyle commented, "We have so much we need to focus on doing and learning as managers to be able to help our sales team get better. Their completing the *Sales Evaluations* can wait."

Coaching Tip #6. Is it best to have your sales team members complete the *Sales Evaluation* this early in your process? The answer depends on their experience, attitude, and seniority. It will most likely be better to wait until later if you have new, inexperienced, and not very skilled salespeople on your team. It is also best to hold off having them complete the evaluations if they are overly negative or resistant to change. But giving the *Sales Evaluation* early to an experienced sales team could help generate positive interest in your change process and training.

Once you have completed the evaluations you have chosen to administer at this point, it is time to move to the next phase: designing your processes, programs, and training.

CHAPTER

22

Design Your Ongoing Sales Improvement Strategy

As we began our next consulting session Kate shared, "I've really been frustrated the last week or so. I now see all these parts and pieces of where our team is right now; I also see all of these gaps and exposures in what we are doing as a sales organization, but I have no idea how to fix them."

I told Kate her frustration was completely normal for a sales leader. There is nothing worse than having a clear understanding of all the problems, gaps, and exposures in a sales team, knowing you want them to get better but having no idea how to fix or improve any of your current problems.

> **Chapter 4** Applying the concepts of *ISO 9000* to improve the consistency and quality of your sales team

The majority of sales organizations have encountered two gaps in leading their sales teams. Most leaders push their sales teams to get better without any idea of what getting better actually involves (the first gap). They also don't have any clarified definitions of the goal skills or best practices they want their people to achieve (the second gap).

Kate and Kyle agreed they had encountered both of these leadership gaps in their company. To help them understand how to develop their change process, I shared the concepts of *ISO 9000* covered in Chapter 4.

They agreed they had already completed the first ISO step of identifying and beginning to track what their people were doing. I pointed out they were tracking where their team's skills and sales dollars were (a history focus), but they still were not tracking the processes and structures of how they needed to change and improve the team to get there (a future focus).

If you want to lead your sales team to a stronger selling position, you need to provide them with the detailed steps and structures of how to get there. To help them understand how critical the need for a common set of steps and structures is, I suggested Kate and Kyle try this evaluation of their sales team.

I told them to ask each sales team member to write down the answers to the following 10-question survey. Be sure to explain to your team that this survey will help them better understand what their team is currently doing and is not a test.

1. What do you feel are the most critical selling skills necessary for success as a sales professional?

Expected answers: There will be little consistency among answers of sales team members. Most of the answers will be simplistic or vague focusing only on operational selling skills. The majority of answers will also be reactive with them just responding to customers rather than proactively driving their selling process.

2. Can you write down the steps of a sales call? (Ask this question as a timed test of your team as in Chapter 1 Test #2.)

Expected answers: The majority of salespeople cannot write the steps down because they either don't know them or have forgotten them due to a lack of regular use.

3. What are the minimum goals you want to accomplish on every customer sales call?

Expected answers: Again expect to see little consistency among sales team members. Answers will be simplistic or vague, focusing on more reactive functions involving satisfying the customer and being of assistance. Ideal answers include proactive activities such as, "Look for new business opportunities," "Do something to improve my customer's satisfaction or interest in my company," or "Talk to more than one person." Notice how low the minimum expectations are for most of your people.

4. What indicators or tools do you use to identify and modify your communication style to better fit each of your unique customer/prospect's personalities?

Expected answers: There will be few indicators or tools utilized. The majority of sales people communicate with others intuitively, hoping they will know what to say when the time comes.

5. What are the tactical selling processes or steps you implement from the time you identify a new prospect or application opportunity to sell until the time you close on the business?

Expected answers: There will be few tools or structures understood or being utilized. The majority of salespeople think only one move ahead and function like the "Hellarewe" bird mentioned in Chapter 1.

6. What are the most important sales tools available to you (brochures, product samples, tours, meetings with senior management, events, or outings)? When or under what conditions are they most valuable?

Expected answers: The answers will cite only the physical, "printed" sales tools available to them. Most will not identify intangibles such as meetings with their manager, tours or outings as sales tools. Expect a low level of complexity and multiple steps ahead thinking about how to utilize these sales tools.

7. Once a prospect agrees to your proposal what are the steps between "Yes, I'll buy" and the point at which they are installed, delivered, and stable?

Expected answers: There will be few tools or structures understood or being utilized. Expect to see very few multiple stepped answers from your sales team members.

8. What are the most critical activities your sales manager can do to increase your selling success?

Expected answers: The majority of answers will focus on administrative, pricing, and problem solving issues. A few responses will suggest their managers should be pushing them, coaching them, or helping them achieve more than they would achieve if just left alone.

9. What are the most important time and territory skills every sales rep needs to be utilizing?

Expected answers: Responses will contain detailed analyses of how to be more *efficient* including how to be organized, how to manage their schedules, and how to get as much done as possible in the least amount of time. A few answers will focus on how to be more *effective* in their jobs including ways to be more proactive or to think multiple moves ahead.

10. What are the three or four most important selling ideas we need to communicate to customers or prospects when they ask, "Why, based on all the competitive alternatives available to me, do I want to buy from you?"

Expected answers: Expect to see a wide variety of answers. Also expect most of the responses to be competitively weak as discussed in Chapter 3 (Question #2).

The answers themselves are not a critical part of this 10-question exercise, but they enable you to evaluate two major factors of your sales team's abilities:

1. *Are your salespeople intuitive or structured?* How clear are their definitions of the steps and structures you expect them to have a solid understanding of? A sales rep with an intuitive style will at best only be able to provide vague or rambling responses. But a structured and more consistent sales rep will be able to answer these 10 questions with the steps or structures they are using. Do your sales reps even understand any of the basic steps or structures of selling?

2. *How consistent are your sales reps with their selling steps and structures?* If your sales team provides logical answers to any of these questions, then the next issue to evaluate is if there is any kind of consistency in the answers from your sales team.

When Kate had everyone complete this 10-question survey, two-thirds of the team either left sections blank or provided vague answers. The other third were able to at least attempt a description for some of the questions though none were impressive. It was evident Kate's entire sales team lacked any kind of structure or process in their selling efforts. "At least they are functioning as a consistent team," Kate laughed.

This survey is an effective way to prove to sales leaders that their sales team members have little or no best practices or consistent steps and structures in place.

How to Develop and Define Your Selling Best Practices

The overall goal of defining and implementing a set of best practices is to help increase your team's consistency, effectiveness, and coachability. Adding consistency and defined standards to processes and procedures will enable you to track feedback and results. As the leader of your sales team, you would have no way to track what was working if each salesperson on your team was prospecting with a completely different set of steps and processes.

Increasing the effectiveness of your team will help you improve results, shorten the selling process, and lower your chances of failure. Your goal as their sales leader is to help them see and understand how they could be doing something better or faster. Once you have consistent processes in place, you can start measuring results and determine which variation or change generates greater success.

And finally you want to increase the *coachability* of your team by building the kind of SWAT Team relationship discussed in Chapter 1 so "What one member learns, benefits all."

To develop a specific best practice or to clearly define the best way to do something means you and your team have to work through the following planning and evaluation process:

Step 1: Understand what your team is currently doing or how they are using this skill. How much consistency or variance exists within your team?

Step 2: Measure the efficiency and effectiveness of each alternative being implemented by a team member to see if anyone is generating better results than the others.

Step 3: Research if there is anything published or defined by others that can help clarify the best practice you are working to design and improve.

Step 4: Work with your team to design what you feel are the "best practices" of this area of study. Quantify and define the steps, components, skills, or philosophies that make up this newly defined "best practice." Since your team is more likely to accept and adhere to the best practices if they have input in the design, it is important to get as many members as possible involved in this step.

A steps-of-a-sales-call best practice can be as simple as listing the five steps that need to take place during a sales call. Those steps are (1) lower their resistance, (2) ask questions to learn and qualify the buyer, (3) present your solutions in an interactive dialogue with your buyer, (4) ask for the order or some type of commitment, and (5) agree and set up your next contact to continue the persuasive selling process.

For more complex skills, processes, or structures your defined best practices could be multiple selling steps that need to be consistently followed.

Simply put, defined "best practices" are the instruction manual or roadmap for the skill or process being discussed. It is the guide to help keep your sales reps consistent in their efforts, effective in the way they apply this best practice, and thinking in a proactive, multi-stepped manner.

Step 5:   Test your newly defined "best practice" to see if it is indeed the best way to be doing this task or process. Continually identify ways to improve or fine tune the identified best practice.

Step 6:   Train all members of your team on the new "best practice," allowing time for discussion of how utilizing this new "best practice" can increase the effectiveness and success of each team member.

Step 7:   Be sure all members of your team commit to using these new best practices and to accepting your coaching and guidance.

Step 8:   Establish tracking and coaching systems to monitor and implement these new best practices to insure they are successfully and consistently utilized. Determine how frequently you need to fine tune and reevaluate the effectiveness of these "best practices."

While defining the detailed components of the various sales and sales leadership best practices is beyond the scope of this book, it does provide the basic structures and process of *how* to go about developing best practices. The goal of this book is to help define the major skill best practice categories required to lead your sales team. Once you have defined the range of "best practices" you need, the details can be researched and identified from a wide range of sources (books, experts, Internet, etc.).

What kinds of "best practices" does your sales team need? Some that you will most likely need and benefit from include:

Sales leadership best practices.   The *Sales Leadership Evaluation* and the *Central Leadership Values* can help determine the most effective areas to be defining and developing your sales leadership best practices.

Sales skills best practices.   The *Sales Evaluation* can help identify the most effective operational, tactical, and strategic skills of your selling best practices.

249

Sales tools best practices. You also will need to develop the defined "best practices" for

- Selling tools.
- Message of uniqueness.
- Selling processes.
- Sales team education plans.
- Sales coaching process.
- Sales skills, training, and development tracking process to be utilized with each sales rep.

Once you have designed what you need, it is now time to *prioritize* what to work on and implement in your sales team

---

By the time you get this far in your evaluation and design, it is guaranteed you will have identified multiple times the number of best practices projects you need for the time and funding you actually have to complete their development and implementation. What is the next best best practices project you can work on now that will generate the most significant results for your team?

The majority of businesses do not have the time, resources, personnel, or awareness to be able to fix everything at once. What are your priorities? What do you and the members of your team feel needs to be fixed/improved first? Which areas, if improved, will generate the greatest revenue and/or profit improvements? And which skills are the most fixable given the current resources and leadership time you and your team have available? These are always tough questions for you as the sales leader to answer.

"Prioritizing the importance of 'best practices' we need to work on is driving me nuts!" complained Kate. "We have so many areas that need work and help it seems almost impossible to prioritize the next best area to invest in improving."

There is no one right or best answer to this question. Just remember there are a lot of things you have to do to be competitive but only a few that will actually increase your competitive advantage. Try to work on the big stuff first that will have the greatest impact on your quality, customer service, selling effectiveness, or competitive advantage.

Once you finish analyzing the evaluation responses and designing your best practices, it's time to implement these new skills, tools, structures, processes, and awareness with your sales team.

CHAPTER

23

Implement a
Learning Growth Strategy
for Each Sales Team Member

After several months of work Kate and Kyle were both satisfied with how their sales leadership skills, sales tools, selling structures, and philosophies had improved. "I feel like I'm starting to get a handle on how selling is really supposed to work and what our team needs to do to increase our competitive edge and start winning more business!" said Kate.

When a sales organization is in as much disarray as Kate's was it is very common to want to start fixing and improving their organization in the wrong order. At the simplest level, improving a sales force requires you to improve your sales leadership skills and awareness, improve the sales tools available to your team to help communicate your competitive uniqueness, and train your people on how to utilize all of the newly discovered and defined skills and awareness. This is the best and most consistently effective way to improve a sales team.

Working on your management skills first will help you more effectively lead your team through the rest of the change process. Working on your leadership skills first will ensure that through your leadership and coaching, new skills and procedures stay implemented and utilized.

Next, you need to work on defining and improving the sales tools

253

your team needs to be successful. It is essential to clearly define the sales tools before you begin the skill training necessary to use the tools.

Once you have improved the sales leadership and coaching structures as well as the sales tools, it is time to begin aggressively training your team on the new selling system you have developed.

Most sales leaders who come to me for consulting and training assistance almost always want their first step to change to be conducting a sales training class.

Recently, I received a call from Mike, the VP of Operations for an application software company. I was recommended to him by one of his sales team members who had been through my training more than 10 years ago. Mike's company sells a very complex and customized software package specifically designed for managing all aspects of a doctor's office.

Mike explained he was asked to spearhead efforts to improve their selling process and assist in helping their new sales manager. The company employs 8 outside sales reps responsible for finding and selling to new doctors offices and 12 customer service technicians, who are in charge of installing, maintaining, and growing their existing customers. Mike explained that both departments considered their function to be sales and both were compensated based on how much they could grow their assigned territories (either new business or existing).

Mike called me wanting to schedule sales training for his team. He explained that the owner had hired a close friend to head the sales force several years ago and since joining the company had pretty much destroyed the sales team. Just like Kyle had with Kate at the printing company, Mike's company promoted the best sales rep to sales manager hoping to turn the sales team around. Bill, the new sales manager, had never managed a sales team before but was excited about his new job. Bill was also amazed at how screwed up the entire sales department was. "It reminds me of that old television comedy series called *F Troop* about a screwed-up military post in the Wild West. It seems like little about our selling processes seems to be done the right way."

I asked Mike why he wanted to begin by implementing sales training, and why he was interested in fundamental, or operational skills at that. His answer was, "Well, we need to start somewhere and only have the funding to do one day of training for now."

With no effective leadership structure or awareness in place, no sales tools or selling processes defined or stabilized, and a sales team who didn't seem to be able to do their job right, what would be the long-term impact of conducting a day of operational foundation selling skills for this team?

I explained the three components of changing a sales culture (sales leadership skill improvement, rebuilding of sales tools, and then finally sales training) and convinced Mike his company would receive a faster payback on their training/consulting investment if they conducted their sales training last and not first.

We scheduled a two-day consulting session with Bill and Mike during which we reviewed the concepts covered in this book and discussed how to improve their sales leadership environment, redefine the sales tools they would need, and then lead their team through sales training.

In just two days they were able to identify and even start outlining all of the factors they needed to change for their salespeople to be motivated and skilled in their selling efforts. They did not have the funding or the time to implement all the structures outlined, but they now had a plan and an understanding of the next best things to work on first. When they do begin conducting their sales training, they will be aware of what the training needs to focus on and how to coach and lead their sales team to a stronger selling position.

Establishing the Best Environment to Help Your Sales Team

The best learning and growth environments tend to share the same four attributes:

1. *A safe and affirming open team learning environment.* Resistance to change or growth is in direct conflict with your ability to receive and implement new ideas. The stronger your resistance and higher your level of stress, the lower your ability to learn. How comfortable do your team members feel sharing what's really going on in their territories? How important do they feel they are to you, your team, and your company?

   The first step in increasing the selling skills of your team is to make sure they feel comfortable taking risks and telling you that they have made mistakes. You, as the sales leader, are the greatest contributor to building and maintaining that trust and comfort level with your sales team. You do that by making sure your feedback and comments are supportive and at least partially positive. To help establish this open environment be sure your salespeople feel they contributed to either the design or development of their upcoming training and obtain their commitment to participate in this new process.

The difficulty of leading independent individuals, especially the *very* independent, self-sufficient individuals who tend to be in sales is that training and coaching will not be successful unless both the coach and the person being coached agree these efforts are necessary and productive.

Another idea is to end every training meeting with a discussion of, "Did this training help and was this a productive use of our team's time?" If you receive negative feedback from your team, then something needs to be changed or improved. No sense cramming training down their throats against their will. You need them to want to learn. You can handle in private any discussions with one or two individuals, especially the more senior members of your team, expressing negative feedback on your training.

As explained in Chapter 2, everyone needs to feel important, included, and a part of your team's commitment to sales training for this to work. As Kyle said to his printing company salespeople, "We're all in this lifeboat together and everyone in this boat rows."

2. *A positive environment.*   The second element necessary to create a positive learning and growth environment centers on you and the interactions you have with your team. What percent of your comments and training feedback is positive versus negative? Your sales team will be more affirming and positive with each other if they feel those same behaviors coming from you as their leader.

One way to establish a positive learning environment is to allow mistakes. You need to focus on what people are doing, or trying to do right instead of focusing only on what they are doing wrong.

You also need to celebrate progress and milestones. Keep in mind it is the attempts that matter. Results are secondary. As the sales leader you need to make sure you have created an environment where your people feel it is safe to make mistakes as long as they and the rest of the team are able to learn and grow.

3. *A proactive, forward-focused environment.*   The third element necessary to build a positive learning and growth environment

requires clear communication that your sales training is focused on improving the team's skills and future success, not on past mistakes and placing blame.

4. *An organized and planned out environment.* The fourth and final element essential to building a positive learning and growth environment is earning your sales team's trust in your ability to implement your planned training and coaching process. Be sure to share with them the anticipated outcome of the changes: what you expect them to learn, why these are the most critical next best skills to work on, and how you expect them to implement the ideas covered.

   You need your team's agreement that you have an effective design and they agree with your prioritization of topic training. Without this type of agreement and support from your team you are just wasting training funds. No learning or behavior changes are likely to occur under a stressful or uncomfortable environment.

How to Conduct Effective Training and Adult Learning

An important characteristic of training is the type of training structure or process you select to best communicate your new learning ideas. To best understand the benefits and trade-offs of any specific training format, you need to first understand the steps of adult learning. To select the best training format for your sales team you have to also understand the steps necessary for long-term learning and change. Any training program you are considering should be evaluated against the six steps of the adult learning process. Your sales training will not be successful unless all members of your team are able to complete each of these six steps. Keeping these steps in mind as you evaluate various sales training formats can help you make the best selection for your team.

1. *Increase awareness.* This is the step where you teach a lesson or provide a corrected or improved insight. There are several training process alternatives available to help increase your team's awareness. The benefits and trade-offs of various training formats are covered next.

2. *Increase the comprehension of the ideas covered.* You have just presented a new sales idea to your team. Just because they have this

257

new information doesn't mean they will actually do anything with it. To move their learning process forward, you need to help them digest the ideas so they understand you are talking about them and what they need to change.

This is the "Yea, we mean you and your territory" part of the sales training. One of the main reasons otherwise successful training programs fail to generate long-term change is that attendees have not made the connection between developing better awareness and then actually applying this awareness in their territory.

Awareness digestion needs to occur both during the actual training class and in your ongoing role as coach and leader of your team. After the completion of a training class or program, you as the coach need to work with members of your team to be sure they understood the training. You also need to help them process this new material by asking questions such as, "How do you see that idea working with your accounts?" or, "How would you say that so it gets the attention of your customers?"

A lot of solid sales training on the market does a good job, but if no one from your leadership team follows up to help team members process the ideas covered, then the new information evaporates within a few months and is forgotten.

What have you done since your team's last training experience to insure all team members understood and processed the new information? Consider how effective the prospective training is at helping your team process information. Then decide how easy it will be for you to continue that digestion process through your ongoing coaching efforts.

3. *Increase raw implementation.* This is the step where you get your sales team to begin implementing. You are not looking for perfection here, just some kind of action. This is where most training falls apart. Even when a sales team has new awareness and understands what to do with their new information, getting them to take action and actually do something is where most training stalls.

You, as coach, play a critical role in this raw implementation phase of learning. Your job is first to help get them to at least attempt to utilize what is being discussed. Your second critical role in this step is to provide affirming feedback and encouragement. This is where a lot of sales leaders fail as coaches. They provide their people with great new information and even show them how relevant it is to them and their job—and then just wait for results.

Scientists say inertia is the strongest force in nature. Helping create change in a sales team means you need to be the leader here to get your people out of their routine and into some type of action.

4. *Increase refinement.* Once team members are taking action, the responsibility of a coach is to help them refine, or get better at what they are doing. This is also the continually quality improvement fourth step of *ISO 9000.*

5. *Increase permanence.* Once your sales team is improving their skills it is time to lock this new skill in so it becomes habit without their having to even think about it. Repetition of action, positive feedback, and ongoing coaching are the three best ways to help someone move to a permanent level of change.

6. *Go back to the first step and start increasing awareness in a different area.* A philosophy of lifelong learning is based on the idea of always reinvesting and moving to the next level. Once members of your team have reached permanence with a skill it is time, as their coach, to help them identify the next best skill (or skills) to work on next.

How much time and attention are you investing in your sales team to help them increase their awareness? Their comprehension? Their raw implementation? Their refinement, improvement, and permanence? How much time are you investing in helping your people identify new skills and awareness they can improve?

Skill Training Alternatives to Help Your Sales Team Learn and Grow Their Skills, Structures, Processes, and Philosophies

Are you ready to start conducting sales training with your team? You have a number of sales training avenues or approaches to choose from. Listed next are the six major alternatives to training a sales force. Which works best for you will depend on the size of your sales team, how experienced they are in selling, the size of your training budget, and your time and meeting constraints.

These six training alternatives are in addition to your role as a sales leader and coach. All six of these training alternatives are strengthened if you are able to provide management coaching and follow-up to help make any ideas covered stick. These six approaches are listed by degree of flexibility and customization to your unique environment and requirements with the least flexible training options discussed first.

The benefits and trade-offs of the six sales training alternatives available to you include:

1. *Public sales rallies.* These are large sales meeting events or rallies. The sales rallies could be as large as 10,000 attendees and are characterized by lots of excitement, high energy, and motivational messages. They usually comprise multiple (normally celebrity) speakers each presenting their ideas in a very condensed time frame.

   Benefits of public sales rallies:
   - Lots of fun and very motivational.
   - You can send as many or as few of your people as you wish.

   Concerns or potential negatives of public sales rallies:
   - Presentations and training materials tend to be heavy motivational and attitude focused with little actual how to skill training.
   - Usually lots of time is spent at these programs pushing products for sale in the back of the room.

   Best usage for public sales rallies:
   - Great for entertaining or working to motivate someone.
   - Public rallies are a nice break from your territory.
   - Very rarely considered real skill training.

2. *Public or university seminars.* These are training seminars conducted as noncredit courses. The vast majority of university seminars have less than 100 attendees. Most public or university seminars are at least a full day of training. Like the large meeting sales events or rallies you are still meeting in a general audience setting (little customization to you, your company, or even

260

your industry). Program presenters do not tend to be celebrities or even well-known experts.

Benefits of public or university seminars:

- Inexpensive training.
- You can send one or more people.
- Usually involves fairly skilled and experienced trainers or facilitators of the material

Concerns or potential negatives of public or university seminars:

- This type of environment involves general skill training across multiple industries and/or companies minimizing talking about your unique industry, situations, or customers.
- Most of the established public or university programs tend to focus on foundations or operational skills.
- It is difficult for a sales leader to understand the new skills being learned by the sales rep or to be an effective coach to understand how to apply the new material if they did not attend the training.

Best usage for public or university seminars:

- Great for training one or two people at a time.
- A great training environment for sales leaders to attend.

3. *Hiring outside consultants or experts.* These are training seminars or consulting sessions with outside experts normally conducted in your offices.

Benefits of hiring outside consultants or experts:

- Allows you to bring in an outsiders extended view to offer you and your team fresh or unique ideas.
- These presenters are usually more effective and entertaining with their presentations so they tend to hold their attendee's attention.
- These people promote themselves as experts who can defend and prove their views and suggestions (unlike a number of in-house trainers who may have never personally worked a sales territory).

Concerns or potential negatives of hiring outside consultants or experts:

- These experts are normally expensive. You may need to have a larger sales force to be able to justify the expense of bringing in one of these experts.
- Can be only event focused training instead of allowing your training to be a process.
- These presenters are less effective if they do not do any homework or research in advance of your training to learn the unique aspects of your business.

Best usage for hiring outside consultants or experts:

- These experts are great within a specific skill area.
- Tend to be best training alternative when teaching advanced skills and insights.

4. *In-house training departments.* This is sales training taught by members of your in-house, or internal training, department.

Benefits of utilizing your in-house training department:

- Usually effective if provided with the proper training materials and are focused and knowledgeable in the topics you need trained.
- Inexpensive since these people are already employees of your organization.

Concerns or potential negatives of utilizing your in-house training department:

- You have to be a fairly large company to be able to afford an extensive in-house sales training program.
- A large number of in-house trainers (even in-house sales trainers) are in their position because of their training expertise and experience and may never have personally sold. They have no credibility in front of your sales reps.
- Programs tend to focus on the more fundamental or operational skills.

Best usage for using in-house trainers:

- Product and fundamental sales training skills (unless trainer has sales background with your company).

- Can be effective helping your sales team process the training information covered by another training alternative.

5. *You conducting in-house sales training with your team.* This is sales training taught by you for your sales team.

   Benefits of conducting in-house sales training with your team:

   - Inexpensive training.
   - Allows you to conduct your training with multiple process times between classes to allow you to assign homework assignments and to help coach them through the digestion and raw implementation phases of their training.
   - Allows the most digestion and processing of ideas of any of these training alternatives.
   - Coach is also active as a trainer.

   Concerns or potential negatives of conducting in-house sales training with your team:

   - Sales leaders tend to make inexperienced trainers who are new to the material.
   - Most sales leaders are not trained in how to conduct effective sales training (the blind leading the blind).
   - Coaches leading these classes tend to blend in operational meetings, discipline feedback, and training into the sales class killing the attitude and focus of the sales training.

   Best usage for you conducting in-house sales training with your team:

   - Great alternative to helping provide sales skill training to your team.
   - This format is great for teaching foundation or operational skills though they tend to have a tougher time handling advanced or complex sales training topics.
   - This alternative is a great effort to incorporate or to wrap around any of the other five training alternatives. Important way to provide process and digestion to any training conducted for your team.

6. *Self-study.* This training involves the individual working alone with only minimal coaching. This can include self-study courses in a book, on the Internet, or in audio or video format.

Benefits of self-study training programs:

- Very inexpensive to conduct training.
- Doesn't require attendee to travel or be out of their territory.
- Easily customized or adjusted to the skills, awareness, and pace of student.

Concerns or potential negatives of self-study training programs:

- Hard to keep students disciplined enough to complete training program.
- Misses most of the digestion efforts.
- Hard to understand complex topics, structures, or ideas if no one to help digest with you.

Best usage for self-study training programs:

- Depends on budget, speed of change, distance to travel, strength of in-house and coaching training skills, topics to be addresses, time frame to be completed.
- Best when training dollars and time are really tight or you have lots of remote staff.

How to Conduct Your Own In-House Sales Training

There is a simple structure to increase the effectiveness of any training you conduct as a sales leader.

1. Design your sales training to center around an audio, video, or written sales training piece. It might be an article out of a sales training or association membership magazine, an audio or video product that you bought, or a few workbook pages from a seminar or presentation you attended.

2. Give your team the selected materials and strongly encourage that they read or listen or watch this material prior to your scheduled sales meeting.

3. During the training session you need only to ask your team members the following four questions:
   - What success have you had so far (since the last training meeting)? This is the time to generate positive comments

264

and to keep your team excited about the success they are having to the ideas being presented.

- What did you think of the ideas covered in the assigned article, audio, or video?
- How relevant did you think the ideas covered in this article, audio, or video were, and how do you see applying these ideas to you current territory?
- So what are you going to try implementing before we meet again (next week)?

4. Coach and lead your sales team as they take on this new skill or awareness.

How do you know if your training is actually working?

Too many sales managers dump a few days of sales training on their team, do little to no implementation coaching, and then sit and wait several months for sales to increase.

But it is possible to keep stronger control of your sales team and receive more immediate feedback even while they move through their change process. You can begin observing and tracking their commitment to change while still in your first training session. There are four steps to generating long-term change in an individual:

1. *Change in Attitude.* Are they at least giving you feedback that they are excited about these new ideas and suggestions? If you are receiving negative feedback from the beginning about the training, then you need to deal with the negative issues before continuing your training efforts.

2. *Change in Effort.* Are your people even trying the ideas or skills proposed? Saying "great ideas Boss" is great for the first few days but now it's time to get to work and actually try doing something.

   The goal in this second step is to get them to initiate the effort. Are they trying anything new? Are they at least attempting to use or apply the new terms and language you are training them to apply?

265

They will likely not be very effective or successful in their attempts of new skills, processes, or philosophies. You need to affirm their efforts as you coach them on how to improve and recognize that they may not be successful at first.

3. *Change in Progress.* Now things are starting to build and accumulate. After measuring their attitude and efforts, you can now start looking for positive progress. Are they starting to issue more proposals? Are there more requests for information? Is your team giving more plant tours or arranging visits to customer sites? Once your team has begun actively implementing the new processes, you can start looking for provable progress in their efforts.

4. *Change in Results.* Once you have worked your team through focusing on their attitude, their efforts, and their progress it is time to start looking for this fourth and final step in measuring change.

As a coach and leader it is our job to help our team member's work through these four stages of change. You can't shortcut the process by just pushing through to results. As the leader of your team you need to help coach them on an ongoing and consistent basis through each of these four steps of change.

Now that you are implementing a solid sales training process and skill building to help increase your team's skills, it is time to discuss how you will keep them focused on their assignment.

CHAPTER

24

Track Sales Team Members' Improvements by Utilizing a Comprehensive Sales Performance Tracking System

To begin, or improve your sales team improvement strategy you need to initially *Evaluate* (Chapter 21), *Design* (Chapter 22), and *Implement* (Chapter 23) your training process. Now that you are implementing your training you also need to begin tracking your team's progress.

It is best if your tracking begins before you implement your training. You need to first understand and identify where your people start to be able to recognize if they have made improvements. Tracking your team's progress and skill levels has been discussed throughout this book as part of the *ISO 9000* concepts of improvement.

What kinds of tracking systems are you currently utilizing for your sales team? Most sales organizations only have sales performance tracking systems in place. They track only how much you sold and at what profitability. But to strengthen and improve a sales force you also need to be tracking the sales skills of your team as well as their progress through the outlined assignments and training. Bottom line: You need to be tracking not just *what* your team has sold (the traditional model) but also *how* they are performing their job. Though these two tracking systems will be integrated in the information and value they can provide, they are two separate, yet complementary, tracking systems.

In this chapter I present only a *skills and improvement* tracking system.

Tracking the Performance of Your Sales Team

You need three integrated components or tools to have a comprehensive tracking system in place for your sales team.

1. *Tracking Tool #1: Sales and Sales Leadership Evaluations.* It is imperative both of these evaluations be completed by both you (the sales leader) and each of your team members before initiating any type of training or change efforts.

   The goals of beginning your sales improvement process with the *Sales Evaluations* is to gain a clear and detailed understanding of the current skills, and gaps, of each individual and to introduce your upcoming sales training direction and focus.

   A third goal is to also gain consensus within your team. You, as their leader, need to have a solid and detailed understanding of the skill balance of each team member. You also want to make sure each team member has an accurate and detailed evaluation of their own skills that both of you agree and accept.

   As you complete all of the individual sales team evaluations, you also want to start a full team discussion of where they see the entire team's skills are. Having them discuss and evaluate the skills of the entire team helps strengthen each rep's commitment to working as a single SWAT team and helps them understand why your upcoming sales training can be of such value.

   Once you have a consensus on the beginning or base line skills of your team it is important to remind them this evaluation tool is an integral part of their ongoing skill development. You also want to go back and reevaluate anyone who has made significant improvements to help them see how much progress they have actually achieved.

2. *Tracking Tool #2: Informal sales leader feedback and coaching.* The second integrated component of a comprehensive tracking system involves your role as an active and involved coach and leader of your team. In your role of sales leader you need to constantly observe, evaluate, and coach each team member toward improved skills and awareness. How involved and present are you as their sales leader? Are you constantly being a proactive coach by asking questions, offering encouragement, and suggesting ideas? You don't have to sit down and complete the entire 20-question evaluation as a formal meeting every month. You can also have a positive impact working through this evaluation one question at a time as you see discussion opportunities throughout the year. You will increase your team's success if you can keep referencing and focusing on these 20 evaluation questions.

3. *Tracking Tool #3: Formal annual performance plan.* Does your company have a formal annual performance plan evaluation system in place? An ideal annual performance plan is one initiated at the beginning of the year between a sales rep and their manager that outlines all of the expectations you and your company have for that rep. It also includes expected sales performance numbers and specific goals for accounts in one's territory. The better plans also define expectations for personal and professional development and continual improvement. The form is discussed and then signed by both the manager and sales rep and everyone gets a copy.

   Once this plan or roadmap for the year is completed, it is time for the sales rep to get to work. During the year there are then periodic informal discussions between you and the rep about their plan, their progress to date, and their plans to successfully complete all of the assigned or identified tasks.

   At the end of the year the performance plan is again reviewed in a formal meeting. The sales manager and the sales rep each go through and now score (usually a one to five scale) the sales rep's performance for the year. As part of the discussion on the rep's success last year are discussions and suggestions of what needs to be incorporated into next year's plan. By the end of this meeting last year's plan has been evaluated, reviewed, discussed, and signed off (showing agreement) by both the rep and manager and the next year's plan has also been completed and signed.

Though complex and time consuming, a formal performance plan provides a tremendous amount of agreement of both current and potential performance levels between a rep and her manager.

The 20-question *Sales Evaluation* is not in conflict with a formal annual performance plan review process. The *Sales Evaluation* tool can be a great precursor to developing and formalizing an annual performance plan. Through discussions the rep and manager can prioritize what skills the rep performs best and what areas would most benefit from increased attention over the next year. Areas to be worked on or to receive additional emphasis can then be written into their performance plan.

What kinds of tracking tools can you put in place to help you lead your sales team? The reality is that if you don't measure and track it, it won't change.

CHAPTER

25

Lead Your Sales Team by Ongoing Coaching of Your Defined Selling Best Practices

Improving a sales force requires you to implement a multiple stepped process across your entire sales organization. In the vast majority of organizations it is never just one simple isolated problem causing lower than desired sales levels.

This chapter presents one additional concept of sales leadership: how to actually be a leader and coach of a sales team. The reality is we are only going to cover a brief overview of what it takes to be an effective leader and coach; otherwise this chapter would equal the length of the rest of this book.

As stated in Chapter 5

> The job of a sales leader is to help each of your people achieve more than they would have achieved if just left alone.

So how do you actually apply all of this to really make a difference in your sales team, your upper management, and the rest of your organization?

The Evolution of a Sales Manager

To understand what it takes today to successfully lead a sales team requires brief reflection on how the job of a sales manager has evolved. During each of these past phases sales leaders tended to focus the majority of their leadership style and focus on this latest skill of leadership. Though in general they are accurate the following listed dates are not exact. Different industries evolved through these levels at slightly different times.

Sales Leader as Intimidator (prior to the 1970s)

The goal of the Intimidator style of leadership involved generating results by scaring your team into success. These sales leaders would yell and scream—the drill sergeant mentality of leadership. They created the illusion that if they got angry enough they might actually hit you. Members of their sales team responded to this style with fear, but the fear did tend to generate at least a short-term increase in results.

So why did this style of leadership stop working? Around the 1970s as our collective legal awareness increased, salespeople began to realize "Hey, you really can't hit me!" When the fear was removed it now meant only they were just watching their sales manager jump up and down and scream. Not an effective leadership model.

Sales Leader as Motivator (the 1970s and 1980s)

When sales leaders realized the "yelling thing" was no longer effective, they turned to being a "motivator" of their team. Now they viewed the goal of their job as sales leader was to energize their team—really pump everyone up. They would hang motivational posters throughout the office and would give their team Monday morning motivational lectures saying things like "You can do it," "Make it happen," "Never give up," and "See you at the top of the sales mountain!"

These are positive statements to share with a sales team but tended to be the only thing most sales leaders were sharing.

So why did this style of leadership stop working? Sales teams and their leaders started to realize they needed more than just a positive attitude to be successful. How frustrated would you be as a sales rep if you went to your boss asking for help on an account and your manager's response is only, "You can do it!"?

Sales Leader as Administrative Assistant (1990s)

Most businesses in the 1990s were concerned with maximizing profitability, increasing efficiency, and somehow figuring out how to reduce all of the bureaucracy and paperwork overwhelming their business. Since the majority of sales leaders had never been trained on how to be effective managers, most reverted back to their sales roots. A large number of sales managers decided the most productive contribution they could make to the team's success was to personally take on some accounts acting as account rep. They also decided the best way to maximize the selling productivity of their team was to do anything they could to keep their sales reps out selling in front of their customers.

So most sales managers shifted to a leadership style of becoming an administrative assistant. The idea was if I, as your manager, can help handle some of your paperwork, problem solving, and expediting then you as the rep can now spend more time selling in your territory. Most managers also felt this a productive effort since they, as a manager, could get problems solved and orders expedited faster than their sales reps could.

This philosophy did tend to make the sales team more productive, but the productivity occurred at the expense of any sales leadership, coaching, or guidance. In a lot of cases the sales reps were doing more managing and directing of their boss than the sales manager was of their reps. Under this administrative assistant structure sales reps would dump stacks of folders detailing all of the current problems they were having on their manager's desk, then go back into their territory confident all of the problems they had given their manager would be solved.

But look at the opportunity cost of this structure! Now the sales manager/leader was spending all of their time on administrative and scheduling issues, a lower paying job than that of a sales manager, and there was no leadership of the sales team occurring. Remember this was also when the concept of experience = trained was a strong belief of both sales reps and their manager.

Sales Leader as Coach and Strategist (2000 and beyond)

About 2000 there was a realization that increasing efficiency might not actually translate to increased effectiveness. Sales leaders also began to realize their sales team's didn't have the answers they needed, didn't know what they were doing, didn't understand how they were winning sales or where they were going.

Sales leaders realized the only way to significantly increase their sales volumes was by training, coaching, and leading their team to success. Most had no idea how to accomplish this but they did realize the critical role they needed to take in their sales team's selling efforts.

What does it take to successfully lead a sales team? The reality is you need all four of these leadership attributes to be effective as a leader. You need to communicate the need for discipline, structure, and order (the Intimidator style without all the yelling). You also need to motivate even the most experienced reps (the Motivator style).

But you also need to realize that even though you could help expedite customer issues in the short term, longer term results will be achieved only when you train and coach your people to solve customer problems on their own. Their job as a sales leader was to then help each of their people achieve more than they would have achieved if just left alone.

As discussed in Chapter 6, most sales leaders are working harder and putting in more hours than all but the most senior and successful members of their sales team. Do you want to be a better leader to your team? How much time do you have available in your current schedule to actually work one-on-one with each team member? How many meetings can you schedule this week to help lay out selling strategies and multistepped plans to sell your team's most important accounts? The sad reality is most sales leaders are just too busy with their own accounts, internal management meetings, and paperwork to be able to work as a coach and strategist to their sales team.

Becoming a better coach, strategist, and leader by reshaping your entire sales organization will require you to reorganize, refocus, and delegate so you can free up time to be an actual leader to your team. How much time can you free up to invest in growing your team?

How do you help your team members achieve more than they would have achieved if just left alone? There are a number of skills outlined in the 20-question *Sales Leadership Evaluation*. But the two most critical responsibilities of a sales leader are (1) leading and motivating your entire team and (2) leading your team's selling process as a coach and strategist.

Sales Leadership Responsibility #1: Leading and Motivating Your Entire Team

An old leadership concept states "You *manage* processes but you *lead* people." Look at the bias or focus of most sales organizations. They call the people in charge of their sales teams "managers" focusing attention on the paperwork, administration, and processes. Wouldn't it be both better and more accurate to be calling these people "sales leaders" to help them understand where they need to be investing their energies?

The Four Points of Motivation

Bill McGrane, Sr., a self-esteem consultant from Cincinnati, Ohio, identified four absolute rules of motivation:

You Cannot Motivate Anyone to Do Anything. The concept of trying to motivate someone is invalid. It is impossible for you to motivate anyone.

All People Are Already Highly Motivated. If you are alive then you are highly motivated. Are you thinking of any of your relatives whom you feel are the unmotivated exception? The problem is not *if* they are motivated, but *where* their motivation is compared to yours.

People Are Motivated for Their Reasons—Not for Yours. And they are motivated because of their biases and not yours. They are motivated by their life experiences, their culture, their heritage, their peer groups, and their beliefs. Everyone is highly motivated. Everyone gets fired up and excited about something even if that something is to do as little as possible, they are *still* motivated.

All You Can Do Is Create the Environment for People to Motivate Themselves. Most sales leaders' problems are not due to the lack of motivation within their employees. It is caused by their lack of understanding of what most motivates each member of their team. The job of a leader is to create such a positive environment for their sales team so that all members are fired up, energized, and highly motivated. But the motivation only comes from within the employee. You are not motivating them but instead are only redirecting, refocusing, or channeling that motivational energy into contributing to your team's and organization's common good.

How to Create an Environment for People to Motivate Themselves

How are you redirecting, refocusing, and channeling that motivational energy within your team? There are five major categories or ways you can enhance each team member's motivational environment.

Recognition by Management/Company. Question #10 of the *Sales Leadership Evaluation* (Chapter 14) stated the best way to generate positive energy (or motivation) in someone is to make them feel loved and important.

So many managers just don't understand their role as leader. I've actually had several owners and senior leaders of companies over the years tell me they don't need to get involved in a lot of this "touchy feely" stuff of telling everyone "Great job" on a regular basis because, "We only hire experienced sales pros."

Everyone wants to feel highly valued and important. It is a universal truth of leadership. What kind of positive feedback and recognition are you providing your people?

One alternative to creating a stronger motivational environment is to help provide them with extra job perks like personal use of their cell phone minutes, not having to attend certain meetings, or even extra days off. Other motivational environment enhancers include any kind of personal attention for a sales rep from senior management, extra flexibility, or even input in company or sales team decision making.

Look how successful the airline frequent flyer and hotel frequent stay programs have been. They are able to generate high customer loyalty just by giving their customers no cost upgrades to first class seating or an upgraded hotel room. How are you making your team members feel loved and important? And what can you do to help organize your senior management team to provide more ongoing and varied positive feedback and recognition to your team members?

What kind of recognition can you help generate for your team members and the other departments within your company to help people feel more valued and important so they are more motivated?

Increased Responsibilities or Challenges.   Some senior sales reps tend to brag about how much more territory or quota they carry than the others. They talk with pride about this added responsibility. How are you helping your people motivate themselves by empowering them to be able to get their job done? And how much recognition do they receive when they are carrying the largest territories or quotas?

Advancement/Promotion.   Advancement and promotions within a career used to be a significant motivational environment builder. But the flattening of corporate America in the 1980s reduced the ability of management to recognize and motivate employees by promoting or giving them a more important title. This is still a significant motivator of sales people; it's just not an option as available to a company as it used to be.

If you have at least 10 sales reps working in your company, do you have different job titles based on seniority or proven performance?

Ability to Achieve Fair and Clearly Defined Goals.   This is a motivational environment area management tends to ignore. One of my customers sold large computer equipment. Management assigned the annual quota performance expectations to the sales team each January. The reps were paid a fairly sizable quarterly bonus based on percent of year to date quota achieved, so this quota number was a significant focus of the entire sales team. The year before Max, the top performing sales rep experienced a spectacular year finishing more than 200 percent of his assigned quota. When asked how he did it, he talked about how he had reorganized and refocused his selling efforts. Max explained, "Half my performance last year was because of my hard work and creativity" but he also identified luck, which played a significant role when some unique one-time orders came his way.

Even though he shared all of this with his management, a distant uninvolved management team by the way, they still doubled his next year's quota. Max talked to several co-workers about how unfair he felt his quota assignment was, how there was no way he could make those numbers again this year due to the absence of these special one-time orders, and how hard this out of line quota was going to hurt his earnings.

277

After complaining to the company owner several times but seeing no adjustment he took a job working for the competition.

Are all of your quotas and assignments fair and clearly defined for all members of your team? Are your quotas actually assigned at the beginning of the year? I've seen some companies not assign annual sales quotas until as many as two or three months into the year. If a large order is closed in January the rep will feel the final quota assigned was perceived as being increased due to the large sale the beginning of the year.

An Affirming Work Environment with a Feeling of Team Purpose. The fifth and final way to help create (or strengthen) a sales team's environment is to be sure to not play one rep against another. Every member of your team has to feel they are on the same SWAT team where "what one learns benefits all."

The ways to create a stronger SWAT team feeling is to first make sure each team member feels important and second, don't encourage a "star" system of team recognition.

A star recognition system is based on promoting negative recognition programs like "sales person of the year" where the only way you can have one winner is to first announce the rest of the team are losers. All rewards and contests need to allow for multiple winners (Anyone selling over X receives this award). This way one person winning can be celebrated because the winner did not take anything away from the other reps. The only way a "salesperson of the year" award can occur is if it is first taken away from all nonwinning team members so one winner can win. How supportive would you be of the person sitting next to you if they had just won the salesperson of the year award from your company, preventing you from winning it yourself?

What can you do to strengthen your team's motivational environment where they feel valued, loved, important, with fairly defined goals in an affirming team environment?

> What can I do if I have a worker who doesn't seem to be highly motivated?

Just because all workers are highly motivated doesn't mean they will be highly motivated working for you. Part of your interviewing and hiring responsibility as sales leader is to evaluate and understand the personal motivation of every candidate interviewed. It doesn't matter how good a salesperson is. If your environment doesn't fit either their expectations or needs they will probably underperform in the job. And if someone is not fitting into your culture or environment you have to decide "are they fixable to our environment?" If the answer is no, then you need to help them find other work either within your company or with someone else. You cannot condone incompetence or allow a disruptive force to continue to destroy the motivational environment of the rest of your team.

It is very common for a new head of sales to join a company, implement the types of enhancements and improvements suggested in this book, and then realize several sales reps no longer fit the company and its new selling environment. Now the only question is how long will it take you as the leader to fix it and help both of you find something better?

> How do you motivate the very senior, very successful, but excessively eroded performer?

It is normal to have your top performing reps also be your most challenging to deal with and keep motivated.

Chapter 3 discussed how most of the better sales professionals have a strong ego and those huge egos are one of the best defenses against all the risk and rejection inherent in the job of selling. Unfortunately the stronger the ego, the more challenging and time consuming it is to create an environment for them to keep motivating themselves.

Some ideas to help you successfully lead a "high ego-high performer":

Understand how a strong ego is natural and even preferred in a top performer. The first suggestion is to stop fighting this problem of "dealing with our "prima donna reps." Ego'ed sales reps are a natural reality of most selling environments.

"Keep the reins loose—but in control." High ego'ed sales reps need to feel they are special (it's one of the ways they feel highly valued and important) and get to do more than others in their company.

Pick your battles with your top performers. Allow them to get away with the small stuff while you still control and demand conformance to the big stuff you need from them to keep your team functioning properly.

In some states they teach traffic cops who stop and give speeding tickets to allow the driver to "fire off one last shot" after they have been given a ticket. They have learned the ego and anger of someone just getting ticketed is such that the driver will likely "fire off" a final comment as the officer is walking back to their patrol car. The one liner said just out of earshot of the officer is accepted as the way a high ego person tends to try saving face in this embarrassing situation. The officers are taught, if at all possible, to let the remark go. It's one of the ways they manage this type of "high ego" behaviors.

Define the out of bounds you will allow. Simple rules of a high ego'ed person: "The higher your ego the more you want and need attention and recognition." One of the ways they feel loved and important, and get recognition from their peers, is by rocking the boat and testing the current rules and environments established by you, their leader. You want to take a proactive role and define the boundaries before they test you. You need to show them you are flexible due to their great selling success but that there are still minimum performance or rule requirements expectations. High ego-ed individuals will test everything to see where the out of bounds lines really are. You can take control by clearly delineating these lines and also clarifying what things are nonnegotiable.

Sales Leadership Responsibility Leading Your Team's Selling Process as a Coach and Strategist

In addition to the sales leadership responsibility of leading and motivating your entire team, the second critical responsibility is to also lead your team by being a strong coach and strategist.

How strong a coach and strategist are you? A successful sales coach will offer the majority of their communications to their sales team in the form of questions. Instead of telling or edicting you need to be asking questions and allowing them to discover for themselves what you most likely already know.

Your job as a coach and strategist parallels the definition of a sales leader. Your job is to help each member of your team achieve more than they would be able to achieve if just left alone. You can accomplish this by helping to change the awareness, focus, and skills of a salesperson, especially a senior salesperson.

The majority of this book presents tools to help your sales team modify their skills and awareness of the new best practices of selling defined in this text. Both of the 20-question evaluations were also developed to help provide detailed "best practices" of both sales and sales leadership.

Your role as a coach and strategist is also tied to these concepts. A successful sales coach needs to utilize coaching language to help their reps understand how they are doing, what they can do better, and where you want to direct their outsiders coaching expertise. The goal of this coaching language is to help your sales reps understand, in advance, some of the questions you will want to ask. You can increase a sales rep's stability and comfort level by utilizing these terms in your coaching and strategy sessions. All of these terms (or questions) have already been explained throughout this book. As a coach you want to be asking questions like:

- "What are you doing to communicate a stronger strategic competitive message to this customer?"
- "Walk me through the selling steps you plan to use from the time you identified this prospect until you close the sale."
- "How many moves ahead are you thinking with this account? What can you start doing differently to help provide this additional information?"
- How are you working to better understand your customer's political environment by getting higher, wider, and deeper within their account?
- "What can you be doing to be more proactive in your ideas and efforts at this account instead of just waiting for your rep to call for help?"
- ". . . and then what?"

How good are you at asking these types of "stretch" coaching questions on a regular basis with your team?

> When is the best time for a sales manager to jump in to a challenging selling situation?

Each sales rep needs a different amount and type of coaching help. Your job as their leader is to understand them well enough to be able to push them to change without having them bolt and run.

Your job is to proactively ask the tougher questions or offer to help instead of just waiting for them to ask (by which time it is usually too late to do anything to save the account).

Increasing your awareness and skills of both your sales leadership and selling abilities will help you better understand when it is good to jump in and get involved. Utilizing both 20-question evaluations will help contribute to a positive selling environment. How well did you and your team do on the 20-question evaluations? What can you do to work to increase your selling and leadership skills?

Coaching Does Not Have to Be Scheduled to Be Effective

Your job as a coach and strategist is to proactively look for opportunities where your help and guidance can be of productive help to a salesperson. That can occur when you are in informal discussions about an account, when you are out making sales calls with the rep, or during any regularly scheduled account briefings or planning sessions.

Your value as a coach to a sales rep could involve your actively assisting them on an account you have not even visited. Effective coaching involves assisting in pre-call planning as well as postcall debate and planning for their next call.

What can you do to help your sales team by understanding more about the selling process (as outlined in the 20-question *Sales Evaluation*) and your role as a coach and strategist (as outlined in the 20-question *Sales Leadership Evaluation*)?

Your Job as a Sales Leader

The goal of a sales leader is to help each of your people achieve more than they would have achieved if just left alone. The process to accomplish this goal is based on you working to lead and motivate your people as well as to manage your team's selling processes.

The collective tools outlined in this book are meant to help you accomplish all of this. These tools are meant to help you, as a coach, to stay:

Proactive focused to help you initiate discussions and efforts with your team instead of just waiting for them to identify a problem and then to ask for help.

Tactical focused to help you improve your team's understanding and control of your selling processes and structures.

Strategic focused to help you improve your team's ability to communicate a stronger, coordinated philosophy and competitive positioning in your markets.

Future focused to help you improve your team's ability to think and plan more than one move ahead

Political focused to help you improve your team's ability to increase their competitive advantage through a better understanding and working of your customer's political environment to get higher, wider, and deeper.

You know you and your team are good. Are you now good enough, and equipped with the right tools to help them get better?

Section

VI

Are You and Your Sales Team Ready to Get Better?

Section Overview

CHAPTER 26   So Now What?

This book has laid out detailed step-by-step processes to help increase your team's competitive advantage. Providing a multistepped plan is the easy part. Actually implementing all of the necessary components and leading your team to higher performance levels is where the real challenge lies.

The proven tools, structures, and concepts offered have been researched and developed to provide you and your team with the tools necessary for success, and you also have www.GreatSalesSkills.com as an additional resource.

You can still be successful leading this change process even if your senior management isn't interested. Though it will be difficult to implement long-term success, it is still possible for you to improve your sales team's selling environment by working on your own sales leadership skills to become a stronger coach and strategist. You can also work to improve the selling skills of your team.

The key here is to do something. Too many organizations keep talking about wanting to change, but they never do. You know you and your team are good. Is it now time for you to help them get better?

26

So Now What?

Selling continues to become tougher. Competition is getting better, customers are more informed and aware of the competitive alternatives available to them, and business in general continues to become more complex and demanding. As the leader of your sales team, your job is to help your sales team figure out how they can continue to win profitable business in this new reality.

The proven tools, structures, and concepts offered in this book have been researched and developed to help provide you and your sales team with the tools necessary for success.

You also have www.GreatSalesSkills.com as a resource. Both of the 20-question evaluations outlined in this book can be completed online at no charge. You can also receive a free customized report based on your 20 answers that will offer you suggestions to help increase your skills and awareness.

How to Begin

Where is the best place to begin? It depends on your organization. To implement the entire process outlined in this book you need to start by getting your senior management's approval and support. The next step requires working on your personal leadership skills and your ability to generate success and results for your organization.

Once you have gained the support and commitment of your senior management and understand how you can contribute as a leader to your team, it is time to conduct sales training and coaching to help each of your team members develop and implement these advanced selling ideas.

What if your senior management doesn't really care and is not interested in changing anything? Though it will be difficult to implement long-term successful programs and change, it is still possible for you to improve your sales team's selling environment by working on your own sales leadership skills to become a stronger coach and strategist and by helping to improve the selling skills of your team.

The key here is just do something. Too many organizations state they want to make improvements, but they never do. Or even worse, once they make the necessary changes and start to see some results the entire team moves onto the next and latest theory or training concept, and these new ideas then begin to decay ultimately disappearing completely from your team's language and focus.

> What can I do to increase the long-term "stickability" of these ideas within my company and sales team?

Do You Want to Become a Sales Manager or a Sales Leader?

Most sales managers are good at maintaining what they already have. They work to increase the efficiencies and productivity of their team but do not push their team to do things differently or better. They are reactive generators of change within their sales team waiting for someone else to initiate the communications or changes necessary to generate increased sales and profitability.

A sales leader though is different. They are proactive in what they do, maintaining a tactical, strategic, and future focused leadership communications style and process. They are also positive and affirming communicators with a vision of how good their entire team can really be.

Which do you want to be? A sales manager or a maintainer of business? Or do you want to be the more proactive leader of a team of fired up change agents?

There are two promises with this material. The first promise is this stuff does work and has been researched and proven in others' organizations. The second promise is that this material will only become effective when you do.

It's the old consulting joke that this information is guaranteed to work within your sales organization or we'll give you all your old skills back.

You know you and your team are good. Is it now time for you to help them get better?

APPENDIX

Sales Leadership Evaluation
Evaluate yourself by circling a number for each question:

1 Unaware * **2** Weak * **3** "Just Average" * **4** Leading * **5** "Best Practice"

Your Role as an Administrator, Problem Solver, and Disciplinarian		
1 2 3 4 5	#1	Your skills as an organized administrator are ____?
1 2 3 4 5	#2	Your skills coaching your sales reps through problem solving are ____?
1 2 3 4 5	#3	Your skills managing and coaching the pricing and profitability decisions of your team are ____?
Your Ability to Build and Retain a Sales Team		
1 2 3 4 5	#4	Your *"new sales person"* searching and interviewing skills are ____?
1 2 3 4 5	#5	Your *"new hire"* sales training program is ____?
1 2 3 4 5	#6	Your *"Performance Plan"* program in place for each member of your team is ____?
1 2 3 4 5	#7	Your ongoing *"experienced sales team"* training process is ____?
1 2 3 4 5	#8	Your accessibility to your sales force is ____?
Your Ability to Lead		
1 2 3 4 5	#9	Your sales team would rate their satisfaction level working for you as ____?
1 2 3 4 5	#10	Your amount of *"positive focused"* communications with your team is ____?

(Continued)

1 2 3 4 5	#11	Your ability to initiate new ideas and account planning conversations with your team is _____?
1 2 3 4 5	#12	Your ability to delegate to your sales team is _____?

Your Ability to Be a Coach and Strategist of Your Selling Process

1 2 3 4 5	#13	Your ability to organize and lead your team as a single market force is _____?
1 2 3 4 5	#14	Your team's ability to communicate a single message of market leadership is _____?
1 2 3 4 5	#15	Your ongoing new business prospecting process currently in place is _____?
1 2 3 4 5	#16	Your marketing and promotional skills are _____?
1 2 3 4 5	#17	Your ability to commit time to individually coach and strategize with each of your sales reps is _____?
1 2 3 4 5	#18	Percentage of time spent talking *"future focused"* with your reps is _____?
1 2 3 4 5	#19	Your ability and time committed to talking *"tactical and strategic focused"* with your sales reps is _____?
1 2 3 4 5	#20	Your ability to communicate with customers to help your sales reps get *"higher, wider and deeper"* is _____?

Years in Leadership (Circle One)

Less than 1 Year   2–5 Years   6–10 Years   11–20 Years   Over 20 Years

Total Years in Sales and Leadership (Circle One)

Less than 1 Year   2–5 Years   6–10 Years   11–20 Years   Over 20 Years

Sales Evaluation

Evaluate yourself by circling a number for each question:

1 Unaware * **2** Weak * **3** "Just Average" * **4** Leading * **5** "Best Practice"

Evaluating Your *Operational Selling Skills and Abilities*

Understanding the Technical Side of Your Business

1 2 3 4 5	#1	Your technical knowledge of your products/services and how they relate to your industry is ____?
1 2 3 4 5	#2	Knowledge of your competitor's products and their customer success stories is ____?

Understanding the Fundamentals of Selling

1 2 3 4 5	#3	Your knowledge and daily usage of the steps of a sales call is ____?
1 2 3 4 5	#4	Your understanding of personalities and ability to identify and then mirror your customer's communications style is ____?

Understanding How to Manage Your Time and Information

1 2 3 4 5	#5	Your personal *"time and territory"* organizational skills are ____?
1 2 3 4 5	#6	Your ability to utilize technology to increase your productivity and effectiveness is ____?

Evaluating Your *Tactical Selling Skills and Abilities*

Maintaining and Growing Your Business

1 2 3 4 5	#7	Your ability to proactively manage, control, and resolve customers' problems is ____?
1 2 3 4 5	#8	Your ability to keep your existing accounts stable and under control is ____?
1 2 3 4 5	#9	Your ongoing new business prospecting process is ____?

(Continued)

293

Managing Your Selling Process

1 2 3 4 5	#10	Your ability to think and plan multiple moves ahead with each of your customers and prospects is ____?
1 2 3 4 5	#11	Your knowledge/understanding of competitors' pricing practices are ____?
1 2 3 4 5	#12	Your ability to utilize company support resources in your territory is ____?

Maintaining and Controlling Your Customer

1 2 3 4 5	#13	Your ability to communicate what your customers want to buy instead of just what you have to sell is ____?
1 2 3 4 5	#14	Your understanding of the political environment and decision process of each of your accounts is ____?

Evaluating Your *Strategic Positioning Skills and Abilities*

Ability to Manage the Strategic Aspects of Your Selling Process

1 2 3 4 5	#15	Your ability to communicate what your customers want to buy instead of just what you have to sell is ____?
1 2 3 4 5	#16	Your knowledge of your competitors' strongest *"value points"* they use to sell against you is ____?
1 2 3 4 5	#17	Your ability to win business at a higher price/margin by communicating your stronger value is ____?

Your Philosophy Toward Ongoing Personal Development and Improvement

1 2 3 4 5	#18	Ability to represent yourself in a professional, truthful, and ethical manner is ____?
1 2 3 4 5	#19	Your ongoing commitment and efforts to grow and improve your selling skills and awareness are ____?
1 2 3 4 5	#20	Your ongoing use of one or more coaches or mentors to help you get better is ____?

Years in Sales (Circle One)
Less than 1 Year   2–5 Years   6–10 Years   11–20 Years   Over 20 Years

INDEX

Accessibility, of sales manager, 134–135
Account loss review, 14–15, 30
Account planning, with sales organization, 140–142
Administrative assistant, sales leader as, 273
Administrative skills, 119–122
Adult learning, 114, 257–259
Advancement, as motivator, 277
Amiable personality type, 184
Analytical personality type, 183–184
"And then what" question, 99–100, 199

Best customer, defining, 147–148
Best practices:
  coaching and, 231, 271–273
  developing and defining, 247–251
  ISO 9000 and, 46–47
  leadership values and, 67–68
  prioritizing of, 250–251
  sales manager's role and, 71–72
Biases:
  identifying company's, 17–19, 22
  identifying sales manager's, 69–72
Blanchard, Ken, 33, 89

Coaching, *see also* Coaching bias; Training
  of best practices, 231, 271–273
  evaluation of improvements and, 269
  leadership responsibility and, 280–283
  sales leader as coach, 122, 145–165, 274–275
  use of coach, 224–225
Coaching bias, 70
  of customers, 76–77
  of other departments and workers, 78–79
  of sales organization, 81–82
  of senior management, 72–73
Commitments, needed for successful change, 2–3, 23–39
  to communications structures, 29–31
  to focus and strategy, 35–38
  in improvement strategy, 237–238
  to leadership, 26–29
  to responsibilities and expectations, 31–33
  to rewards and consequences, 33–35
  to values, 24–26
Communication:
  about competitive uniqueness, 212–217

Communication *(Continued)*
 about what customer wants to
  buy, 203–207
 with customers, 163–165,
  182–184
 evaluation of positive, 139–140
 importance of commitment to
  structures, 29–31
 importance of positive, 87–92
 of product's value, 219–220
Company:
 coaching, number crunching,
  disciplinary bias of other
  departments in, 78–81
 using support resources of,
  200–203
Competitive pricing awareness,
  199–200
Competitive uniqueness message,
  149–152, 212–217
Competitors:
 knowing explanation of their
  competitive advantage,
  217–219
 knowledge of value points of,
  217–219
 technical knowledge about,
  177–180
Computer skills, 121, 187
Consequences, *see* Rewards and
  consequences
Consultants, for training, 261–262
Continuous quality improvement,
  ISO 9000 and, 48
Core values of selling, 206–207
Customer Relationship
  Management (CRM)
  computer systems, 74,
  187

Customers:
 coaching, number crunching,
  disciplinary bias of, 76–78
 communicating about what they
  want to buy, 203–207
 communication styles of,
  182–184
 communication with, 163–165
 invalid assumptions about
  relationships with, 11–13
 keeping accounts stable,
  193–194
 resolving problems of, 191–192
 technical knowledge about,
  176–180
 thinking ahead about, 196–199
 understanding decision process
  of, 207–209
 winning new, with stronger
  value, 219–220

Data, *see* Number crunching bias
Decision process of customers,
  207–209
Delegation ability, 142–143
Disciplinarian bias, 70
 of customers, 78
 of other departments and
  workers, 80–81
 of sales organization, 84–85
 of senior management, 75–76
Discovery phase, of ID to
  Close process, 202
Doers, 50, 60
Doing manager, 60–64
 defined, 50
 problems with, 65–68
Driver personality type,
  183

Ego:
  controlling own, 28–29, 30
  leading of salesperson with
    strong, 279–280
  role of in selling, 54–55
Empathy, *see* Trust,
    demonstrating in sales
    organization
Ethical behavior evaluation,
    221–222
Evaluating your sales force,
    233–240
Evaluation phase, of ID to Close
    process, 202
Expectations of salespeople, *see*
    Responsibilities and
    expectations
Experience:
  invalid assumptions about, 8–9,
    21–22
  necessary for sales manager,
    54–57
Expressive personality type, 183

Focus and strategy, importance
    of commitment to, 35–38
Four quadrants of personality,
    183–184
Future, focus on, 160–161

Goals, ability to achieve, as
    motivator, 277–278
Growth strategy, *see* Learning
    growth strategy

"Hellarewe" birds, 10, 245
Higher price/margin, winning
    business with, 219–220
Hiring skills, 108, 127–131

Identification and tracking, *ISO
    9000* and, 42–46
Identify to Close selling process,
    197–198, 201–203
Improvement strategy steps:
  develop strategy, 230,
    243–251
  evaluate sales force, 229,
    233–241
  implement learning growth
    strategy, 114, 230, 253–266,
    285–289
  lead by coaching best practices,
    231, 271–283
  track improvements, 231,
    267–270
Informational power, 27–28
Information controls, 120–122
Information management,
    operational selling skills and,
    185–188
In-house training, 262–265
Internet, marketing with,
    155–157
Interviewing skills, 108,
    127–129
Intimidator, sales leader as,
    272
Intuitive selling skills, 9–11,
    46–47, 175, 244–247
Invalid leadership assumptions,
    8–16, 235–236
ISO 9000, 41
  prospecting efforts and,
    153–154
  quality improvement steps of,
    4, 42–48
  using to improve strategy, 230,
    243–251

Leadership:
  coaching and, 280–283
  determining best practices for, 249
  importance of commitment to, 26–29
  invalid assumptions about, 8–16, 235–236
  motivation and, 275–280
Leadership skills, evaluation of, 119–126, 238–241
  administration, problem solving, and pricing, 108, 119–126
  determining best practices for, 249
  form for, 291–292
  how to use, 107–108, 110–117, 167–168
  leadership ability, 109, 137–143
  sales team building and retention, 108, 127–135
  selling process coaching and strategizing, 109–110, 145–165
  tracking improvements and, 268
Leadership values:
  balancing coaching, disciplining, number crunching, 50–51, 69–86
  believing in structures of selling, 52, 101–106
  leading, not just doing, 50, 59–68
  leading with vision, 51, 93–100

right to lead team and, 49–50, 53–57
  showing empathy, loyalty, and trust, 51, 87–92
Learning growth strategy, implementing, 230, 253–266, 285–289
  conducting effective training for, 114, 257–259
  establishing best environment for, 255–257
  evaluating success of, 265–266
  training alternatives, 259–264
Listening versus talking time, 203–207
Loyalty, see Trust, demonstrating in sales organization

Managers, see Sales manager; Senior management
Managing manager, 50, 61
Marketing and promotional skills, 154–158, 205
McGrane, Bill, Sr., 90, 275
Mentors, use of, 224–225
Motivation, 275–280. See also Rewards and consequences
Motivator, sales leader as, 272–273
Mountain men/women, 13–14
Multiple steps ahead selling philosophy, 196–199

NeuroLinguistic Programming (NLP), 184
New hires:
  interviewing of, 127–129
  training of, 129–131

Number crunching bias, 70
    of customers, 77–78
    of other departments and
        workers, 79–80
    of sales organization,
        82–84
    of senior management,
        73–75

Operational selling skills,
        101–104
    improvement of, 169–170,
        173–188
    selling fundamentals and,
        180–184
    technical knowledge and,
        176–180
Outside consultants, for training,
        261–262

Performance plan, 33, 131–132,
        269–270
Personal development, 221–225
Personality types, 182–184
Personal life, balance in, 140
Personal power, leadership and,
        27, 29
Planning:
    account planning with sales
        organization, 140–142
    performance plan, 33, 131–132,
        269–270
Political environment of
    customers, 207–209
Positional power, 27–28
Positive communication
    environment, 7, 87–92,
        139–140, 256

Pricing and profitability:
    decision making skills and,
        124–126
    knowledge of customers',
        199–200
Proactive sales environment,
        256–257
    leadership and, 51, 93–100
    sales organization and, 11–13,
        191–194
Problem solving skills, 122–124
Productivity, improving with
    technology, 186–188
Profitability and pricing decision
    making skills, 124–126
Promotion, as motivator, 277
Promotional and marketing skills,
        154–158, 205
Prospecting skills, 152–154,
        194–196
Public sales rallies, for training,
        260
Public seminars, for training,
        260–261

Recognition, as motivator,
        276–277
Reports, see Number crunching
    bias
Responsibilities and expectations:
    importance of commitment to,
        31–33
    increasing of, as motivator, 277
Rewards and consequences:
    importance of commitment to,
        33–35
    increasing, as motivator,
        276–277

Sales call, steps in, 181, 244–245, 248

"Sales hours required to fulfill" report, 80

Sales Leadership Evaluation, 44, 107–110, 111–113, 167–168, 227

Sales Leadership Question 1, 119
Sales Leadership Question 2, 122
Sales Leadership Question 3, 124
Sales Leadership Question 4, 127
Sales Leadership Question 5, 129
Sales Leadership Question 6, 131
Sales Leadership Question 7, 133
Sales Leadership Question 8, 134
Sales Leadership Question 9, 137
Sales Leadership Question 10, 139
Sales Leadership Question 11, 140
Sales Leadership Question 12, 142
Sales Leadership Question 13, 145
Sales Leadership Question 14, 149
Sales Leadership Question 15, 152
Sales Leadership Question 16, 154
Sales Leadership Question 17, 158
Sales Leadership Question 18, 160
Sales Leadership Question 19, 162
Sales Leadership Question 20, 163
Sales manager:
    definition of, 49
    evolution of, 272–275
    experience necessary for, 54–57
    as in-house training conductor, 264
    responsibilities of, 5–8, 15–16, 159, 231
Sales organization:
    ability to build and retain, 108, 127–135
    ability to lead, 109, 137–143
    coaching, number crunching, disciplinary bias of, 81–86
    competitive uniqueness message and, 149–152
    creating best environment for, 255–257
    evaluation of, 1–2, 5–16, 112–113, 229, 233–241
    evaluation of company support for, 17–22
    improvement strategy, 244–247
    manager's support for, 65
    marketing and, 154–158
    motivation and team purpose, 278
    prospecting skills of, 152–154
    showing empathy, loyalty, and trust to, 51, 87–92
    as single force, 145–149
    tracking improvements of, 231, 267–270
    working with individual members of, 158–160
Salesperson Question 1, 176
Salesperson Question 2, 177
Salesperson Question 3, 180
Salesperson Question 4, 182
Salesperson Question 5, 185
Salesperson Question 6, 186
Salesperson Question 7, 191
Salesperson Question 8, 193
Salesperson Question 9, 194
Salesperson Question 10, 196
Salesperson Question 11, 199
Salesperson Question 12, 200
Salesperson Question 13, 203
Salesperson Question 14, 207
Salesperson Question 15, 212

Salesperson Question 16, 217
Salesperson Question 17, 219
Salesperson Question 18, 221
Salesperson Question 19, 222
Salesperson Question 20, 224
Selection phase, of ID to
    Close process, 202
Self-esteem, of salespeople, 90
Self-study, for training, 263–264
Selling skills, improving:
    operational skills, 101–102,
        169–170, 173–188
    strategic positioning skills,
        102–104, 171–172, 211–225
    suggestions for, 172, 227–228
    tactical skills, 102–104,
        170–171, 189–209
Senior management:
    changing expectations of sales
        manager of, 66–67
    coaching, number crunching,
        disciplinary bias of, 72–76
    evaluation of support for sales
        organization, 2, 17–22
    positive sales culture and,
        236–237
Showcase accounts, 177–180
Strategic positioning selling skills,
    171–172, 211–225
    managing, 212–220
    personal development and,
        221–225
Strategic selling skills, 102–104
Strategist, sales leader as, 274–275
Strategy for selling, evaluation of:
    communication with customers,
        163–165
    competitive uniqueness,
        149–152

focus on future, 160–161
leadership responsibility and,
    280–283
marketing skills, 154–158
prospecting skills, 152–154
single market force, 145–149
tactical focus, 162–163
work with individual reps,
    158–160
Structures of selling:
    importance of, 9–11, 46–47
    leadership values and, 52,
        101–106
    skills evaluation and, 180–184
SWAT teams, 13–16, 146, 278

Tactical selling skills, 102–104,
    170–171, 189–209
    maintaining and growing of
        business, 191–196
    maintaining control of
        customer, 203–209
    managing selling process,
        196–203
    prospecting for new business,
        194–196
    strategy and, 162–163
Talking versus listening time,
    203–207
Team:
    building, 127
    delegation and, 142
    satisfaction, 138
    SWAT approach, 146
    tracking performance, 268–270
Teamwork, importance of,
    13–16
Technical knowledge of market,
    176–180

Technology, ability to use, 186–188

Telephone prospecting, 196

Territory organizational skills, 186

Time management skills, 121–122, 159–160, 185–188

Tracking, of sales organization's improvement, 231, 267–270

Training, *see also* Coaching
conducting effective, 257–259
importance of, 8–9, 21–22
ISO 9000 and, 47
six approaches to, 259–264
skills for experienced team members, 133–134
skills for new hires, 129–131

Trust, demonstrating in sales organization, 51, 87–92

University seminars, for training, 260–261

Values, *see also* Leadership values
four core values of selling, 206–207
importance of commitment to, 24–26

Visionary leadership, 51, 93–100

Website, marketing with, 155–157

"Why buy" question, 150–151, 216–217

Win-Loss review, 148–149

Ziglar, Zig, 84